The Muse of
Modernity

The Muse of Modernity:

Essays on Culture as Development in Africa

Edited by
Philip G. Altbach and
Salah M. Hassan

Africa World Press, Inc.

P.O. Box 1892
Trenton, NJ 08607

P.O. Box 48
Asmara, ERITREA

Africa World Press, Inc.

P.O. Box 1892

Trenton, NJ 08607

P.O. Box 48

Asmara, ERITREA

Cover Design: Aaron J. Wilson
Cover Illustration: <u>Mother and Child</u> © Ibrahim El-Salahi

ISBN: 0-86543-560-X Cloth
       0-86543-561-8 Paper

This book is dedicated to

Alberta Arthurs—

For her commitment to cultural development
and the civil society

Contents

PREFACE

The Muse of Modernity: Essays on Culture as Development in Africa brings together a group of the best thinkers on African cultural topics. All of the contributors to this volume have been both leaders in key cultural areas and thoughtful advocates for African culture. They reflect on the "state of the art" in their respective fields, and point to directions for future development. Thus, this book is a combination of thoughtful analysis of the current state of culture in several key areas in Africa, with suggestions for improvement. The authors are united by a conviction that culture and its various related enterprises and institutions are of central importance, not only for Africa's intellectual and emotional life, but also for socioeconomic development. We are convinced that culture is central to development and that the institutions that support culture are just as central as factories, airlines, or banks.

We focus here on some key areas of culture—visual arts, music, publishing, radio, and film, among others. The issues discussed in this book apply not only to the cultural spheres analyzed here, but to other areas of cultural endeavor as well. Realities differ among African countries, but the problems discussed here are common across the continent. It is our hope that the essays in this volume will serve as a guide for cultural workers and institutions concerned with culture and development in Africa. These essays are intended to stimulate a genuine interest in cultural development in Africa, moving beyond the issue of culture's relevance to economic development. The essays also help confront deeply entrenched Western stereotypes and misconceptions about contemporary African arts and culture, in general. Above all, they help familiarize the reader with theoretical issues at the heart of the discourse on African culture—in the hope of providing a better vision for engagement in such a field. While our authors come from different parts of the continent and represent different cultural arenas, they are all united by a conviction that culture is central for African development.

This book stems from a conference held at the Rockefeller Foundation's Bellagio Study Center in Italy, in May 1995. Alberta Arthurs of the Rockefeller Foundation, Anita Thorell of the Swedish International Development Authority, and Mora McLean of the Ford Foundation helped to conceptualize the conference and provided needed support. Katherine Salahi of the Bellagio Publishing Network's Secretariat in Oxford, England, organized the event, which included the participation of all of the authors in this book except for Professor Ali Mazrui, as well as representatives of international organizations concerned with culture and development in Africa. Editorial assistance on chapters was provided by Edith Hoshino. Daniel Halpern and Catherine Priser translated two of the chapters from French into English. The Center for International Higher Education at Boston College also contributed to the completion of this volume. We appreciate the cooperation of the contributors to this book, who worked closely with us on revisions.

We would like to recognize the vision and the commitment to African culture and to civil society of Dr. Alberta Arthurs, director for the arts and humanities at the Rockefeller Foundation. Her concerns have helped to shape the scope of this volume, and her enthusiasm for African culture and the relationship between culture and development have been instrumental in this project, as well as in countless others. Her approach combines the timely inclusion of cultural experts in development discussions with relevant scholarly research and support for cultural activities themselves. Dr. Arthurs' vision of a community of people in development was instrumental in building the Bellagio Publishing Network, a successful community of publishers, donor organizations, and others committed to publishing and book development. This book reflects the ideas that Alberta Arthurs expressed at the 1992 conference held at the World Bank on "Culture and Development in Sub-Saharan Africa":

> It becomes clear that there is much learning to be done, much reciprocity to be achieved, among African professionals and other professionals, among African peoples and other people. . . . In the realm of cultural production, . . . historians, artists, cultural observers and theorists, social scientists, writers, are at par. They share the world; they do not divide it; their boundaries are porous; their influences are mutual; their transfers are two-way. There is in this sense an interesting disjunction between the terms "culture" and "development." Although we conventionally think of development as moving from North to South, we must think of culture differently. It moves in many ways. It is unpredictable. It will not go in a single direction.

Philip G. Altbach
Chestnut Hill, Massachusetts

Salah M. Hassan
Ithaca, New York
March 1996

CHAPTER 1

Perspective: The Muse of Modernity and the Quest for Development

Ali A. Mazrui

INTRODUCTION

Let us confront issues like culture, development, modernization, and dependency frontally. What do they all mean? What is their significance for African societies? Let us first deal with the complex role of culture.

Culture is relevant for development because of the seven functions that culture has in society. When culture functions as a lens of perception, it influences how people view themselves and their environment. For example, African cultural concepts of immortality have influenced attitudes regarding family size and population growth. Many Africans believe that no person is really dead as long as the person's blood flows in the veins of the living. Having many children, therefore, improves a parent's chances of immortality. Translated into modern terms, no person is really dead as long as the person's genes are still among the living. It is, therefore, rational to maximize one's genetic legacy by having many children. This concept of immortality has contributed to making the rate of population growth in Africa the highest in the world, with implications for development—for better or for worse.

Another function of culture is when it serves as a spring of motivation. What people experience as incentives or disincentives for certain patterns of behavior is greatly influenced by culture. For this reason, the work ethic, for example, is very often a product of such cultural configurations as Max Weber's concept of "the

Protestant ethic" and the more recent phenomenon of workaholic behavior among Japanese executives.

Is the work ethic in Africa cultivated or stifled by culture? Has the work ethic been damaged by the consequences of the colonial experience? Is the work ethic among African women stronger than among African men? Have African men been more damaged, culturally, than African women? Needless to say, the work ethic has enormous implications for development. In the final analysis, the work ethic is a cultural imperative.

Culture also serves as a standard of judgment. What is right or wrong, what is virtuous or evil, what is beautiful or ugly are all greatly conditioned by culture. What constitutes corruption? Why is taking a chicken to a chief in traditional society acceptable as a form of salutation but rejected as bribery in modern society? Is the problem of corruption in Africa compounded by the clash of standards of judgment between the traditional and the modern? Is moral fluidity itself a consequence of a clash of cultures?

The fourth function of culture concerns its role as the basis of stratification. Rank, caste, and class are all profoundly conditioned by—if not created by—culture. There is, in addition, traditional gender stratification. In most sub-Saharan traditional cultures, for instance, women were thought to have a triple custodial role—as custodians of fire, water, and earth. As custodian of fire the African woman finds herself in charge of rural Africa's most important source of domestic energy—firewood. She treks long distances to collect it. As custodian of water, the African woman ensures the water supply for the home and for the extended family. Again, she often walks a mile or two to the lake or river (unless a well is more readily available).As for the woman's role as custodian of earth, this is linked to the concept of dual fertility—the fertility of the womb (woman as mother) and the fertility of the soil (woman as cultivator). To this day, in many African countries, women make up the majority of farmers—as well as being major suppliers of domestic water and firewood.

What role does culture allocate to *men*? In societies of mixed husbandry, males (both boys and men) are in charge of the larger domestic animals, such as cattle or camels. Some cultures allocate responsibility for all domestic mammals (goats, sheep, etc.) to males—leaving only poultry in the hands of women. Men fell trees so that women can use branches for firewood. Men go to cities or mines to work as wage laborers, while their womenfolk remain on the farms.

A new division of labor emerged in some colonial economies—women cultivated food crops like yam and maize, while men took charge of cash crops like cocoa, cotton, and coffee. But in places like Karicho, in Kenya, it is still women who pick the tea leaves at harvest time. Considerations such as these make cultural awareness indispensable for effective development planning.

The fifth function of culture is as a means of communication. Culture provides all sorts of nuances in communication and intimation. But above all, culture provides language in the literal sense of the legacy of words and lexicon. We shall return to this function of culture more fully in relation to the potential of indigenous African languages in development. Can any country approximate first-rank economic development if it relies overwhelmingly on foreign languages for its discourse on development and transformation. Will Africa ever effectively "take off" when it is so tightly held hostage to the languages of the former imperial powers? We shall return to this theme later in this analysis.

The sixth function of culture is precisely in defining and influencing production and consumption. Cultures differ widely in productivity—not only in the world as a whole but also within Africa. Are the Kikuyu, in Kenya, really more productive than the Maasai? Are the Igbo, in Nigeria, really more productive than the Tiv? Are the differences between the groups cultural? Clearly, development planners cannot ignore such considerations.

This brings us to the final function of culture—that is, culture as a basis of identity. Culture is crucial in defining who "we" and "they" are and in marking the frontiers of solidarity. Indeed, what constitutes a Kikuyu or a Maasai, an Igbo or a Tiv, is preeminently a function of such cultural variables as lineage systems, kinship, and language. How can development tap into the fountains of identity to achieve results?

These, then, are the seven functions of culture, and—whether those in charge like it or not—development is caught up in the complex configuration of those functions. But our conceptual problems are by no means over. We still have to grapple with what the process of development is all about. There are issues of definition, process, and goals involved that require a closer look.

BETWEEN DEVELOPMENT AND MODERNIZATION

What is development? One possible answer is that development is modernization minus dependency. But what is modernization? One possible answer is that modernization is change that is compatible with the present stage of human knowledge, that seeks to comprehend the legacy of the past, that is sensitive to the needs of the future, and that is increasingly aware of its global context. This is the positive interpretation of modernization.

If development equals modernization minus dependency, and we have defined modernization, what, then, is dependency? Dependency could mean either surplus need or deficit control. Country *B* is dependent on country *A* if country *B* needs country *A* more than the other way round (surplus need). Or, alternatively, country *B* is dependent on country *A* if country *B* has less control over their relationship than country *A* has (deficit control).

Where does culture enter into all this? If development equals modernization minus dependency, there is no doubt about the relevance of African culture in at least the part of the equation that concerns "minus dependence." African culture is central to this process of reducing dependency in the dialectic of modernization.

IDENTITY AND INDIGENIZATION

One strategy of transcending dependency is **indigenization.** This includes greater utilization of indigenous techniques, personnel, and approaches to purposeful change. Indigenized modernization would include greater use of African languages in the pursuit of economic and constitutional change. As stated earlier, no country has ascended to the level of a first-rank economic power by excessive dependence on foreign languages. Japan rose to dazzling industrial heights by "scientificating" the Japanese language and making it the medium of Japan's industrialization. Korea has done this for the Korean language, making it the medium of its own technological takeoff. Can Africa ever "take off" technologically if it remains so overwhelmingly dependent on European languages for discourse on advanced learning? Can Africa look to the future if it is not adequately sensitive to the cultural past? Culture as communication and culture as production need to converge.

When two Japanese physicists meet to discuss a problem in physics, it is now possible for them to discuss it in the Japanese language. When two African economists (let alone physicists) meet to discuss economics, even if they come from the same linguistic group in Africa, the chances are that they can only discuss advanced economics in a European language. Overcoming this linguistic/cultural gap may be critical for reducing dependency in Africa's experience.

But languages are not enriched only by their capacity as a medium for scientific discourse. The soul of each language is ultimately in creative literature—among the poets and dramatists, among the writers and storytellers. Taking African languages seriously would have to include a patronage of the literary arts and an effort to sustain the infrastructure of publishing in indigenous languages, as well as in international languages.

In the twentieth century, no language is automatically a scientific language, but every language is automatically a poetic language. African languages need to be made purposefully more scientific. But with poetry, the focus should not be on the language of poetry but on the poets themselves—not on making the language artificially more poetic, but on making the poets more naturally productive and engaged. The two policies—"scientification" of African languages and support for African poets and writers—have to be jointly pursued as part of long-term national development. Culture as communication and culture as identity should find a meeting point in literature.

Three Africans have won the Nobel Prize for literature since 1986. It was possible for an Arab—Neguib Mahfuz—to win it for literature in his native Arabic. It was possible for a South African white—Nadine Gordimer—to win the Nobel Prize for books written in her native European language. But it was not possible for the only Black laureate—Wole Soyinka—to win the Nobel prize for literature written in his native Yoruba. Soyinka could only be in the running for the prize through the imperial language of the "other." Europe's linguistic domination of sub-Saharan African cultures is more uncompromising than Europe's domination of, say, the Arab world. Is this a case of culture as stratification? Is this a rank order of races? Or a stratification of cultures?

A Japanese may win the Nobel Prize for works written in Japanese; a South Asian for masterly use of Bengali, Urdu, or Hindi; a Frenchman for genius of expression in the French language; and an Egyptian did win the prize for creative accomplishments in Arabic.

However, for the foreseeable future, the Nobel Prize for literature is unlikely to be awarded for brilliant use of an indigenous African language. Are we waiting for modernization to come? Or are we waiting for dependence to leave? In this domain the linguistic "other" has precluded the linguistic "self" from ever being noticed as being of literary relevance. Is this "great chain of being" racial or cultural?

Rabindranath Tagore won the Nobel Prize in 1913, when India was still decidedly a British dependency. The works for which he won the Nobel Prize were in Indian languages, especially Bengali. He created from his linguistic womb. But in Africa the European "other" still inhabits the African "self." When does race end and culture begin? They say African languages are not modernized enough. Or is this a case of Africa itself not being independent enough?

When Tagore won the Nobel Prize for literature written in Bengali before the first intra-civilizational war (World War I), it must have looked like a major step toward a "concert of cultures," a step toward a partnership of civilizations. Even after making allowances for the influence of W. B. Yeats behind the scenes, even after allowing for the fact that the award of the prize was probably aided by the fact that Tagore had personally translated a number of his works into English, the award signalled not a clash of civilizations but the potentialities of parity of esteem across cultural divides.

But progress in cultural parity since the Tagore award of the Nobel Prize has been slow and painful. The functions of culture in almost every society continue to feel the hegemony of Western power and the omnipresence of Western civilization. Has the stumbling block been Western racism? Linguistic dependence continues to be particularly severe in Africa. We need to elevate African languages. The global culture of stratification needs to be challenged.

THE IDIOM OF RELEVANCE

Next to indigenization as a strategy for transcending dependency is the related strategy of **domestication**. This second strategy involves making imported institutions more relevant to Africa. For example, the Western-style university is basically a foreign institution in Africa, and yet every African country has attempted to reproduce it, often in unabashed imitation. Some of those African campuses were previously overseas extensions of European universities. Makerere in Uganda, Legon in Ghana, and Ibadan in Nigeria started as overseas colonial extensions of the University of London, producing graduates with degrees of the British university. Université Lovanium in Belgian Congo (now Zaire) was conceptually an extension of Louvain University in Belgium.

The strategy of domestication involved trying to make those African extensions more and more relevant to Africa in terms of the subjects they taught, the methods they used, the goals they sought to realize, and the actual people who taught the courses and made policy. In reality it has not been easy to Africanize African universities. In fact, many of them are now decaying, partly because they were not adequately relevant to the needs of their societies, and partly because they were not culturally designed in the image of their societies. They remained "undomesticated," in our terms.[1]

If indigenization includes greater use of indigenous languages, domestication includes making the Euro-imperial languages in Africa more relevant for African needs. The imperial culture of perception needs to be changed. Instead of using the French language to promote French culture and civilization, domestication would make the French language a servant of African culture and literature. Great African novels in French are achievements in domestication.

There are times when the achievements of domestication come at the expense of indigenization. In the second half of the twentieth century it is often much easier to let the Euro-imperial language be the main language of national journalism, national politics, and national education—without bothering to develop indigenous languages for the same roles. Domestication becomes the soft option as compared with the tough alternative of indigenization.

In such situations, domestication may cease to be a method of transcending dependency but rather serve to deepen that dependency. In the former French colonies, the French language is still much more part of the problem (dependency) than it is part of the solution (transcending it).

The muse of modernity is elusive in conditions of acute dependency. Is "negritude" in Senegal a case of using the French language to serve African needs? Or has it been a case of deepening Senegal's cultural dependency upon France? The poetry of Senegal's Leopold Senghor has been both a garland of African negritude and a chain of cultural dependency. The deep Senegalese dialectic between cultural dependency and cultural liberation continues. Perception is affected by culture conflict.

In secondary schools in Africa, the literature taught to many African children is sometimes still European literature. But what is more to the point is that the African literature taught to African school children is almost never in indigenous languages. The European "other" haunts the African "self" from a young age in postcolonial schools. Have we been witnessing a clash of civilizations in African schools? Or does literature provide a cover for dependency?

The format of the literature is also often heavily European in derivation. The novel is of course a European invention in any case, but even other literary genres in Africa have been profoundly affected by the legacy of colonialism.

Felix Mnthali of Malawi once wrote a poem about "The Stranglehold of English Lit.," a poem dedicated to Molara Ogundipe-Leslie.

> Your elegance of deceit,
> Jane Austen,
> lulled the sons and daughters
> of the dispossessed
> into calf-love
> with irony and satire
> around imaginary people.
>
> When history went on mocking
> the victims of branding irons
> and sugar plantations
> that made Jane Austen's people
> wealthy beyond compare!
>
> Eng. Lit., my sister,
> was more than a cruel joke—
> it was the heart
> of alien conquest.[2]

> —Felix Mnthali,
> "The Stranglehold of English Lit."

Is this a clash of cultures in the classroom? Is it racism in disguise? Or a hopeful beginning of cultural convergence? Alamin M. Mazrui has reminded us that three of Shakespeare's plays have been translated into Kiswahili—*Julius Caesar*, *The Merchant of Venice*, and *Macbeth*.[3] Shakespeare is being domesticated.

But what has not been translated is at least as significant. What has not been translated into Kiswahili is the only play by

Shakespeare with a Black hero, albeit a tragic hero. Why has it not been translated? Because in the play a Black man was married to a white woman, Desdemona. What is more, the Black hero killed the white woman in a fit of jealousy. The villain of the play is a white man, Iago, who manipulated Othello's jealousies. The play is, of course, *Othello*.

Why did Julius Nyerere not translate the only Shakespearean play with a Black hero into Kiswahili? Why was Nyerere's compatriot, Samuel Mushi, not fascinated by Othello's wife, the fair Desdemona? We are still in the shadow of colonial dependency.

Without realizing it, neither Julius Nyerere nor Samuel Mushi had confronted what colonial education had left out of their Shakespearean agenda—*Othello*. This play virtually never featured in the syllabus of the Cambridge School Certificate for the British colored empire. Nyerere and Mushi did not translate it mainly because it was not part of the Shakespeare to which they were exposed in their colonial textbooks. Domesticating Shakespeare in Africa has had its colonial limits. The subtle censorship of imperial racism had censored a tempestuous love affair between a white woman and a black man.

If Alamin Mazrui's research findings are correct, these Swahili translations of *Julius Caesar*, *The Merchant of Venice*, and *Macbeth* have now become legitimized as part of Swahili literature itself (rather than simply as Swahili translations of foreign literature).[4] Is this a deeper domestication of Shakespeare and a hopeful trend toward cultural synthesis? Is this another arena where the European "other" inhabits the African "self"? Why should translated Shakespeare become Swahili literature proper?

Here a comparison is appropriate with *The Rubayat of Omar Khayyam*, by Edward Fitzgerald (1859). Although Khayyam was a Persian, the *Rubayat* is definitely part of *English* literature. Is this the equivalent of Nyerere's translation of *Julius Caesar* becoming part of Swahili literature? Of course, the main difference was that *The Rubayat of Omar Khayyam* was not a *translation*. Fitzgerald breathed his own literary genius into an independent interpretation of the worldview of the Persian poet of the twelfth century: "A jug of wine, a loaf of bread and thou"; "The moving finger writes, and having writ moves on. . . ."

A mere translation of *The Merchant of Venice*, on the other hand, does *not* give us a piece of Swahili literature. Only an indifference to Shakespearean literary authenticity and a readiness to engage in a drastic Swahili reinterpretation of the play would have justified listing the work within the corpus of Swahili literature. Only then would it have been cultural synthesis—and a deeper domestication of Shakespeare.

Nevertheless, a great area for cultural domestication is precisely such translations of distinguished foreign works into African languages. Civilization has grown out of mutual intellectual and cultural stimulation. Under another strategy we shall later refer to the need to make African cultural achievements available abroad. But under this strategy of domestication, the most relevant translations are from foreign to indigenous languages. Machiavelli has already been translated into Kiswahili, but the translation is not widely available.

Much more widely used are those Swahili translations of Shakespeare's *Julius Caesar*, *The Merchant of Venice,* and *Macbeth*. If modernization includes the trend toward globalization, the Africanization of Shakespeare is part of the process of wider modernization.

DIVERSITY AND INTEGRATION

A third strategy for transcending dependency is that of **diversification**. In agricultural production, that could mean diversifying the range of crops that a country cultivates for both domestic consumption and export. It could mean diversifying a country's markets abroad, to make sure that the country is not too dependent on one or two overseas outlets for its products. Multilateral aid is a form of diversification as compared with bilateral aid. During the Cold War, nonaligned countries were even able to diversify their "masters," and play one off against the other. Competitive imperialism like that of the Cold War can sometimes give smaller countries more space for maneuver than monopolistic imperialism allows.

Africa must also diversify the foreign cultures from which it seeks to learn. There is excessive reliance on the West as the only "other." And yet, what is there in Japanese culture that enabled Japan to beat Westerners at their own industrial game?

In 1868, after the Meiji restoration, the Japanese asked themselves if they could modernize *economically* without Westernizing *culturally*. They embarked on a crusade of selective industrialization under the slogan of "Western technique, Japanese spirit." Years later, they had become an industrial power to reckon with. Their culture of motivation was highly stimulated. What was it in Japanese culture that enabled them to remain so Japanese culturally and still pull off an industrial miracle before World War II? How did culture as *identity* and culture as *production* converge?

Japan was subsequently briefly occupied by the Americans following the country's surrender after the use of the atomic bomb on Hiroshima and Nagasaki. When the occupation ended, Japan started its second industrial miracle—less culturally selective than the first, but even more technologically triumphant. What was there in Japanese culture that made such miracles happen?

Japanese industrialization has not been without its costs. The culture of production has been allied to Japan's culture of stratification. The environment has often paid dearly, Japanese women have remained marginalized, and ethnic minorities in the country have been exploited without adequate recognition. But Africa *needs* to look eastward toward the Japanese experience, as well as northwards toward Europe and westward towards North America, for cultural insights relevant to modernization and development.

Africa should also swallow its pride and look more closely at countries like South Korea, Malaysia, Indonesia, Singapore, and others in Asia that had the same per capita income as Ghana in 1957 and have since left most of Africa far behind in per capita income and industrial growth. To what extent are the economic achievements of the Asian "Tigers" due to cultural factors? Can foreign cultures be studied for lessons that are relevant for others?

Of course, Africa has been studying *Western* culture for decades in the hope of stimulating its own development. It is time that Africa diversified the cultural models it examines for developmental lessons. Such diversification may help reduce Africa's dependency upon the West in other areas of endeavor as well.

A fourth strategy in the fight against that dependency is the strategy of **horizontal integration**. This involves not only *national* integration within each country but *regional* integration as well. Pan-Africanism therefore becomes an instrument of horizontal integration, and Pan-Africanism is partly rooted in cultural and racial identification.[5] The culture of identity is central.

In reality, such movements are born out of a combination of nightmare and dream, anguish and vision. What nightmare and dream released the forces that culminated in the formation of the European Union as a success story?

Pan-Europeanism had two parents—poetry and war. The poetry provided the vision and the sensibilities of being European;

war provided the practical impetus—either through conquest (as European nations expanded and contracted) or through a desire to avoid some future war. That was the combination of nightmare and dream.

After World War II, the Schuman Plan and the European Coal and Steel Community illustrated the creation of deliberate Pan-European interdependence to avoid the future risk of war.

The Cold War both divided Europe (between East and West) and united Europe within each camp. Once again nightmare and dream played their paradoxical integrative roles.

The poetry of Pan-Europeanism goes back at least to the European Renaissance, when Europeans were stimulated by a new sense of shared civilization. By the time of the French Revolution from 1789 onward, William Wordsworth across the Channel in England could proclaim passionately:

> Bliss was it in that dawn to be alive
> But to be young was very heaven.

> —William Wordsworth,
> *French Revolution*

However, the French Revolution was a combination of both poetry and war—the two major stimuli of Pan-Europeanism. The French Revolution was both nightmare and dream.

Does Pan-Africanism have a comparable stimulus of poetry and war? The real stimulus for Pan-Africanism has been the combined power of poetry and imperialism, rather than poetry and war. The poetry includes legends of past heroes and makers of history. More recently, there have been two schools of Pan-African cultural nationalism—romantic primitivism and romantic *gloriana*.

Romantic primitivism celebrates what is simple about Africa. It salutes the cattle herder rather than the castle builder. In the words of Aimé Cesaire:

> Hooray for those who never invented anything
> Hooray for those who never discovered anything
> Hooray for joy! Hooray for love!
> Hooray for the pain of incarnate tears.

> My negritude [My blackness] is no tower and

        no cathedral,
It delves into the deep red flesh of the soil.

                              —Aimé Cesaire

On the other hand, romantic *gloriana* celebrates Africa's more complex achievements. It salutes the pyramids of Egypt, the towering
structures of Aksum, the sunken churches of Lalibela, the brood-
ing majesty of Great Zimbabwe, and the castles of Gonder. Romantic *gloriana* is a tribute to Africa's empires and kingdoms, to
Africa's inventors and discoverers, and to great Shaka Zulu rather
than the unknown peasant. Culture as identity and culture as stratification are intertwined.

Both forms of Pan-African cultural nationalism were a response to European imperialism and its cultural arrogance. Europeans said that Africans were simple and invented nothing. That
was an *alleged fact*. Europeans also said that those who were simple
and invented nothing were uncivilized. That was a *value judgment*.

Romantic primitivism accepted Europe's alleged facts about
Africa (i.e., that Africa was simple and invented nothing) but rejected Europe's value judgment (that Africa was, therefore, uncivilized). Simplicity was one version of civilization, romantic primitivism said:

        Hooray for those who never invented anything
        Who never discovered anything . . .

Romantic *gloriana*, on the other hand, rejected Europe's alleged facts
about Africa (that Africa was simple and invented nothing) but
seems to have accepted Europe's value judgment (that civilization
is to be measured by complexity and invention).

An African country can produce both types of Pan-African
nationalists. Senegal's Leopold Senghor has been a major thinker
and poet in the negritude school. Negritude is associated with romantic primitivism. Senghor's most hotly debated statement is:

        "Emotion is black . . . Reason is Greek."

On the other hand, the late Cheikh Anta Diop, Senegal's Renaissance man, who died in 1986, belonged more to the *gloriana* school. He spent much of his life demonstrating Africa's contributions to global civilization. And he was most emphatic that the civilization of pharaonic Egypt was a *Black* civilization. This was all in the grand Pan-African tradition of romantic *gloriana*.

What of the reality of Africa? It was a fusion of the simple and the complex, the cattle herder and the castle builder. It was more than romantic primitivism and romantic *gloriana*. Real Pan-Africanism must go beyond the twin stimuli of poetry and imperialism.

The Pan-Africanism of economic integration will be led by Southern Africa, with the new community that has added South Africa to the old fraternity of the Southern African Development Coordination Conference (SADCC). The success of this economic subregional integration will rest in part on the fact that one member—the Republic of South Africa—is more equal than the others in the new economic fraternity of the Southern African Development Community (SADC). A pivotal state often helps to assure the success of regional integration. But a shared sense of African identity will also be needed to sustain SADC. The culture of identity needs to be allied to political stratification in the quest for economic development.

In the period immediately after 1958, the old European Economic Community survived partly because some members were definitely more equal than others. In another instance of political stratification, the Franco-German axis was, under Charles de Gaulle, more "Franco" than German. But now German economic might has restored the balance in the new European Union. However, a shared European culture was also needed all along to sustain unification; the culture of identity was invoked.

Similarly, Southern Africa has the advantage of having one member indisputably "the first among equals"—the Republic of South Africa. The pivotal power is the premise of regional survival. But a regional identity has to be culturally strengthened to sustain long-term unity.

The Pan-Africanism of linguistic/cultural integration will probably be led by East Africa, which enjoys the good fortune of a regionwide indigenous language. That language—Kiswahili—is able to play a role in binding together Tanzania, Kenya, (to some extent) Uganda, Somalia, and (potentially) Rwanda, Burundi, and Eastern Zaire. Northern Mozambique and Malawi are also feeling Swahili influence. Swahili is spoken by more people than any other indigenous language of Africa. It will hit its first 100 million people early in the twenty-first century, if not sooner. Kiswahili is expanding more rapidly than any other lingua franca in the continent.

Pan-Africanism of political integration will probably be led by North Africa. There is already a kind of economic cooperation fraternity binding five countries—Libya, Tunisia, Algeria, Morocco, and Mauritania. Economic cooperation has been limping along. However, Egypt has now expressed an interest in joining this movement toward greater North African regional integration. The subregion is still a long way from political integration, but it is the best place in Africa for such an adventure—since it shares a religion (Islam), a language (Arabic), a culture (Arabo-Berber), and a substantial common history across the centuries.

Part of the stimulus for North Africa's integration will be European integration. The economies of North Africa and Southern Europe are to some extent competitive. The closer integration of Spain, Portugal, and Greece into an enlarged European Union is ringing economic alarm bells in North Africa. This could help to promote Pan-Africanism in Arab Africa.

The Pan-Africanism of military integration is likely to be led by West Africa—with the precedent set by ECOMOG under the Economic Community of West African States (ECOWAS). In spite of the difficulties and inconclusiveness of ECOMOG's attempted rescue operation in Liberia, the effort has been a major pioneering enterprise in the history of *Pax Africana*.

But this issue is precisely the Achilles' heel of Pan Africanism as a whole. Who will keep the peace in Africa as we approach the end of the millennium? Many institutions will be needed, and sustaining those institutions will require greater and greater horizontal integration and cultural synthesis. Again, a culture of identity needs to be tapped for regional cooperation.

COUNTERPENETRATION: A GLOBAL STRATEGY

The fifth strategy for fighting dependency is that of counterpenetration. This strategy involves infiltrating the infiltrators—counterpenetrating the citadels of power. Since we have defined modernization partly in terms of sensitivity to the global context, counterpenetrating the powerful is a search for a more balanced globalization. It is a quest for a more symmetrical interdependence.

In the second half of the twentieth century, Japan has so effectively counterpenetrated European and North American markets
that it is no longer clear who is exploiting whom. South Korea's
counterpenetration of the American economy has also been impressive, though on a much smaller scale.

It is also possible for a Third World country to use its raw
materials as a source of influence in the world rather than as the
basis for continued dependency. For a brief decade (1973–1983)
the Organization of Petroleum Exporting Countries exerted some
leverage over the world economy on a significant scale. Petro-
power from the Third World briefly counterpenetrated the com-
manding heights of the world economy.

Then there is demographic counterpenetration. Irish Americans are a demographic lobby for Irish interests in the United States;
Jewish Americans are a demographic lobby for the state of Israel.
Some African Americans, like those who support TransAfrica, are
a demographic lobby for Africa on Capitol Hill. All of these are
cases of demographic counterpenetration—as is the case of African professors teaching young Americans in U.S. colleges and universities.

Making African culture available on equitable terms to the
wider world could also be not only counterpenetrative but also
modernizing for that wider world. The globalization of African
culture is a modernizing imperative, provided it is done without
exploiting Africa.

Progress is being made in the teaching of courses on African
literature, African art, African philosophy, and African aesthetics
in Western colleges and universities. One day, particular African
works will no doubt be included in courses on *world* civilization,
and not merely in courses on African culture.

CONCLUSION

We have redefined the once-discredited concept of modernization
to mean change that is consistent with the present stage of human
knowledge, encompasses the legacy of the past, is sensitive to the
needs of future generations, and is responsive to its global context.

We have defined development as modernization minus dependency. But what is dependency? It is either surplus need or
deficit control. Country *B* is dependent on country *A* if country *B*
needs country *A* more than *A* needs *B* (hence surplus need). Al-

ternatively, dependency is a situation in which country *B* has less control over its relationship with country *A* than country *A* has (hence deficit control). The two kinds of dependency do not always pull in the same direction. In the history of imperialism, the imperial power often needed the colonies more than the colonies needed the imperial power. But the colonies had deficit control over the relationship.

If development equals modernization minus dependency, how is the dependency to be subtracted from the modernization? We have suggested five strategies for ending or reducing dependency—indigenization, domestication, diversification, horizontal integration, and counterpenetration. Underlying them all is the continuing salience of culture and its seven functions—as lenses of perception, as means of communication, as a basis of stratification, as a spring of motivation, as a standard of judgment, as a pattern of production and consumption, and as the foundation of identity. This essay has ranged from poetry to Pan-Africanism, and from sculpture to the "scientification" of African languages. The "muse of modernity" is trying to articulate a stanza vibrant with Alexandrian echoes:

> A little modernity is a dangerous thing
> Drink deep or taste not the Western spring.[6]

What is needed is more of modernity and less of "the Western spring." A non-Western route to modernity is possible for Africa—provided African culture is fully mobilized as an ally in the enterprize.

NOTES

1. See Ali A. Mazrui, "The African University as a Multinational Corporation: Problems of Penetration and Dependency," *Harvard Educational Review* 45 (May 1975):191–210. See also Ali A. Mazrui, "Afrocentricity Versus Multiculturalism? A Dialectic in Search of A Synthesis," James S. Coleman Annual Lecture, University of California, Los Angeles, May 5, 1993.
2. Felix Mnthali, "The Stranglehold of English Lit.," in *Modern*

African Poetry, ed. Gerald Moore and Ulli Beier (London: Penguin, 1989), 139–40.
3. Alamin M. Mazrui, "Shakespeare in Kenya: Between English and Swahili Literature" (paper presented at the annual meeting of the African Literature Association of the United States, Columbus, Ohio, March 17, 1995.
4. Ibid.
5. The section on Pan-Africanism draws on material presented in Ali A. Mazrui, "Pan-Africanism: From Poetry to Power" (closing address to the conference on "Africa in the Contemporary World," sponsored by Espace Afrique and Centre de Recherches Entreprises et Société (CRES), Geneva, November 13–17, 1994.

6. This is a paraphrasing of Alexander Pope's famous lines:

> A little knowledge is a dangerous thing
> Drink deep or taste not the Pyrean spring.

—*Essay on Criticism*, 1711

CHAPTER 2

Arts and Humanities Capacity Building in Africa: Problems and Prospects

Damien M. Pwono and Jacques G. Katuala

INTRODUCTION

While the link between culture and development is increasingly recognized by both national development agencies and the donor community as one of the main prerequisites of successful development programs and projects, Africa lacks the human and institutional capacity to use cultural knowledge in the development process. Moreover, the lack of appropriate cultural development strategies and funding opportunities has undermined people's creativity and participation in cultural life. Here, culture refers not only to the arts but is viewed in its broadest sense: as heritage, a framework for guiding social and economic development, and as a dynamic in itself. This essay assesses the situation of African arts and humanities, identifies and discusses a number of capacity constraints on African cultural institutions, presents some opportunities for building the needed capacity in the arts and humanities, and suggests some general strategies for building and/or strengthening institutional and human capacity in the arts and humanities.

In retrospect, the strategies adopted by many African governments for the development of the arts and humanities can be seen as a shift from the use of culture for national unity by liberation movements, some of which took over power after independence, to its current misuse by politicians to manipulate the people. This use of cultural knowledge for the maintenance of political power—as opposed to its use for guiding development policies— has affected the growth of viable cultural institutions as well as the creation of effective strategies to promote people's well-being. This situation of the state of the arts and humanities in Africa was recently assessed during a meeting convened in Nairobi by the Rockefeller Foundation.[1] Although the main purpose of the gathering was to assess the state of the arts and humanities on the continent in order to probe funding opportunities, the meeting served a number of other functions as well.

The Nairobi meeting provided an opportunity for scholars, artists, and development practitioners to exchange information and views on the relationship between culture and development. It provided a forum for scholars and development practitioners to learn more about their common and conflicting views of the roles of the arts and humanities in national and regional development. It also built new bridges between artists and people in the humanities from Northern, Southern, Eastern, Western, and Central Africa who are isolated from each other by factors such as linguistic barriers and lack of opportunities for networking. At the end of three days of presentation of papers and intense discussions in plenary sessions and in small working groups, it became apparent that current impediments hindering capacity building in the arts and humanities in Africa lie not only in the lack or inadequacy of a cultural policy framework and financial shortcomings, but also in the lack of coordination of efforts among artists and people in the humanities themselves as well as within the donor community.

The organization of the 1995 Bellagio meeting of donors interested in African cultural programming during the United Nations World Decade for Cultural Development (1988–1997), therefore, offered an unprecedented opportunity for donors to discuss some of the major challenges facing cultural development in Africa, to enhance communication among themselves and other actors, and to explore possible areas of collaborative action. The need for collaboration is crucial at this critical period, when the cultural dimension of development is increasingly being recognized, both domestically and internationally. The promotion of the new approach to development that places culture at center stage and sees awareness of local sociocultural conditions as assets in identifying, designing, implementing, and evaluating development programs and projects, requires the crafting of sound strategies and the participation of all actors, including artists and people in the humanities. Although the need for such strategies has been strongly expressed, especially at several meetings during the World Decade for Cultural Development,[2] not much is being done to translate the new development thinking into practical activities. This is a big challenge for Africa, given the current socioeconomic and political conditions of the continent.

In this essay, to borrow from James Coleman, capacity is broadly defined as being an institutional and human procreative force—one that generates developmentally positive outcomes, including increasing levels of capacity itself.[3] It is integrative, responsive, adaptive, and innovative. Capacity building then is defined as a comprehensive process; a methodology, an approach, and related strategies; a set of concepts that includes the building, rebuilding, strengthening, utilization, and sustainability of capacity; an enabling environment to support capacity building; and the technology used in the process. Ideally, any macrolevel strategy to build institutional and human capacity for cultural development in Africa has to be based on two critical prerequisites that determine the success or failure of the strategy: the existence of an enabling environment, and a better knowledge of the capacity constraints on African cultural development.

In his article on an enabling environment for capacity building, Joel Samuels defines that environment as a set of political, economic, social, and cultural conditions and factors that exist and/or should be created to support activities related to capacity building.[4] In this context, the basic components needed in order to launch any capacity-building action plan include: political stability; the continuity of economic and social policies; a clear demarcation between the sphere of the "state" and that of "civil society"; professionalism on the part of the actors in society; good governance (accountability, transparency, predictability, the rule of law, etc.); the nurturing of a group of elites; confidence and/or belief in capacity building; allocation of adequate resources; and proper utilization of arts and humanities outputs. Yet, under the present circumstances in Africa, many of these key components of the enabling environment are in a fragile state. Capacity building in the cultural sector cannot take place in a society in which political instability is prevalent. As a long-term endeavor, arts and humanities capacity building is undermined in an environment of political instability in which the government and cultural actors are focusing on survival and short-term interests.

The interrelationship between culture and the economy shows that stability in economic development policies can be a catalyst for capacity building in the cultural sector. Conversely, political and economic instability can provide a fatal blow to cultural programs and projects. Stability in economic policies, therefore, is a prerequisite for investments in cultural industries. Erratic economic policies cannot create the proper enabling environment for promoting capacity building in the cultural sector.

A clear government policy that establishes and recognizes a demarcation between the sphere of the state and that of civil society creates the conditions for the development of activities related to arts and humanities capacity building. Without this demarcation, the efficiency of both civil society and the public sector is weakened because special interest groups will seek to extract concessions from the government.

Professionalism of all the development actors in a society is an essential ingredient in capacity building for cultural development. The existence of people in a society who are deeply imbued with the values of their profession creates conditions for the development of capacity-building activities. Therefore, the lack of professionalism within the leading cadres of society can doom capacity-building efforts for cultural development since this can lead to an endless cycle of misdirected efforts and funds.

Good governance as a prerequisite for capacity building refers to the normative framework for the organization and management of the state. The five main pillars of good governance are accountability of government and its institutions and officials for their decisions; transparency in decision making; openness and availability of information; predictability; and the rule of law in a society. All these features of good governance are essential in creating the environment necessary for effective arts and humanities capacity building.

Capacity-building activities for cultural development are spearheaded by the existence of developmental and cultural elites. These are elites in public, private, or civil society who can provide the leadership not only in the implementation of activities related to arts and humanities capacity building, but also to those aimed at providing a vision for the society. A widespread confidence across society in the value of the arts and humanities creates the enabling environment for the success of capacity-building activities. Lack of faith creates tensions between different sections of a society about the value of capacity building; in addition, the belief that the professional skills involved will empower some groups rather than others has been one of the main reasons for past failures in arts and humanities capacity-building efforts. Finally, demand for local arts and humanities capacity building creates the conditions for the production of new capacity. The existence of a demand not only creates the conditions for the sustainability of the capacity created, but also guarantees returns for investments undertaken to build it. Quite often, it is this demand that makes it possible to capture some of the attention and effort of those working outside Africa for the benefit of African arts and humanities.

The existence of an enabling environment is a necessary condition but not a sufficient condition for building human and institutional capacity for cultural development. Another important prerequisite for building such capacity is an assessment of the specific needs of the continent because at present there is insufficient knowledge of the specific problems of African artists and cultural researchers for which solutions have to be found. Several of these constraints that contribute to the current state of crisis can be identified at both the macro- and microlevels.

MACROLEVEL CAPACITY CONSTRAINTS

At the macrolevel, the current state of crisis in African cultural institutions is due to several factors, such as the legacy of colonial models of economic development; the increasing maladjustment/divorce between the state and the surrounding culture; the inadequate knowledge of local cultures; brain drain and the absence of the support that would enable existing human resources to be used creatively and successfully; and the lack of a vision for the future.

Colonial Models of Economic Development

The colonial perception of African culture took a heavy toll on African cultural development. African societies and their cultures were studied only as curiosities and valued solely for the profit-making potential of exotic interest in them and their usefulness in establishing the backbone of the colonial system. The main features of the arts and humanities during this period were static ethnography, with a political agenda and highly instrumentalist; the introduction in the school system of programs on the arts and humanities disconnected from the concerns of Africans and their social realities; and ignorance about the humanities in Africa and their founding studies in both the Maghreb and sub-Saharan Africa.

The Attitude of Postcolonial Governments

Since the modernist approach to development and strategies adopted by the colonial regimes identified African cultures with "traditions" that were considered to be static and backward, it is significant to find that after independence, a large number of African policymakers and members of the intelligentsia continued to stick to this view of development, which precluded the utilization of local knowledge, know-how, beliefs and traditions, memory, collective imagination, and aspirations.

African culture, although used by political leaders for personal political gain, was perceived by many postcolonial governments as an impediment to a development that was defined entirely in economic and physical terms and that stressed solving problems such as those of health, sanitation, housing, and roads. Even though one can identify on the policy side a new dynamism in African arts and humanities in the 1960s through the creation of bodies in charge of guiding research on the arts within government bureaucracies, the opening of several research centers and institutions devoted to the arts, and the appropriation of generous budgets for the arts and humanities, the narrow intellectual conformism to the former colonial powers' perceptions continued with the rise of dictatorial regimes.

Considerable evidence presented at the Nairobi Conference on the State of Arts and Humanities in Africa shows that the current crisis in African cultural institutions also finds its origin and its main features in the continent's overall context and the increasing maladjustment between the states and the cultures that surround them. Whatever the ideological orientations of the past and current regimes in power in Africa, African cultural institutions were progressively marginalized and brutally choked.

This marginalization of culture took on the same format everywhere: the idea that cultural development is an "expensive luxury" not needed in the current situation in Africa; undervaluation of departments of culture as evidenced by their position at the bottom of the ministerial hierarchy, where they are usually grouped with, and subordinated to, social services and other agencies; reduction in budget allocations for cultural development; overvaluation of "scientific disciplines"; the closing of many faculties of arts and humanities; the overlooking and demeaning of national cultural productions; and harassment of artists, researchers, and students of African arts and humanities who do not share the official ideology and policies.

The persistence of the colonial legacy, the disconnection between the Westernized elite and their own national cultures, the nonintegration or weak integration of these cultures in effective programs and projects, and the lack of an epistemology of a national culture have contributed to a lack of knowledge about local cultures. This is exacerbated by a lack of an autonomous research agenda and practice—both of which are more and more influenced by the needs of foreign donors. Malika Horchani-Zamiti refers to this as "jet research,"[5] which is a piecemeal research agenda based on the demands of foreign donors and which leads to mostly short-term and utilitarian research producing raw data to be processed for the benefit of researchers from the North.

The Brain Drain and Lack of Support for Cultural Initiatives

The crisis of African cultural institutions is also due to the brain drain of national and regional experts, who continue to leave the continent for economic, political, and professional reasons. The need for qualified and motivated professionals to play a leadership role in a variety of fields cannot be overemphasized. But because of the previously described development ideology espoused by many governments and donors, there is little support for the few individuals who, through their skills, experience, and dedication, could contribute to the creation of a clear vision for the arts and humanities in Africa. The lack of networking between these different groups has also prevented them from interacting with each other and from developing a common consciousness of their role as cultural activists. This situation has left a void in the leadership of cultural development on the continent.

Very few African governments have a clearly formulated cultural policy containing a general perspective on the future, broad objectives, and strategies on how to translate this into reality. Activities are then undertaken on a piecemeal and ad hoc basis. Although culture in Africa is not homogeneous and expresses itself in different forms and with various strengths in different places, many cultural programs, projects, and activities are not systematically tied together into a coherent vision for the future.

MICROLEVEL CAPACITY CONSTRAINTS

The consequences of the macrolevel constraints on African cultural institutions are felt at the microlevel as they affect the capacity of artists and people in the humanities to participate in the cultural development of the continent. At the microlevel, the continued marginalization of those in the arts and humanities who are against donor-driven research has also caused most of them to become the targets of nationalistic ideologies and religious fundamentalism, with the potential for dangerous consequences on the stability, development, and future of Africa.

The low quality of cultural research output reflects the imbalance between pure and applied research and the way in which artists and those in the humanities perceive one another. The lack of utilization (or, at best, the underutilization) of African culture in the development process has contributed to the prostitution of a significant number of artists and researchers who took the opportunity to or were forced to become singers of praises or designers of state ideologies (nationalism, African authenticity, Negro-Africanism, Marxism-Leninism, etc.). In the Maghreb, for example, this has led to requests for exclusive indigenization, quick rehabilitation of founding fathers, Arabization, and passive, uncritical consumption of the arts and humanities.

The lack of exchanges among artists, intellectuals, and researchers, even within the same country or linguistic zone, has led to a narrow nationalism that, in turn, has caused some countries to create institutions or programs whose main objectives have been to ruin regional initiatives. Consequently, ideas, knowledge, and cultural productions do not circulate between countries and regions. This reinforces the breach between intellectual practice and the real life of African societies. Even within the same country, the separation between artists and researchers has led them to ignore each other. The lack of opportunities for disseminating research results and showcasing cultural productions has led to the misuse and the migration of talent. This situation has also caused many of the remaining Africa-based artists and people in the humanities to play the role of data collectors or informers who produce raw data to be processed by and to benefit their colleagues abroad.

OPPORTUNITIES FOR CAPACITY BUILDING

The current bleak picture of the state of the arts and humanities in

Africa does not preclude the existence of a few success stories here and there that need to be revisited. There are examples of innovative and even radical strategies of cultural liberation and development that led to original approaches by a number of personalities such as Kwame Nkrumah and Julius Nyerere or inside liberation movements such as FRELIMO in Mozambique and the ANC in South Africa.

Other noteworthy efforts are the creation of universities and research centers such as the University of Dar es Salaam in Tanzania, the University of Nairobi in Kenya, and the Center for African Studies at Eduardo Mondlane University in Mozambique. However, because of many of the above-mentioned constraints, these institutions, which should have become centers of excellence in the arts and humanities, have declined and are today in the same situation of crisis as many other cultural institutions in Africa. The only exception to this is South Africa, where the end of apartheid has created a stimulating situation for research and networking.

However, regardless of several macro- and microlevel capacity constraints on African cultural development, there are opportunities for building capacity in the arts and humanities. The main opportunities are: a general recognition that culture and development are closely linked; a concern to bring local stakeholders into the decision-making process on development; a recognition that stakeholders need institutional and human capacity to participate in the decision-making process; an awareness of the need for national and regional networking; the existence of African success stories such as the use of culture in South Africa both against apartheid and in helping to build a new identity; the emulation of Southeast Asian success stories of capacity building for development, including cultural development; the push for regional integration; the emergence of civil society and the overall efforts in the democratization process in Africa; the use of technological advances, especially the revolution in communication technology; and the manifestation of donor interest in funding cultural activities.

Strategy for Building Institutional Capacity

With regard to cultural development, it is known that the problem is the lack of strong institutions for people in the humanities and artists to carry out research, to showcase their creations, and to foster networking. An effective strategy for institutional capacity building calls for support to existing institutions that have the potential of recovering their past capacity, reputation, and impact; and the creation of new mechanisms for coordination of efforts. This is why former centers of excellence and publications that were Africa-based, such as *Transition, Black Orpheus*, and *Drum,* need to be revived as a means of disseminating scholarly research. The organization of major international festivals of arts and culture such as FESTAC, which was last held in Lagos in 1978, should be institutionalized in Africa to promote cultural exchanges and networking between Africans and African-derived cultures overseas. Similarly, current donor-supported activities such as the African Publishers' Network (APNET), African Film Festivals, the International Center for African Music and Dance, arts exhibitions, and the development of independent radio and museum education programs should be provided with resources to strengthen their institutional capacity.

As to the creation of new institutions, there is an urgent need to reassess requirements and to institute networks of artists, scholars, and researchers on the continent to enable Africans to take responsibility for the design, development, and destiny of African arts and humanities. The goals of new initiatives should be clearly defined. These new institutions should mainly play the role of coordinating bodies and also of clearinghouses at the national or regional level, taking stock of and disseminating existing knowledge on culture and development.

These bodies should also assist development institutions in proposing general guidelines, as well as specific approaches to better ways of dealing with culture and development in terms of needs assessment, programs, or project design and management. It is at this point that a "forum for culture and development experts" could be developed, at the African level, or a "society for culture and development," at the international level, as a membership organization aimed at uniting policymakers, donors, artists, cultural managers, social scientists, and other development practitioners interested in and committed to the promotion of culture and development.

Strategy for Building Human Capacity

One of the main strategies that has been identified to deal with human capacity constraints is training, both formal and informal. However, there is considerable evidence showing that training is not the best strategy for building human capacity if there is no clear definition of the goal for which people are being trained. There is also ample evidence that training is a good strategy to build human resources if cultural factors are taken into account. Formal training should be combined with informal training as one of the strategies to deal with the paucity of human capacity for cultural development. This is why scholars, researchers, and institutions should accord due recognition to traditional artists, specialists, and experts and integrate them into universities, specific cultural departments, and research centers. At this juncture, regional coordinating bodies should assist in the design of training courses and the development of training materials on cultural policy formulation, finance, and management.

Other strategies to build human capacity for cultural development could include: making direct funding available to finance new and existing capacity-building programs and to leverage funding from other sources; providing institutional bases for African artists and researchers, thus helping reverse the drain of these valuable resources from Africa; encouraging the use of African researchers in promoting the effective use of their outputs by both the public and private sectors; helping to create the development of networks of highly trained professional cultural experts in government, academia, and the private sector; promoting donor coordination and developing greater focus, prioritization, and rationalization in the development of human resources for cultural development; human capacity building through technology transfer; and the establishment of an equilibrium between demand and supply of human resources in the arts and humanities.

Capacity Sustainability

The issue of capacity sustainability should be raised here. The question is how to sustain the institutional and human capacity for cultural development that may be created through all the above strategies. Sustainability has several dimensions that have the same objective: to make sure that capacity (re)built can be maintained after the end of specific interventions. This applies to financial and institutional sustainability and the sustainability of capacity utilization.[6]

It is at the design level and in the evaluation and implementation of the action plan that every precaution has to be taken to make sure that the capacity to be (re)built is sustainable. Capacity sustainability, therefore, calls for solid strategies that will create an enabling environment for cultural institutions to achieve their objectives and for artists and people in the humanities to work to promote culture and development in Africa.

SUGGESTED ACTION PLAN

Based on the constraints on and opportunities for capacity building for cultural development discussed in this essay, it is clear that one of the creative ways for African governments and the international community to respond to challenges in the area of cultural development is not only to acknowledge and to make speeches about the importance of cultural development or the need for taking cultural factors into account in projects management, but also to develop structures and to provide adequate resources that would enable creative minds to work on problem-solving strategies.

Reflecting on the current attention that is being given to culture and development, one would hope that the cultural dimension of development may also become one of the top priorities in the design of development programs and funding policies along similar lines as have evolved with regard to environmental concerns. Achieving this objective would also require the development and implementation of viable policies, the creation of true professionalism in the cultural sector, the mobilization of cultural activists, and the institutionalization of activities and mechanisms to support artists and cultural entrepreneurs and managers, and others in the humanities.

Because of the multiplicity of capacity constraints, there is a need for prioritization and an action agenda that tackles problems in an incremental rather than holistic way—hence the following urgent action agenda for the coordination of previously suggested activities targeting both human and institutional capacity building in the arts and humanities. This action agenda consists of the creation of a center for culture and development, the establishment of a foundation or a fund for the arts and culture, and the development of a consortium of donors to African cultural activities.

African Center for Culture and Development

Although the Pittsburgh experience in running management training programs shows that cultural institutions face almost similar capacity problems throughout the world,[7] it has been noted that in developing countries, especially Africa, cultural institutions would have been far more effective in achieving culture and development goals if their missions were well defined and their managerial capacity improved.

This is an area in which African governments and the international community could make important contributions. In this context one might recommend the creation of a sustainable "African center for culture and development" and encourage the establishment of chairs in culture and development or in the arts and humanities at universities and similar institutions to improve the human capacity of cultural institutions. The main objectives of a center for culture and development could include:

- gathering and disseminating (in Africa) the international body of knowledge on the cultural dimension of development;
- enhancing creativity and the use of artistic expression to promote development programs and projects; and
- improving the managerial capacity and effectiveness of cultural institutions and programs.

To meet the above objectives, the proposed center could undertake a series of activities reflecting a wide range of needs expressed by both cultural and socioeconomic development institutions and personnel. These include: building databases of culture and development thinkers and practitioners in Africa; designing and implementing training programs and conferences; the production and dissemination of educational materials, research and publications, special projects, and consulting services on culture and development.

The training of cultural personnel is an essential building block in improving the management of cultural institutions as well as promoting the sociocultural dimension of development. The goal of short-term training courses could be a multiple-language or degree-granting program in collaboration with selected universities. This program could develop and share strategies and managerial tools that would enable people in the humanities, policymakers, and development practitioners to:

- undertake pertinent analysis of cultural factors in development planning and management;
- seek better ways to communicate cultural, socioeconomic, and environmental issues through artistic and cultural expression;
- evaluate the sociocultural impacts of development programs and projects on community life;
- explore the cultural adjustments necessary to respond to the challenges of the changing environment;

- analyze the potential for using the arts in economic development; and
- establish and strengthen human and institutional capacity of cultural institutions.

Training topics could include: strategic planning; cultural policy formulation, evaluation, and management; cultural projects management; marketing and audience-development strategies; entrepreneurship; fund-raising and capital-formation strategies; and financial management and business-negotiation techniques.

Training materials designed for use during seminars and workshops could be made available for wide dissemination. Similarly, audio and video materials on the interplay between culture and development could be produced in multiple languages for dissemination through radio and television broadcast. Research results from studies conducted by culture and development scholars and practitioners could be collected and reported in a journal on culture and development in Africa. This Africa-based publication could focus on "success stories"—case studies of new methodologies and development policies, programs, and projects that took cultural factors into account, respected cultural differences, introduced useful new practices or shared knowledge across cultures, and led to new and better solutions.

Special projects of the proposed center might consist of joint ventures on culture and development activities with ministries of the arts and culture or other local and regional cultural institutions and field testing of new methodologies; a roster of international consultants to assist cultural institutions and national planning ministries to undertake cultural needs assessment and train personnel; and development of tools for analyzing the economic impact of culture and evaluate cultural inputs and outputs in programs and project management. The proposed center could also assist in the establishment of sociocultural evaluation units in appropriate ministries in order to ensure that development policies, programs, and projects are culturally examined. Such units would be managed by coordinators who would rely on panels of experts mostly drawn from among the local population. Similarly, project funders could consider recommending new guidelines requiring that each proposal contain clear cultural analysis statements in order to be considered.

An African Fund for Arts and Culture

Regardless of the existence of rich artistic and cultural traditions and the political will to bring culture to the center of development strategies, the creation of space and opportunities for research, production, dissemination, and utilization of cultural knowledge, as well as broader public participation in cultural life in Africa, has often been hampered by the lack of adequate funding to implement appropriate strategies or even to sustain the few existing initiatives.

This is also why it is hereby suggested that a fund for the promotion of the arts and culture be instituted at the regional or continent level to support both human and institutional capacity building for cultural development. The proposed structure could function as a grant-generating entity for a number of targeted activities. Such activities could include grants, fellowships, and scholarships to artists and researchers; support for festivals, inter-African cultural exchange programs, arts and humanities residency sites, arts exhibitions, and publications. Institutional support could also include the creation and/or rehabilitation of centers of excellence, regional facilities of education, training, and research in order to upgrade the professionalism and skills of African artists and researchers in all areas related to their profession. Similarly, funds could also be used for networking and advocacy activities to be undertaken to link and to improve channels of communication between artists, humanists, policymakers, and donors.

There is no doubt that appropriate funding for these activities would raise consciousness on the transformative potentials of the arts and humanities in facilitating not only the process of building bridges of understanding across ethnic and linguistic boundaries but also that of shaping the overall development process in Africa.

Network of Donors, Policymakers, and Cultural Practitioners

Recognizing the current critical need for improved lines of communication among donors, policymakers, and doers who are probing new opportunities for partnerships, the establishment of a consortium of donors and policymakers or a network of those interested in promoting African cultural activities could be considered as a crucial step toward this end. Since the lack of dialogue among the donor community has led to the often unproductive, and at times unnecessary, duplication of projects on the ground, and decreased the effectiveness of their efforts, the establishment of the proposed consortium or network would increase the effectiveness and efficiency of donor assistance toward promoting cultural development in Africa by encouraging collaboration.

Much in the way that APNET has enhanced communication among donors and actors in this field, the group could be expanded to include donors present at the 1995 Bellagio Conference on African Culture and Development to constitute a large body that would address broader African cultural funding challenges. What is being proposed here is the design of an organizational framework for donor coordination that could function as does the Association for the Development of African Education, or along the lines of other models yet to be identified. This international network, which should be based in Africa, could serve as a forum for policy dialogue, and an exchange of information for cultural capacity building. Such a task force could be formed to work on details such as a mission statement, mode of operation, secretariat, memberships, and so forth.

CONCLUSION

In this essay, an attempt was made to show that the lack of capacity among African cultural institutions is due to several macro- and microlevel constraints that prevent them from participating in the development process of the continent. It was also argued that there are several opportunities that could be seized upon to build the institutional and human capacity for cultural development on the continent. General strategies related to institutional and human capacity building were briefly suggested and an action agenda proposed. This agenda calls for the establishment of a coordinating body that could be called African Center for Culture and Development, which would not only tackle critical and priority problems related to arts and humanities capacity building, but also serve as a research center for culture and development. The proposed center could also serve as a secretariat for networks of artists, researchers, development practitioners, and donors. Since the funding of cultural activities receives the least attention within both national and international development agencies, it was hoped that the 1995 Bellagio meeting would offer an opportunity to explore the possibility of designing and implementing a new strat-

egy aimed at identifying, mobilizing, and deploying necessary
funds for cultural activities. It is in this context that the creation of
a fund for African arts and culture has been proposed.

What is equally critical to the development of a coherent funding strategy for cultural activities in Africa is the need for collaboration and partnerships among donors. Thus it has been proposed
that a consortium of donors supporting African cultural activities
be created. By strategically implementing the above suggestions,
donors would certainly increase the effectiveness of their support
to viable cultural institutions and activities capable of promoting
a new approach to development that respects the rich diversity of
human societies and cultures and searches for sustainable development through participation and democracy in the form most
appropriate to any given society. It is from this perspective that
African arts and humanities capacity-building strategies might
enable culture to fulfill its two main contributions to development:
promoting an understanding of how best to secure creation of and
adaptation to technological forms of development; and shaping
its own destiny—with regard to identities, social cohesion, group
aspirations, personal well-being and satisfaction.[8]

NOTES

1. International Meeting on the State of Arts and Humanities in
   Africa, Nairobi, Kenya, November 29–December 1, 1994.
2. These include meetings organized by the Swedish International
   Development Authority (Stockholm, 1991), UNESCO (Paris,
   1991; Abidjan, 1993; and Harare, 1994), and the World Bank
   (Washington, D.C., 1992).
3. James S. Coleman, "The Resurrection of Political Economy,"
   Mawazo 1 (June 1967).
4. Joel Samuels, "An Enabling Environment for Capacity Building," *Building Capacity* 2, 1 (October 1994).
5. Malika Horchani-Zamiti, "Contributions des sciences humaines
   et sociales aux transformations economiques et sociales au
   Maghreb" (paper presented at the International Conference on
   the State of Arts and Humanities in Africa, Nairobi, November
   29–December 1, 1994).
6. Some of these strategies are currently being implemented by
   the African Capacity Building Foundation (ACBF) in the area of

policy analysis and development management. For more de-
tails, see the World Bank, *The African Capacity Building Initiative:
Toward Improved Policy Analysis and Development Management*
(Washington, D.C.: World Bank, 1991).

7. The Language and Culture Institute of the University of Pittsburgh used to run short-term international training courses on
the management of cultural institutions.

8. It is this emphasis on culture that has led the Rockefeller Foundation to establish an arts and humanities field office in Africa.
Culture permits concentration on some of the most positive
things Africa has to offer. Rather than always treating the continent as a source of problems and disasters, cultural programming facilitates building on strength and releases underutilized
talent.

CHAPTER 3

The Modernist Experience in African Art: Toward a Critical Understanding

Salah M. Hassan

INTRODUCTION

Today, there is hardly anybody who would deny the relevance of culture to development and the need to emphasize cultural processes and parameters in analyzing Africa's economic problems and political crises. The two concepts, "culture" and "development," which have obviously been separated analytically, are now being reconciled through the relatively novel notions of "cultural development" or "cultural dimensions of development." However, such realization is far from being seriously considered among Western-oriented donors involved in development issues in Africa. This was partially due to predominant profit-seeking, market-oriented capitalist models of economic development, and to equally pervasive Eurocentric models and ideas of progress that resulted in transplanting Western economic, technological, and cultural models (socialist or capitalist) onto African soil with no consideration of relevancy regarding cultural or social issues or the importance of African culture for its own sake.

Back in my native country, Sudan, more than ten years ago, I vividly recall being excluded from an American scholarship program—sponsored by the U.S. Agency for International Development (AID) and targeted for African students wishing to do postgraduate studies in the United States—after I had satisfied all the academic requirements to qualify for it. The reason given was that African art history, the field I wished to major in, was not a "developmental area"; that is to say, studying art history and other humanities fields was not relevant to development in Africa—in view of the primary objectives of the AID programs in Africa. Having succeeded through a program other than the AID scholarship to come to the United States and to study and develop an expertise in the field I wished to study, I for one should be more than pleased to see a shift in perception of culture vis-à-vis development and to see a genuine change in attitudes on such issues.

When approached to present a state-of-the-art paper on my area of interest, which is African art and visual culture, for a conference of "Donors Interested in Culture and Development in Africa," I thought about what to say that would go beyond the relevancy of culture to development—as the very idea of the conference is predicated on the widening acceptability of that proposition. It is easy to sit down and compile a list of recommendations or plan of action in the African visual arts for donors engaged in culture and development in Africa, which is what I initially contemplated doing.

Reflecting on my own experience of teaching and living in the West for more than a decade, I find this to be less crucial if the objective of the conference is to develop a genuine interest in cultural development itself in Africa, and to move beyond the model of "culture's" relevancy to economic development per se. On a day-to-day basis, whether teaching or engaged in an African art-related project in museums or other cultural arenas and institutions, I often find myself struggling with deeply entrenched Western stereotypes and misconceptions about African arts and African culture in general. Moreover, I have come to realize that contemporary deveopments in African arts and culture have been profoundly misunderstood even among the most liberal scholars, students, and art specialists in the West. Contemporary African cultural forms (mostly perceived as those forms produced during the colonial and postcolonial period) are often regarded as second-rate and second-hand distorted copies of their Western counterparts. The colonial experience is often regarded as detrimental to the fate of Africa's "authentic" classical and traditional arts. Modernization, often perceived as Westernization, is believed to have led to the near extinction of Africa's great traditions in the arts. Such perceptions, distorted and based on misconceived ideas about the nature of the contemporary experience in African arts, have led to an emphasis on preservation and conservation of cultural and artistic forms deemed to be classic and traditional and of historical value within the few programs and initiatives of cultural development in Africa. The contemporary forms, especially in the visual arts, continue to be underestimated and neglected, with no serious efforts to study, collect, stage, or exhibit them.

For the above reasons, I chose to provide a critical look at the contemporary experience in African art, focusing on the modernist experience in African art and related issues. I thought it would be more beneficial to donors and cultural workers in Africa to be familiarized with theoretical issues at the heart of contemporary African culture, in the hope of providing a better vision for engagement in such a field. Better insight into cultural development requires a critical understanding of the field in question. Realizing the need for practical solutions that in the end will enhance the theoretical debate, I opted to provide in a separate appendix a list of specific suggestions and recommendations that may be useful to donors and cultural workers interested in the visual arts in Africa.

AFRICAN ART: THE FIELD AND ITS BOUNDARIES

To this day, the study of African art has remained largely a Western discipline. The scholarship on African art has been the product of Western sensibility and an expression of Western aesthetic responses to African visual culture. This should partially explain the disparity between African art in written texts and African art in reality.[1] As argued by Jan Vansina, "African art" is usually the label given to the visual arts of people south of the Sahara, and in particular those of western and central Africa.[2] Perceived to be authentically less "African," Northern Africa—almost half of the continent including Egypt—has been excluded from the discourse on traditional African art history.[3] Moreover, students of African art have focused primarily on the sculpted form and its aesthetic appeal to the neglect of other forms. Even when more serious students turned to the study of style and cultural and social contexts of African art forms, they have focused primarily on the description of the function and uses of objects in an ethnographic context. Hence, their written texts, often presented in a typical "ethnographic present" mode, have expressed no concern for history, time scale, or change in African art.

It is this approach to African art and creativity that has evolved into what Sidney Kasfir has called the "one tribe/one style"—a paradigm and a model theory that has dominated African art studies to date.[4] It is also due to this approach that African art, mostly presented as traditional masks and wooden sculpted figures, has been perceived as a product of a universal unchanging "tribal" essence and communal sensibility, within which the creative individual remains largely anonymous and in fact less important. Moreover, reading a text on African art or seeing a display of African objects in museums or galleries, one gets the impression that "creativity in Africa had been frozen after some genesis when the known type of icons were crafted by the hands of some hero of a founding myth."[5] In other words, not only have scholars of African art primarily focused on the sculpted form of certain regions, but they have egregiously neglected the contemporary experience in African art and its implications.

Of all the categories of African art, modern art, especially that of Western-trained artists, has received the least attention from art historians and other scholars of African art.[6] This is evident in the few existing exhibitions and publications on the subject, which in turn impacts the field of African art negatively. Most exhibitions and publications were dedicated to traditional and so-called "classical" African art forms to the neglect of the modern ones. Of the intermittent and sparse exhibitions of contemporary African art, mounted in Europe and North America or even in Africa between the 1960s and 1980s, few provided critical analysis of art works or their historical and sociocultural contexts. The majority of exhibitions were mounted with poor documentation, if they were documented at all. Most Western museums still refuse to acquire or exhibit contemporary African works because they do not fit in or measure up to stereotyped standards of African art. Even after some Western museums changed their collection and acquisition strategies, making room for contemporary African or other Third World art, the policy became: "only as long as the contemporary art of a region bears some relation to the 'traditional' art."[7] The works of many contemporary artists from Africa and other parts of the Third World are still dismissed by many museums, galleries, and art experts in Europe and the United States as second-rate. According to Wolfgang Bender, a European museum official made the following statement, when referring to contemporary non-Western art:

It seems like third-rate artwork to us because the art presented here emulates the Western tradition—this is a criterion for selection, and because it is always lagging behind—regardless of how commendable the efforts might be basically. Every comparison with the present international art scene is therefore not in its favor. It cannot escape the critical eye of the Western art world, thus it is superfluous—if I might put it so bluntly, it is an open secret that museums have always refused to take over such displays and always managed to find a new excuse and friendly reasons to dismiss them courteously and painlessly.[8]

However, one should acknowledge an increasing interest in contemporary African art in terms of exhibitions and publications, the latest being the exhibitions and their companion volumes organized by the Center for African Art in New York (now the Museum for African Art), the Studio Museum in Harlem, New York and, most recently, the current exhibition of works by Amir Nour and Mohammed Omer Khalil at the National Museum of African Art, Washington, D.C. The anticipated Africa 95 Festival of African Arts in London has given appropriate weight to modern artistic expression within its programming. In comparison to other international bienniales, the recently initiated Johannesburg Biennale of International Contemporary Art has accorded modern African art the equal status it deserves. This should definitely be saluted as an encouraging departure from the traditional approach to African art.[9]

The following pages provide a historical and critical analysis of the modernist experience in African art. This should help in understanding and appreciating the work produced by African artists today in Africa or in their diaspora in Western centers of modernism. With the growing interest in contemporary African art forms that has been evident in the last decade, it is imperative to provide a critical evaluation of the approaches followed thus far in studying these forms, especially those of the modern African artists. In addition, the field of African art in general requires new frameworks for understanding its forms and the aesthetics that engender them. To achieve this goal, it is important first to investigate the relative neglect of *contemporary* forms of African art within art history and other fields of inquiry that have included the study of African arts.

THE MODERNIST EXPERIENCE IN AFRICAN ART

Today, the story of European artists—Braque, Klee, Leger, Picasso—seeking inspiration from African and other non-Western artistic traditions is well known. In contrast, not as much is known of African artists' journeys into Western centers of modernism, journeys that exemplify a construct Ali Mazrui has often designated as "counterpenetration." Not only have African artists lived or been living in Western centers of artistic production, but they have also been in the forefront of contribution to modernism and even "postmodernism." Informed by their artists' own past and present predicaments, these works express differing approaches to modernity, various responses to colonialism and postcolonialism, and persistent resistance to Western hegemony. Moreover, the history of modernism, solely from a Western perspective, tends to exclude from its recognition not only the fact of plurality of cultures, but any objects of "high" culture produced *by* the "other" as well.[10]

To be sure, the history of modern expression defined by Western standards is relatively short in Africa and differs from one part of the continent to the other. But three factors provide important connections. One is the rise of European and Western patronage and intervention. This was characterized by the establishment of art workshops by European expatriates, mostly colonial administrators, liberal colonial educators, or missionaries.[11] A second and related factor is the establishment of formal art schools and academies, often fashioned on the Western art-educational model, which can be traced to the 1940s or later. Third, and most important, is the nationalistic cultural resurgence that swept many newly independent African countries, where government patronage and interest in the arts became part of building—in some cases inventing—a "national culture" and identity.[12] In the 1970s and 1980s, new African art movements and initiatives emerged either in reaction to or as a rejection of Western schooling in art offered through workshop and art academies in Africa or acquired by travel to study in the West. The basic quest of these new movements and initiatives has been to establish a more culturally rooted, self-conscious, and "African" aesthetic expression. Rejecting the homogenizing effect of Western cultural imperialism, especially its neo-primitivizing and exoticizing tendencies, African artists have repositioned themselves as creators of an autonomous, more global art. The net result has been the creation of new African artists, art movements, and art associations and festivals, all attempting to construct new tropes of self-representation. Today, a myriad of Western and "traditional" African influences have been synthesized and continue to be used within a modern idiom in African art.

It has been argued that the neglect of contemporary forms in African art is due to the preoccupation of Africanists with "traditional" art forms, or so-called "indigenous" and "authentic" art. Yet, in reality this neglect has been caused primarily by the widespread misconception that contemporary African culture is a distorted copy of Western culture, and therefore lacks authenticity. Contact with Western culture is seen as a source of decay—indeed, the extinction—of Africa's great traditional arts. Within this context, contemporary African artistic expressions are perceived as mere imitations of their Western counterparts. Consequently, contemporary art forms have been excluded from the ongoing discourse of art history in Africa.

Although slavery, colonialism, and postcolonial conditions in Africa have disrupted cultures rich in the visual arts, religions, oral traditions, and social and political formations, this disruption was not complete, especially in the artistic and creative domains. A serious look at the contemporary African art scene contradicts assumptions about its authenticity and creative essence. Recent scholarship on contemporary African culture has demonstrated that Africa's encounter with the West has been far more complex than previously thought. In the realm of art, as argued by Susan Vogel, African assimilation of Western techniques, materials, ideas, and forms has been creative, selective, meaningful, and highly original.[13] It has resulted in a continuous recreation of forms and styles. In short, Africa's creative impulses remain alive and continue to contribute great works of literature and masterpieces of visual and performing arts to the world cultural scene.

DEFINING THE FIELD: A PROBLEM OF TERMINOLOGY

Most current scholarship on African art pioneered by scholars and patrons of Western-trained artists in Africa[14] has adopted a Manichaean scheme and continued to define "contemporary" African art within the same parameters set by Ulli Beier.[15] Like modern art elsewhere, "contemporary" African art—meaning art of Western-trained artists—is recognized as individualistically oriented rather than communally centered.[16] It is also perceived as less subservient to dominant socioreligious structures than "traditional" art forms. In other words, "contemporary" art becomes a category reserved for works of those African artists who are mostly urban based, who produce work according to the norms of Western modern art, and who exhibit in galleries, museums, first-class hotels, or foreign cultural centers.[17] These artists are to some extent internationally known, and their patrons include their governments and related institutions, foreign expatriates, and a largely Western-educated native bourgeoisie. Works produced by this category of artists are classified as "elite," "fine," or "high"—as opposed to other forms referred to as "traditional," "tourist," "commercial," or "popular." Considered more intellectual, this fine or high art is contrasted to "traditional" art as a totally separate entity. In this scheme, traditional arts are perceived as consensual, communally based, and created according to rigid and unchanging conventions. Today, few accept the characterization of "traditional" art as representing societies that are unchanging, static, closed, or village-based as argued by Beier.[18] Recent scholarship on the "traditional" art of Africa has clearly demonstrated that it is as intellectual as the work of Western-educated artists. Such a dichotomy—problematic, simplistic, and ahistorical—is inadequate for the study of contemporary African art. This dichotomy—traditional versus contemporary—is created by the colonizing structure in Africa, and it is equally rooted in the epistemological origins of African art scholarship, which is basically Eurocentric.[19] Any serious effort to define contemporary African art forms must start by examining this dichotomy and its validity.

"TRADITIONAL/CONTEMPORARY": THE DICHOTOMY AND ITS IMPLICATIONS

The confusing implications of "traditional versus modern or contemporary" arts can best be explored by raising several related questions. How, for example, can we classify as "traditional" forms of African art that continue to be produced presently in Africa? Are they not "contemporary" art too? The usual dichotomy creates an illusion that forms of African art designated "traditional," or studied as such, are artifacts of the past, although in reality traditional forms of art continue to be produced today within the burgeoning urban as well as rural sectors of Africa. Another methodological question that arises is how to classify these "current" traditional forms? Is the designation "neo-traditional" critical enough to distinguish such forms from either the "plain traditional" or the new art of the educated elites? Still more relevant is the paradoxical realization that so-called "contemporary" art has in fact been in existence for more than a half century—that is to say, since at least the 1920s, if we accept the proposition that the genesis of contemporary art forms was associated with the second decade of colonial rule. Is not that sufficient time to label these forms "traditional" in the original sense of the word or enough time to establish a "tradition"? Or, as some would have it, are "traditions" more often than not actually "invented"?

Recently, categories such as "international," "self-taught," "studio trained," "popular," "tourist," "commercially oriented," and so forth have been proposed to distinguish among the different types of contemporary African artists.[20] Such classifications cannot withstand rigorous analysis and prove problematic when tested against the realities of the contemporary art scene in Africa. As new propositions, they represent old wine in new bottles. African art forms are still subjected to a static system of classification and are perceived to exist outside history.

The predominance of this dichotomy in the field of African art, despite the clear contradictions and paradoxes it entails, is partially due to *an outdated sense* of terms such as "tradition," "authenticity," and "originality." In recent scholarship, the concept of "tradition" is no longer viewed in a "naturalistic" sense as it had been previously. Many students of culture and society have concluded that tradition is no longer an "authentic" body of knowledge handed down from one generation to another with only minor alterations due to the malfunctioning of memory or skill.[21] It has been recognized that society does not treat tradition passively. It often creates its own traditions through the selection of certain historical events and heroes and even through invented pasts.[22] Although the past is a powerful authority in culture, human societies selectively add to the past, subtract from it, or mold it in their own images. The notion of tradition should be rooted in social life rather than in time alone, and tradition should not be used simply as a naming of objects, but also and more fundamentally as a naming process. As noted by Dan Ben-Amos, "the process is no longer the process of delivery, or handing down of themes, symbols or forms, but of selecting and constructing a narrative that would become part of a canon, projected into the present and from an imagined or real past."[23] Hence authenticity is no longer the quest for basic essence of tradition or traditionality. Accordingly, what makes a certain artifact or cultural item "African" or "non-African" is to a great extent dependent on how the Africans themselves perceive it.

The recent debates in anthropology and in other even more emergent fields have challenged conventional ways of perceiving "tradition" and "authenticity." As James Clifford has pointed out, new definitions of authenticity (cultural, personal, artistic) are making themselves felt, definitions no longer centered on a salvaged past.[24] Rather, authenticity is reconceived as hybrid, creative activity in a local present-becoming-future. Non-Western cultural and artistic works are implicated by an interconnected world cultural system without necessarily being swamped by it. Authenticity in that sense is something produced, not salvaged.

Despite newly critical perceptions of notions such as "authentic," "traditions," and the like, that dichotomy still persists in areas of inquiry related to African culture, art, and history. The origin of this dichotomy lies in the unique history of the African continent characterized by two of the most tragic episodes in the history of humanity—slavery and colonialism. As argued by V. Y. Mudimbe, the colonizing structure has resulted in a dichotomizing system with a great number of paradigmatic oppositions: "traditional versus modern; oral versus written and printed; agrarian and customary communities versus urban and industrialized civilizations; subsistence economies versus highly productive economies."[25] It is important to notice that "modernity" itself is a European construct that was articulated initially and most forcefully at the same time "traditional" Africa was being colonized.

In contemporary scholarship on Africa, so much emphasis has been put on the transition from traditional to modern that the paradigm has become misleading. Between the two extremes there is, as Mudimbe has argued, an intermediate diffused space in which social and economic events define the extent of marginality. It is the nature of this space that calls into question the dominant perception in contemporary scholarship on Africa.

It can be argued here that this condition, at least on the theoretical level, has been in part a consequence of the anthropological discourse—a discourse in which an explicit political power was endowed with authority over a scientific knowledge and vice versa.[26] Anthropology, as characterized recently, is a dialogue or (more accurately) a monologue between the presumed cultural "self" and the ethnographic "other." The "other" is perceived here as static, nonchanging, and ahistorical, while the "self" is viewed as universal, dynamic, changing, and historical.

An alternative model for understanding and defining "contemporary" African art, and in fact all other forms of African art, is urgently needed. Within this model, African art forms must be perceived as expressions of a more complex African reality. Within this reality these forms can be seen as existing in one contemporary space and interacting with each other in a "dialogic" manner. Invoking the Bakhtinian concepts of "intertextuality" and "dialogic" principle in relation to the study of literary genre, this dialogic relationship is assumed to exist on temporal as well as spatial and historical levels.

Crucial to this alternative model will be the investigation of the relationship between the artist, his/her art work or product, and the audience or patrons (respectively, "makers," "objects," and "users" or "consumers")—that is, the "social relations of intellectual production" within each art form or tradition. It has been said that African art should be viewed as "a complex process in which society articulates and communicates its consciousness of its origins, its past and its present predicament."[27] Hence, the production of African art is viewed as a complex process in which artists, audiences, or critics communicate and articulate their consciousness, aesthetic values, and judgments.

In that sense we can avoid the "contrastive" manner, by which genres or art forms are defined as separate categories in terms of what they are or what they are not. Hence, each category is defined as a basic relation of intellectual production, which governs the relationship between elements of the creative artistic process, which in turn can be viewed as a communicative process. In any case, all categories must be examined carefully before being applied to the African situation.[28] Further, these categories should be understood as analytical categories constructed by scholars for organizing their material or texts. They may or may not be incongruent in relation to the culturally based ones (or let us say "ethnic genres," using the language of the folklorists), namely those in the mind of the actual creators (artists and audience) of the art object itself.

TOWARD A GENUINE AFRICAN MODERNITY

The search for a new identity expressed in modern forms has been the common denominator of most contemporary art movements in Africa. It is a goal most African artists trained in the Western tradition have shared. Despite the postcolonial aspirations among non-Western nations and neocolonial ambitions of capitalism, which brought new conflicts and challenges to modernism, modernism remains a basic issue of debate for the "other." This should not be interpreted as a "passive" reception of foreign influences by African people, for Africans (like other non-Western people) have long been questioning as well as resisting such Western domination.

Such a quest for modernity as an attitude among African artists is reflected in a statement by Amir Nour, the Sudanese-born sculptor whose works were recently featured in an exhibition at the National Museum of African Art:

> There is nothing wrong with using technology; we need it. But the forms have to come from within the society itself—from the tradition and background we have. . . . You can't have a culture isolated from the rest of the world. Cultures have always developed by being fertilized by new elements from other cultures. I mean the whole modern art movement came about because some (European) artists saw African art. And yet Moore, Picasso, Modigiliani are never labeled Africanist, as I am labeled Western.[29]

Mohammed O. Khalil, another Sudanese who has lived and worked in New York City since 1967 (featured in the same recent exhibition with Nour at the National Museum of African Art), considers his work an embodiment of all his individual experiences as a human being and as an African living in New York. As he asserts, "my roots are as close to me as my limbs." Yet, he prefers to follow his own private creative intuitions rather than deliberately to portray elements of his African heritage. Khalil perceives his art as part of the past—indeed a continuation of it—but he also affirms that there are many other influences on him, and that they are part of all of us as human beings. Khalil and Nour's views echo an early assertion of many modern African artists of their right to use all the sources and mediums available to them and have thus defied and subverted an expectation that their art should look a certain way.

The failure to recognize the above dialogue, despite the statements articulated by African artists, is due to the prevailing dichotomies of "modern/traditional," or "Western modern/non-

Western traditional," and all their implications explained above. It is the failure to recognize that long ago Africans and other Third World people entered the dialogue on modernism and have challenged it on their own soil.[30] Hence, despite recent negative connotations associated with the term "modern" in Western intellectual circles, the term "modern" is more suitable for such new African artistic expressions, because it symbolizes the experience and practices the art forms embody. To call them "modern" distinguishes them from the merely "contemporary"; for where the contemporary refers to time, the modern refers to sensibility and style, and where the contemporary is a term of neutral reference, the modern is a term of critical judgment. Moreover, modernism in the African context, as it is elsewhere, entails a self-conscious attempt to break with the past and a search for new forms of expression.

However, in defining the identity of this new art we find differing perspectives and trends among the artists. Without simplification of a rather complex process, a number of trends and perspectives can be delineated.[31] First, there are artists who advocate rejection of Western influences and a return to traditional sources. Second, we find artists whose works incorporate the latest styles, trends, and techniques of contemporary Western art and who have thus become objects of criticism for rejecting their traditional culture and heritage. There are also artists who advocate in their work a synthesis between traditional heritage and modern Western art and techniques. Viewing these perspectives as part of a dialectically related process, we find that the central matters of contestation have been: how "African" are these new forms of art? To what extent has the exposure to Western art forms and ideas tainted the "Africanness" of these new art forms?

Many scholars of contemporary African art have been quick to justify the preoccupation of modern African artists with the "Africanness" of their work as a reaction to the crisis of identity those artists are facing as products of Western educational systems. In a sense, these scholars have so far dealt with the symptoms but not the causes. What they have failed to explain is why such issues have occupied a central place in the ongoing debate on modern African art.

WHO IS THE MODERN AFRICAN ARTIST?

The majority of modern artists in Africa belong to the first or second generation of a Western-educated elite class that emerged in many African countries after the second decade of colonial rule. That group was a minority—even today—due to the limited education made available by the colonials. Many of these elites lived in colonial or postcolonial capitals and urban centers and experienced the influence of the colonial power's culture—an influence that was almost nil beyond the urban centers. Historically, this new class felt its "marginal" situation—that is, found itself caught in the middle between the masses of urban and rural workers or farmers whose culture and identity are kept intact, and their own aspiration to a way of life similar to the colonial, foreign ruling class. They were prisoners of the contradictions in the social and cultural reality they inhabited. That "marginality," as explained by Amilcar Cabral, constitutes "the socio-cultural drama" of the colonial elites or native "petty bourgeoisie."[32] Against such a background—the basic aim, under colonial rule, to destroy the native's culture, and to assimilate the rising minority "lower middle class" into its own culture—this new group or class gradually became aware of its "marginal" situation. In reaction to that situation, the "return-to-the-source" or other native intellectual movements began redefining (African) "identity." We should note here that "return-to-the-source" movements in the realm of art and literature, or the intellectual reaction to the colonial situation in general, do not reflect an even and unified process. This process ranges from total rejection of and resistance to the Western "colonial" culture or rule, to advocacy of a synthesis of the native culture and Western elements.

The development of a modern idiom in African art is closely linked to modern Africa's search for identity. Most of the works of contemporary artists have apparent ties to traditional African folklore, belief systems, and imagery. The only way to interpret or understand the work of those artists is in the light of the "dual" experience of colonialism and assimilation into Western culture in Africa. Their work reflects that urge and desire: the search for a new identity. This can be seen in the works of many artists who emphasized the use of local materials, techniques, tools, or colors despite varying content; it can also be seen in those artists who have shown a preference for urban or rural genre scenes. Likewise, it can be observed in some artists' uses of motifs and decorative elements borrowed from their countries' ancient, folk or "traditional" arts and crafts.

In nearly all of his writings and public statements about his art, the Sudanese painter Ibrahim al-Salahi has stressed his goal of keeping "Sudanese" motifs in his art—even if its technique may be basically Western. Al-Salahi, who studied at the Slade Art School in London in the late 1950s and early 1960s, found, upon his return from England, that many of the ideas he had acquired from abroad isolated him in his own country and that his work seemed meaningless and without character in Khartoum.[33] Salahi summed up his experience and, to a greater extent, the experience of most modern African artists, in the following statement:

> I left Sudan and came back, then suddenly I started to look around and I started to look for things, for patterns. I have always been fascinated with patterns in local Sudanese handicrafts and what simple peasants were doing and carving and decorating and painting. And suddenly I think that the beauty of it came to me and hit me—it's so strong. I lived with it all my life and yet I never saw it before, until I went outside and came back, with a different outlook towards things. And this is when I started looking—just traveling all over the Sudan and looking at whatever people did—at their homes, their beds, the praying carpets, the way they put the saddles on their camels or oxen. And this fascinated me a great deal and I started just to observe and to draw. But although I said my painting now seems Sudanese in locality, in flavor, I don't deal with it in terms of locality—that it should be Sudanese art, there is no such a thing as Sudanese art. But I mean as a Sudanese individual coming from the Sudan could do something. I find the color in its particular looks very much like our earth, and maybe that's why I feel it's Sudanese.[34]

The Ghanaian artist Al Anatsui's deliberate use of wood burning, a traditionally known technique in African art, to make symbolic political and social statements provides evidence of this urge. Magdoub Rabbah, another Sudanese artist, is known for his use of a technique he termed "solar engraving" to etch beautiful low-relief engravings on hardwood boards mixed with locally made colors and dyes such as henna. Solar engraving is achieved by using commercial lenses to capture the rays of the sun into a single beam to burn the wood surface. Although Rabbah justifies the use of solar engraving, henna, and wood as "a new and cheap source of materials," all the techniques and material he uses can be traced to traditional origins.[35]

Even works of those African artists who most closely conform to norms of the Western artistic tradition reflect a clear relationship to their artistic heritage as Africans. The work of Skunder Boghossian, the Ethiopian artist, for example, should be viewed within such a context. Skunder uses the most diverse techniques and media from Africa and the West to enhance the power of expression in his paintings. His work entitled *Time Cycle II* (1982) offers the finest example of his innovative techniques and media experimentation combining relief with bark cloth (a local African material) and oil color. Skunder's work, vibrant in color and rich with symbols and motifs, synthesizes his country's rich and powerful traditions—wall and scroll paintings and illuminated manuscripts dating back to the eighth century—with European techniques.

To the uncritical eye, the sculpture of Amir Nour may appear nonfigurative and highly abstract. Yet, Nour's work consists of geometric forms, domes, and rectangles drawn from the images of his childhood and youth in the Sudan. These images include domes and arches, cattle horns, calabashes, and sand hills; all are part of the landscape of his homeland, which became part of his aesthetic concern as an artist. These forms are recognizable in Nour's work, especially if one is familiar with the adobe architecture of northern Sudan. In some of his works, the shapes are more formalized and highly abstracted, such as *Grazing at Shendi,* a stainless steel sculpture composed of 202 semicircles of varying sizes. It is a piece inspired by his childhood memories of watching goats grazing on the outskirts of his hometown. Arrangements of the repetitive units suggest the sloping hills and the animals' backs. Repetition of the shapes and the variation in their sizes suggests a sense of distance. The polished surfaces of the units reflect Nour's concern with light in relation to form. A dominant theme in Nour's work has been that of the gourd or calabash, which he later simplified to plain hemispheres. *Expanded Gourd* and *Split Gourd,* as explained by the artist, are two works inspired by his early days while growing up watching calabash artisans in village market places "shining their domed-shaped gourds with animal fat."[36]

The installations of Houria Niati, an Algerian woman artist who has been living and working in London since 1979, shed some light on the untold and complex experience of African artists in their confrontation with the West, in which they sometimes live. Like many other Algerians of her generation, Niati lived part of her childhood under the French occupation toward the end of the war for independence and was a witness to the cruelties of the French and the heroic resistance of the Algerian people. Moving to the West in the late 1970s to study art and later on pursue a career as an artist in London, Niati found herself in another form of confrontation with the West, this time with images of her country and people as fictionalized, exoticized, and constructed by Western artists (orientalist, mostly French painters) in paintings or photographs from the nineteenth century or early part of this century. This new experience plus her complex background as a woman, an Algerian of Arabo-Berber heritage, and Islamic influences are all reflected in her style and the multiple references in her work. Her mixed-media installation entitled *Women of Algiers* was a deconstruction of Delacroix's famous painting of the same title. *Bringing Water from the Fountain Has Nothing Romantic about It* is another installation in which Niati continues to explore the orientalist's constructs of romantic images of Algerian women in popular postcards and photographs from the French colonial period in Algeria. Both installations are composed of series of paintings, mixed with a vibrant environment of sound and color, and accompanied by recitation of expressionistic poetry and performances of song by Niati herself, who was trained as a singer in the Andalusian tradition.

In his recent work, Mohammed Omer Khalil explores more abstract compositions focusing increasingly on issues of light and darkness in addition to color and patterns. The dominant imagery is a combination of transfers of found materials—often stamps, letters, and envelopes with press type—in addition to Khalil's own geometric rendering and patterns. This is clear in Khalil's series of large etchings, *The Bob Dylan Series,* featured in the above-mentioned exhibit, the best example of which is the one titled *Tombstone Blues.*

In conclusion, the style of modern African artists, like their subject matter, is highly heterogeneous and varies according to their artistic and ideological training, and the medium in which they work. Yet, regardless of the differences among their works, these artists share ideological, intellectual, and formal concerns, which they seek to express through consistent and, in fact, related visual devices and vocabularies in terms of style, iconography, symbolism, and technique. Accordingly, we should pay special attention to the vocabulary of visual forms, color, and style used in the works of these artists as well as to the syntax and semantics that order them into final works of art. For in any work of art, ideas and programs are translated into forms, and the quality of those forms determines their effectiveness in transmitting ideas.

It is important to examine new directions in African visual arts, especially the modernist experience. Nigerian artist Bruce Onobrakpeya once asserted that modern African art is "growing in strength, and it has arrived. It is equal to any art being practiced anywhere in the world."[37] It is time to appreciate modern African artistic expression on its own terms. This should be the way to approach the study of contemporary African art forms and the intellectual premise upon which that study should be based.

This approach to African art will offer a fresh look at modernism, and even postmodernism, from an African standpoint, and at issues of cross-cultural and transnational aesthetics. It is important to emphasize the reciprocal flow of influences and traffic that has existed between Africa and the West. This will make it possible to reverse the erroneous perception of unilateral influence, according to which Africa and African art serve as recipients of Western culture and artistic influence, a narrative in which African artists have been projected as passive, silent, and invisible. It is also important to see how African artists have interpreted and translated the aesthetic and social experiences of postcolonial, contemporary Africa into new idioms of artistic expression that are both related to their cultural heritage *and* connected to Western modernism. This will offer new critical perspective on "modernism" as a concept in twentieth-century Western art history, and on cross-cultural aesthetics in general.

The many political and economic problems in Africa have deprived African artists of access to art materials, modern techniques, and facilities such as foundries and print workshops, in addition to venues for exhibiting or marketing their artistic products. To these problems some artists have responded creatively by adopting new formats and using locally found material resulting in products and movements worthy of studying. For the same reasons, many artists have been kept from participation in international exhibitions, publications, and artists' gatherings, thus depriving the art world of their insight and creativity. On the other hand, many of Africa's most talented artists have, voluntarily or involuntarily, been living in major Western metropolises since the early 1940s, and some have even integrated into established African diaspora societies in the United States or Europe. Both groups are crucial to understanding African modernism and its responses to Western culture. Their experiences provide a first-hand look at strategies of negotiations these artists employ in their daily confrontations with persistent borders in an art world that continues to marginalize them, as well as illuminating questions of exile, primitivization, and "otherization" of African artists within the dominant cultural discourse. This is the advantage of such an open-minded approach to the contemporary experience in African art.

Finally, a special emphasis on gender balance would also be crucial to a comprehensive understanding of the contemporary experience in African art. Primarily, this will help redress an egregious imbalance in current rising scholarship on contemporary African artists, which has conspicuously omitted, or only cursorily included, women in favor of an emphasis on male artists. Most important, African women artists living and working in Africa or in the West should be studied to help us understand the dynamic interplay of gender representation and creativity. While acknowledging the problematics of gender-specific representations in the arts, the nature of contemporary gender discourse allows gender as a criterion of representation of artists in written forms or exhibitions. This would not only provide the dynamic interplay of gender and creativity, but also foreground the right of women artists to have an equitable space in a male-dominated scene. It would reaffirm the centrality of African women as creative contributors to their own societies and to the global contemporary cultural scene.

APPENDIX: SUGGESTIONS AND RECOMMENDATIONS

From the outset, I feel the need to emphasize two points in relation to culture and development in Africa. First, the idea of aid for development in Africa has to move from a reliance on models built on a Western sense of "benevolence" or "charity" and on Western ideas of progress that have created dependency, to models that support indigenous and local initiatives and that will create a sustainable development based on capacity building, establishing solid institutions, and a sound infrastructure. Second, development should be tied to African democratization initiatives and respect for human rights in Africa. Donors should support these initiatives by engaging in a dialogue with democratic forces in African societies on issues related to cultural development and making the targeted aid work toward benefiting and facilitating such initiatives in Africa. The following are some suggestions and recommendations that are practical in nature, but rooted in theorizing about the contemporary political and social history of Africa:

Funding and Resources

Enhancing funding and financial resources is a major priority and will certainly lead to more accessibility and dissemination of African artistic products. Shortage of funding and resources available to African artists is symptomatic of deeper levels of crisis in the African continent. African artists and art workers have to move beyond the structures of dependency and domination imposed on them by the heritage of decades of colonial domination and postcolonial oppression.

One suggestion is to develop a practical regional collaboration among African institutions and individuals involved in the arts. This will require a move beyond the limitations of "nation-statism," as suggested by the British progressive scholar Basil Davidson, toward establishing a new form of Pan-Africanism that is realistic and not built on grand illusions or romanticism. Today, many of us Africans are questioning whether the structure of the nation-state, as inherited from the colonial power, is the way for the African continent to move forward. The objective here is to create new regional spaces for art and artists and to pull together resources of art-related institutions already established in one region without building new beaurocratic structures. My suggestion is to establish "regional centers of excellence" in the visual arts and other related areas. These centers can be affiliated with one existing institution or if need be a new one can be built, to serve as centers for study, research, and training in the arts. They can also serve as residency programs for African artists and could provide studio space for work and interaction of the artists with each other. Such centers can also serve as a magnet for repatriating (even on a part-time basis) the African talent exiled or living in the West, who could return to teach, work, and benefit younger rising artists.

African Forums

There is an urgent need for African-based forums in the visual arts. Examples of these forums are conferences, festivals and Pan-African art exhibitions that can serve as platforms for Africans to interact and help create a renaissance of artistic creativity. African visual arts are celebrated more in the West today than in the African continent. African-based platforms such as FESPACO, the Ouagadougou Annual African Film Festival, have proven to be beneficial to African filmmakers and scholars to meet, interact, and show their work. Other African visual artists need a similar platform. The First Johannesburg Bienniale might have been an interesting beginning if had not started out on the wrong footing, focusing more on the international than the regional or African.

Research and Training

The need to encourage research and training in the area of the visual arts within the continent should also be a priority. A lot needs to be accomplished in this area; however, my ultimate objective is to encourage research, documentation, and theorizing by Africans in a field that has been predominantly Western controlled. This will enable more Africans to take control over the discourse about their own history, culture, and arts. If we accept decolonization of knowledge as the first step toward real liberation, the necessary response starts right at this level. This can be achieved through different means. Examples are the building of art institutions engaged in researching African visual arts and the encouraging publication of periodicals and other forums focusing on the field.

Institutions

Encouraging local initiatives in developing and rebuilding established museums, galleries, and other art-related institutions should be a funding priority. There is also a need for creating new art museums, galleries that cater to the new arts and genres in terms of collection, documentation, and dissemination.

Artists Cooperatives

Encouraging establishment of cooperatives of women and men in the folk arts and utilitarian arts that have been traditionally oriented could help in reviving the gradually disappearing rural economic sector and small craft industries, in the face of capitalist market-oriented schemes of development. This could become a source of empowerment for local artists catering to a growing market for African popular and folk arts related to the tourist industry in Africa, and could help avoid the rampant exploitation of their labor by local middlemen and Western art dealers. There are already interesting models from Nigeria and Zimbabwe from which to draw lessons.

NOTES

1. These "texts" consist mostly of coffee-table-type books illustrated with beautiful photographs of art works, printed on
   glossy paper, with short and largely descriptive commentary.
2. Jan Vansina, *Art History in Africa: An Introduction to a Method*
   (London: Longman, 1984).
3. I should add in this regard that the debate on Egypt and its
   exclusion within African art studies is more complex and not
   just a product of the artificial separation between North and
   sub-Saharan Africa within African art studies. As it is contested
   today, the separation of Egypt from the rest of Africa and the
   predominant assumptions of the origins of its ancient civilization as non-African could be attributed to several factors. This
   was largely a product of the mid-nineteenth century
   Eurocentric negative notions about African people and their
   intellectual abilities and cultures, related to the rise of colonialism.
4. Sidney L. Kasfir, "One Tribe, One Style? Paradigms in the His-
   toriography of African Art," *History in Africa* 1 (1984):163–93.
5. Vansina, *Art History in Africa*, 4.
6. Among the few existing valuable works on contemporary African arts we can count Ulli Beier, *Contemporary Art in Africa*
   (London: Pall Mall Press, 1968); *Contemporary African Art* (catalog of an exhibition at the Camden Art Centre, London) (London: Studio International, London and Africana Publishing,
   1970); Dennis Duerden, *The Invisible Present: African Art and
   Literature* (New York: Harper & Row, 1975); Kojo Fosu, *20th
   Century Art of Africa* (Zaria, Nigeria: Gaskiya Press, 1986);
   Marshall Ward Mount, *African Art: The Years since 1920*
   (Bloomington: Indiana University Press, 1973); Judith von D.
   Miller, *Art in East Africa: A Guide to Contemporary Art* (London:
   Frederick Mueller, 1975); Maude Wahlman, *Contemporary Af-
   rican Arts* (Chicago: Field Museum of Natural History, 1974);
   Jean Kennedy, *New Currents, Ancient Rivers: Contemporary Af-
   rican Artists in a Generation of Change* (Washington, D.C.:
   Smithsonian Institution Press, 1992); Susan Vogel, ed., *Africa
   Explores: 20th Century African Art* (New York: Center for Afri-
   can Art, 1991); and the Studio Museum in Harlem, *Contemporary African Artists: Changing Traditions* (New York: Studio
   Museum in Harlem, 1990).
7. See Wolfgang Bender, "Modern Art to the Ethnographic Muse-

ums!" in *The Hidden Reality: Three Contemporary Ethiopian Artists*, ed. Elizabeth Biasio (Zurich: Ethnological Museum of the University of Zurich, 1989), 185. He was quoting a statement issued by an ethnographic museum in Berlin regarding its recent policy of acquisition.

8. Ibid.

9. The exhibition, *Africa Explores: 20th Century African Art*, was organized by the Center for African Art in New York and curated by Susan Vogel. For contributions from several scholars in the field of African arts and the humanities, see the large companion volume, Vogel, *Africa Explores*. See also the Studio Museum's exhibition catalog, *Contemporary African Artists: Changing Tradition* and the National Museum of African Art's catalogue, Silvia Williams, *Mohammed Omer Khalil, Etchings, Amir Nour, Sculpture* (Washington, D.C.: National Museum of African Art, 1994).

10. Rashid Araeen, "Our Bauhaus Others' Mudhouse," *Third Text: Third World Perspectives on Contemporary Art and Culture* 6 (1989):3–14.

11. Examples of such workshops are Oshogbo or Mbari Mbayo Club in Nigeria, established by Ulli Beier in the 1960s, and the Frank McEwen's Workshop School and the National Gallery of Salisbury in Zimbabwe (Rhodesia at the time) in 1957. See dele jegede, "African Art Today," in Studio Museum in Harlem, *Contemporary African Artists* and Grace Stanislaus, "Contemporary African Artists: Changing Traditions," in Studio Museum in Harlem, *Contemporary African Artists*. Despite the positive aspects of European patronage and intervention, there is a point of contention in that these were based on hegemonic and paternalistic attitudes toward Africa and African artists. It is important, as jegede has tried, to reexamine the role of the European expatriate in the light of the myth of the "teachers who do not teach." In reality, those European expatriates and teachers intervened by introducing many techniques and styles that are European in origin, and imposed limitations on the creative potential of those early African artists working with them by having certain expectations of their work.

12. However, governmental patronage in Africa soon faded due to growing economic crises and underdevelopment created by continued dependency on Western capitalism, and the rise of neo-colonialism, among many other problems plaguing African countries today.

13. Vogel, *Africa Explores*.
14. See Wahlman, *Contemporary African Arts*; Evelyn S. Brown, *Africa's Contemporary Art and Artists* (New York: Harmon Foundation, 1966); Frank McEwen, *New Art from Rhodesia* (Salisbury, Rhodesia: National Gallery, 1963); and Beier, *Contemporary Art in Africa*.
15. Beier, *Contemporary Art in Africa*.
16. In some cases, "contemporary" has been used indiscriminately to denote a wide range of African art forms—popular, commercial tourist, fine, etc.
17. Foreign cultural centers are normally related to Western countries' embassies, such as the French Cultural Center, the American Center, the British Council. They are known for their calculated involvement in the native cultural affairs of the host countries.
18. Beier, *Contemporary Art in Africa*.
19. I am using "Eurocentrism" in the sense defined by several seminal works that analyze knowledge in relation to power and power differentials. See Edward Said, *Orientalism* (New York: Pantheon, 1974) and Samir Amin, *Eurocentrism* (London: Zed Press, 1989).
20. For samples of such propositions see, Beier, *Contemporary Art in Africa*; Vogel, *Africa Explores*; Fuso, *20th Century Art of Africa*; and Mount, *African Art*.
21. See the comprehensive review of the concept "tradition" in Dan Ben-Amos, "The Seven Strands of Tradition," *Journal of Folklore Research* 21, 2 & 3 (1984):116.
22. Eric Hobsbawm and Terence Ranger, eds., *The Invention of Tradition* (Cambridge: Cambridge University Press, 1983).
23. Ben-Amos, "The Seven Strands of Tradition."
24. James Clifford, "Of Other Peoples: Beyond the Salvage Paradigm," *DIA Foundation Series* 19 (1987).
25. V. Y. Mudimbe, *The Invention of Africa* (Bloomington: Indiana University Press, 1988), 4.
26. James Clifford, "On Ethnographic Authority," *Representations* 1 (1983): 2.
27. Illona Szombatti-Fabian and Johannes Fabian, "Art, History and Society: Popular Painting in Shaba, Zaire," *Studies in Anthropology of Visual Communication* 3, 1 (1976):17.
28. The tripartite scheme, which has long been adopted for European studies of culture, has been uncritically applied by Africanists to African culture. It divides culture into three lay-

ers: "traditional," "popular," and "elite." As Karen Barber has argued, "This simple typology has shown itself remarkably resilient and tenacious. Even when criticized, it has usually managed to resurface amidst a welter of disclaimers and qualifications; but for the most part it has survived by not being criticized, or even examined. It has simply been applied, as if its correspondence to African social reality were self-evident." See Karen Barber, "Popular Arts in Africa," *African Studies Review* 3, 3 (1987):9.

29. Quoted in Kennedy, *New Currents,* 113–14.
30. Rashid Araeen, "Our Bauhaus."
31. jegede, "African Art Today."
32. Amilcar Cabral, "The Role of Culture in the Liberation Struggle," in *Communication and Class Struggle,* ed. A. Malterart and S. Siegelaub, vol. 1 (New York: International General, 1979), 207.
33. Beier, *Contemporary Art in Africa.*
34. "El Salahi: A Painter from the Sudan: Rhythm and Structure of Arabic Alphabet Underlie Most of His Forms," *African Arts* 1, 1 (Autumn 1967):16–26.
35. Solar engraving resembles the hot rod iron engraving technique that is used by African artists in decorating gourds or calabashes. North and East African women use henna for decorating their hands and feet, creating beautiful geometric and abstract patterns.
36. Quoted in Kennedy, *New Currents,* 114.
37. Stanislaus, "Contemporary African Artists: Changing Traditions," 27.

CHAPTER 4

Rebuilding Africa Through Film, Video and Television

Ben Zulu

It is important to be conscious of the value of African cultures in the framework of universal civilisation, but to compare this value with other cultures, not with the view of deciding its superiority or inferiority, but in order to determine, in the general framework of the struggle for progress, what contribution African culture has made and can or must receive from elsewhere.

—Amilcar Cabral[1]

INTRODUCTION

After three to four decades of independence, most African countries are facing the worst social and economic crisis in modern history. Living standards have dropped to the level where life is an unending struggle for survival, filled with suffering and pain. People feel helpless and hopeless; they lack confidence in themselves and in their governments to change the situation. Why have the majority of African countries experienced reversals in social and economic standards of living when other regions of the developing world have registered significant improvements over the same period?

This chapter argues that Africa's development problems have a long history, rooted in the relationships among culture, development, and progress. This essay will specifically argue, first, that slavery, colonialism, and postcolonial governments undermined the development capacities of African cultures; second, that African governments need to restore the development capacity in African cultures; and third, that Africa's communication industries, particularly the production and distribution of African films and videos, can make important contributions to the restoration of the capacity for development in African cultures.

PROGRESS AND DEVELOPMENT IN AFRICAN CULTURE

In this essay, culture is understood to have a developmental capacity only when people who share its norms and values can demonstrate the ability to survive and progress over time. The history of African survival over the last 300 years since the advent of slavery has sufficiently demonstrated the ability of African cultures to survive. However, African cultures have not exhibited the capacity to both survive *and* progress simultaneously. Since progress is a function of development, why is Africa's development stagnant? Before the advent of slavery and colonialism, African cultures developed and progressed over time, meeting the needs of African people within their sociocultural contexts.

Individual members of communities participated jointly in activities that affected the survival of the social system as a whole. All relationships were supportive of one another through systems of mutual obligations and interest. All members of society were, at some point, members of all institutions, and interactions were direct and frequent. Participation in even the simplest ritual was high, and the values and norms of the society as a whole were embedded and reinforced in the relationships among the participants in their various functions. Each member's participation in the activities of the society tended to guarantee the internalization process of the norms, values, symbols, and ideas of society, and therefore, to guarantee the survival of the society.

African cultures perpetuated norms by providing rules that individuals must obey should they wish to remain within the society. These rules were made legitimate and reinforced by physical force or other sociopsychological means such as ostracism, banishment, imprisonment, and economic sanctions. For example, communities refused to help dissident members plant or harvest their crops; youths identified with norms, traditions, and values through their relationships with adults; and political power was controlled through vested interests of the powerful within the community to preserve their power and maintain the status quo.

THE EFFECTS OF COLONIALISM

Slavery initially and colonialism later undermined the ability of African cultures to develop and progress. The basic form of social and economic organization in Africa is the community. Slavery destroyed communities by taking away healthy and productive men and women. Colonialism introduced and established political systems of control, domination, and economic exploitation. These changes fractured what were once resilient traditional cultures and societies. Colonial governments undermined African cultures through education, information, and religion, effectively colonizing the African mind.

The British Colonial Film Unit produced what they called instructional films, intended to raise the primitive African to a higher standard of culture. These films were made for the colonies, with colonialist hegemonic intentions that propounded and ratified imperialist ideas. They were not only paternalistic in nature but recalcitrantly derisive of African culture and traditions. For example, *Daybreak in Udi* (1948) presented Africans in need of civilizing by a white man, who is a British district officer. In *Men of Two Worlds* (1944), the perennial subject of African witchcraft is depicted. In all circumstances, it was customary to elevate British tradition to the status of preternatural creation, as opposed to mysterious Africa, which was depicted as being immersed in superstitious beliefs, fear, and uncertainty.[2]

In addition to education, information, and religion, colonial governments used coercive measures to undermine African communities. In Southern Africa, for example, colonial governments forcibly removed African people from productive ancestral lands to marginal lands, effectively destroying traditional agricultural systems and transforming African people into cheap reserve labor. With the breakdown of traditional agricultural systems, young able-bodied men were forced to spend their productive lives away from their families and communities, working as migrant labor in the mines, farms, or urban areas of the colonial system, extracting African resources.

This migrant system changed the ways in which African social and economic systems functioned. The majority of people lived in labor reserve areas, dependent on the remittances from male relatives who worked as migrant labor. Social roles and relationships, along with the economic organization that had been passed through successive generations, could no longer function. Languages and religions lost their capacity to communicate codes of behavior that would enable African people to adapt to changes in society. As a result, people became disempowered. This is the nature and character of the societies inherited by postcolonial governments at independence.

INDEPENDENCE AND POSTCOLONIAL ATTITUDES

Most early postcolonial African leaders came to power through liberation movements, which influenced how they governed their countries after independence. The early African nationalist leaders who led their countries to independence had fought mainly for "home rule"—in essence, participation by the local population who had been sidelined all through the colonial period, as opposed to government from the metropolitan country. In the period following independence, these leaders enjoyed a position not dissimilar from that of traditional chiefs—benevolent father figures whose wisdom was unquestioned.[3]

Postcolonial governments did not change the existing political structures. They maintained the institutional arrangements inherited from colonial governments. They used the liberation movement doctrines to formulate policies and programs that sought to extend the availability of government services previously denied to African people. Essentially, postcolonial governments wanted their countries to catch up to developed countries. They believed that Western ideas and technologies could easily be transplanted to African countries through a process of acquiring technical expertise, equipment, and training from developed countries. This belief was reinforced by the former colonial governments, who offered aid support.

The postindependence government styles were not fundamentally different from those of colonial governments. A small elite class, including ruling party politicians and powerful state bureaucracies, used methods similar to those of the colonial governments to control and dominate national populations. For example, postcolonial governments acted to marginalize traditional leaders by creating parallel structures of new leaders at the community level. The new leaders were party functionaries hand-picked by the ruling parties and did not have the legitimacy or the respect traditional leaders had enjoyed. By marginalizing the traditional leaders and cultural institutions, African governments unwittingly perpetuated the colonial attitude that African cultures were not compatible with development.

Postcolonial governments nationalized or controlled the media, placing them under the ministries of information or quasi-government organizations. They valued the media only as a provider of basic education and information, mainly serving their perspectives and political interests. As a consequence, the present media content often includes official government information, music and religious programs, and foreign programs. Local programs that confront the truth of African life are conspicuously absent. Democracy, governance, and development did not change in function. At individual and community levels, people did not become empowered and African cultures continued to be marginalized. This point is made well by C. Berne-Tesfu:

> One major obstacle to efforts to install and consolidate democratic systems in Africa is the all-powerful, highly centralised and hierarchical bureaucratic structures. The organisational imperative of the massive bureaucratic machine is to command and control and is preoccupied with its own survival and enrichment. It is not likely that the powerful bureaucracy will abandon its privileged position and control of the state apparatus to democratically elected political leaders or respect the institutional restraints of democratic rule without struggle.[4]

THE MEDIA AND THEIR RELEVANCE FOR DEVELOPMENT

In most African countries, the media represent a lost opportunity to restore a sense of self-awareness among African people. Accurate self-awareness enables a national population to share the languages and values that allow people to "objectively understand the predetermined elements of their existence."[5] With this understanding, people become active and productive members of society, contributing to progress and development.

The failure to restore the functional and dynamic aspects of African cultures has further undermined African people. The energy and spirit that drove the struggle for independence did not transform themselves into a postindependence force to forge new destinies in which African cultures were equal to other cultures of the world. This is a serious setback because the postindependence period served to reinforce the perception that development cannot be rooted in African cultures. Today, African countries are impoverished and so dependent on external assistance that the notion of independence must be redefined:

> Africa, like other Third World countries, now finds itself under a recolonisation process led by the "big three," the United States, Britain and France. This recolonisation is also made possible by the inability of Africa's leaders to question the unconventional wisdom behind Western-imposed austerity measures. The measures, while supposedly aimed at revamping dwindling economies, are counter-productive, and needless to say, have inflicted heavy doses of pain on the Third World populace.[6]

What does independence mean to the general populations of African people whose culture is in need of empowerment? How can development be restored to African cultures? It is not a matter of imitating other people or transplanting ideas and technologies. These approaches have been attempted, with limited success. Development must come from the living experience of a people and be founded on the shared values of the majority population. Development must confront African life in the modern world. African people live in the modern world and want to see progress in the quality of their lives—a progress that is consistent with their values. These values are not simply traditional or conservative; they are shaped by living experiences, education, and information. To bring about progress requires honest and effective communication and reporting.

To bring the majority of African people into the mainstream of development, African governments must transform education and communication into instruments of enlightenment and empowerment that will lead to social and economic progress. The challenge is how to transform African development from a process driven by governments, political elites, and international development agencies into a force motivated by the cultures of the general populations. This approach has been proven to be effective both in the developed countries themselves and in the newly developed countries of Southeast Asia.

Governments in developed countries have clearly articulated policies to support the work done by deserving cultural institutions such as libraries, museums, schools, and universities, and media such as film, video, and television. Cultural institutions support the process of internalization of the norms, values, symbols, and ideas of the society. They socialize people from an early age to appreciate the achievement of economic resources and mobility. Local cultural institutions serve to develop local languages, diffuse facts and ideas, and promote values important to the society. In this way, the dynamism of a culture is created and recreated, giving a culture the capacity "to adapt itself, modify, adjust abruptly, change, remain stationary—in short, permit what is necessary for the survival of its people."[7] The success of the newly industrialized Southeast Asian countries has shown that the empowerment of ordinary people is important to development and progress. The majority of the national populations have made significant social and economic progress, living within the contexts of their sociocultural institutions.

Postcolonial Africa lacks well-functioning cultural institutions to support adaptation of the cultures. What development there is, is conceptualized and driven by norms and values shared by a very small proportion of the national populations. As a result, there are no commonly shared values that engender "consensus for action, and development of knowledge and skills needed to put material investments to the best use."[8] Many African countries have not overcome the colonial legacy of divide and rule. As a result, real and imaginary differences often get in the way of development or, at worst, create a situation in which countries are at war with themselves. A precondition for shared values is the elimination of these differences through strong communication programs.

The realities of the global environment have made education and communication the most important resources in transactions among people, businesses, and nations across the globe. To be effectively marginalized in education and communication means exclusion from meaningful participation in the global economic system, with consequent stagnation of development.[9] It is necessary to find communication methods that will make education and information accessible to African populations. The present communication capacities found in most African countries are grossly inadequate. Most people rely on oral patterns of communication for their education and information, and therefore new ideas and technologies related to development are very slow to spread. This is a weakness of traditional forms of communication. Yet, the postindependence media process information in elitist ways. The levels of literacy and language proficiency assumed do not exist among the general populations of Africa. Systematically, this serves to perpetuate a colonial system that denied African people access to the education and information needed to enlighten and empower people with knowledge of ideas and technologies to stimulate development.

Postcolonial African governments must move away from development policies that effectively perpetuate colonial legacies. People depend on the ability of cultures to change and adapt to the environment without deteriorating in the process. This capacity is directly related to the way in which education and information enlighten and empower people to deal with their problems. The small or nonexistent role played by education and communication in the lives of the majority of people is responsible for the dominance of other cultures in Africa.

There is a real need for African governments to take action to increase the status of African culture. The policy actions of African governments often propagate the notion of an African "culture that thrives on a simple overglorification of the African past."[10] This approach does "not in any way attempt to contribute to the understanding and the struggle to find solutions to contemporary problems facing African societies."[11] African cultures must be perceived and experienced as interesting and relevant to the realities of the contemporary African situation. For this to happen, education and communication must take on an African character. In other words, African people must develop a capacity to assimilate modern ideas and technologies within their own cultural contexts. This means that African languages, norms, values, and spirituality must be the basis for growth and development.

THE STATUS AND CONTROL OF THE MEDIA

Film, video, and television are universally recognized as the main methods for communicating new ideas and technologies today. These media are so powerful and influential that they are considered framers of modern cultures. For example, African youth of today are often described as a lost generation. They identify more with the youth cultures portrayed in foreign films, videos, and television programming than with the cultures of the adult generations. How will young African people survive in a world in which their inspiration comes from non-African cultures, and in which they are merely consumers and not creators of culture. African youth need to establish a strong identification with their own cultures. It is the only basis for long-term survival in a global system that at present keeps the majority of people in the developing world marginalized. African youth can discover the rich, interesting, and exciting aspects of African culture through media such as film, video, and television, which have the potential to express the dynamism of African cultures. African people must master the film, video, and television technologies to use them to their advantage.

Unfortunately, film, video, and television have remained underdeveloped and underutilized in Africa. The major cause of this situation is government ownership and control of the media. Media are run along bureaucratic lines, lacking the input of the creative and enterprising people required in this industry. As a result, the media do not reflect or express life as lived by ordinary African people. Instead, the media depict the lifestyles of politicians, government officials, and the urban elite. This practice has severely restricted the potential that this industry has with respect to African development.

Film, video, and television are part of the communications industry that combines art, craftsmanship, and business. Specifically, the audiovisual media include the production of films, on the one hand, and the distribution of films to audiences in the form of film, video, and television, on the other hand. Production can either be in film or in video. Although the costs are prohibitive, it is possible to make a film from a video. Distribution is a critical function that is required to ensure that films and videos reach their intended audiences. It requires professional expertise in the areas of marketing, logistical management, and accounting. Specifically, film/video distribution includes the following activities: 1) identification and acquisition of film/video product; 2) promotion of the product; 3) for films, selling rights to theatrical exhibitors or secondary distributors; 4) for videos, selling rights to television broadcasting stations or selling copies to institutions and to rental and retail outlets. Normally, to be successful in distribution, it takes many years of developing personnel, institutional capacities, and knowledge of markets.

The management capacity and financial resources available in African countries have limited the development and growth of the media industry. A regional study conducted several years ago on the film industry in the ten Southern African countries formerly known as the Southern African Development Coordinating Con-

ference (SADCC) showed that film infrastructures inherited from
former colonial governments had collapsed. In some countries,
there were filmmakers trained abroad on government scholarships
who had not produced films since returning home. In other countries, there were well-equipped laboratories and studios built
through donor assistance. However, these facilities worked mini-
mally, if at all.

THE AFRICAN FILM INDUSTRY

There are very few African films made by Africans themselves.
The first film made by an African to be seen by a paying audience
was *Borom Sarret* (1963), by Senegal's Ousmane Sembene, center-
ing on the theme of cultural, social, and economic exploitation.
Prior to the 1960s, sporadic film production initiatives in Africa
epitomized the continent's patterns of colonization. Thus, French
benevolence, while paternalistic, was instrumental in establishing
production facilities, which later introduced Africans to the rudi-
ments of film production.[12] There are now quite a number of recognized French West and Northern African filmmakers: Souleuman
Sisse, Djibril Manberty, and Idrissa Ouadrago—just to name a few.
Their films are funded by the French government through programs that require French participation. This has resulted in films
being primarily produced for European audiences.

Several problems have inhibited the development of African
cinema made by Africans for African audiences. First, the quantity
of films produced by Africans compared to the proportion of films
produced by non-Africans is very small. As a result, film technology does not develop, nor does the proficiency of the production
personnel improve, both of which compromise the quality of the
finished product. Since African products are of lower quality relative to the cheapest internationally available products, their exchange and commercial value is insignificant. This factor affects
the distribution of these films to audiences. Second, Africa has too
many languages. When a film is produced in one local language,
its distribution is limited. To reach wider audiences, it must either
be dubbed or subtitled in international languages, usually English,
French, Portuguese, or Arabic. However, the funding to cover dubbing costs is not always readily available. Even when films are
dubbed, the international languages themselves are not accessible
to the majority of Africans; thus dubbed films reach only a small

number of people, leaving out the vast majority of people, who depend on local languages for their communication. It would be more effective, where budgets are adequate, to dub popular films into regionally spoken African languages.

The challenge for the African producer is to rise to the level of technical and creative achievement that Hollywood has perfected, and attempt to master the same standards of art and presentation. This does not mean that they must spend the same amounts of money or reach the same numbers of people. It simply means that if filmmaking is going to be profitable outside of Hollywood and in any way challenge Hollywood's hold over African audiences, then it must be supported by particular cultures from which the films originate.[13]

Zimbabwe and Burkina Faso are two countries that have shown a potential for African cinema. In Zimbabwe, a local film, *Neria*, broke box office records through attracting new audiences to cinema. Its receipts surpassed the best of Hollywood films released in the country. Burkina Faso is a small, poor West African country. The country hosts the largest Pan-African film festival, FESPACO, every two years. This remarkable achievement is only possible because the government and the people of Burkina Faso value African cinema.

While making films in Africa is very expensive, it must be possible to find ways to increase the number of African films produced. It is important to consider the question of viability. Film budgets will continue to be a major constraint, given the size of the African private sector and the investment incentives offered. Advances in video technology are creating real opportunities for transcending the obstacle of high production budgets. In Ghana, for example, most filmmakers are now using the video medium in place of film. This has increased the number of local productions tremendously.

Video can now be projected on large screens approximating cinema projection. This is a significant and positive development for distribution. Video projection houses have mushroomed in every neighborhood. Filmmakers are producing more local productions, which are being seen by more local audiences. Audiences previously inaccessible are now reachable. With this new capacity, the opportunities for reaching wider African audiences with development-oriented communication are constantly expanding. Video has the added advantage of reaching additional audiences through television. This means that African television audiences could be provided with a wider variety of African productions than is the case at present. African television audiences have been subjected to programming that does not address their development needs. Video used creatively, and with imagination, could deliver education and information in culturally appropriate ways, meeting the needs of African development.

FILM, VIDEO, AND TELEVISION IN A CHANGING SOCIETY

There are fifty-two countries in Africa, with a combined population of over 600 million. Forty-five of these countries have national broadcasting services, with an estimated combined viewership of over 90 million. The number of people reached by the combination of cinema, television, and video far exceeds 90 million. The potential of these audiences to contribute to rebuilding the development capacity of African cultures has not been tapped. The situation will not change until these audiences are provided with a meaningful proportion of African films, videos, and television programs that accurately present African thoughts, ideas, and values within their own sociocultural contexts.

There are changes in Africa that offer hope that African cinema, video, and television industries may effectively serve the education and information needs of African people in the future. These changes are the deregulation and privatization of the media and the return of South Africa to the family of African nations. The liberalization and privatization policies have revived the participation of the private sector in the film and video industry. This allows for the mobilization of private-sector resources to support the growth and development of the African film industry. While this is a positive development, it does not follow that the private sector will give priority to serving the education and information needs of African people. Deregulation and privatization of the media to date have resulted in programming that is devoid of creativity and imagination in regard to local content. In fact, the media has become more dominated by education and information originating from non-African sources. African countries must consider local programming needs and support community media efforts when deregulating or privatizing the media.

With its economic size and the state of its industrial and technological development, South Africa presents a real opportunity for Africa to create a viable film industry. South Africa produces more films than any other African country today, and has producers and distributors with proven international success. These are the factors that have constrained Africa's ability to respond and compete in the global media market in the past. However, South Africa has been isolated from other African countries for a long time and tends to draw its inspiration from industrialized countries. Political and business circles have expressed concern about South Africa controlling and dominating the rest of Africa, in a manner similar to that historically enjoyed by the rich industrialized countries. It is necessary to overcome these perceptions so that Africa can use positively the strengths of South Africa's economy to build an African communications industry that will serve the education and information needs of African development.

There have been several initiatives to promote film, video, and television with South African participation. In July 1994, Media For Development Trust, a nonprofit organization in Zimbabwe with support from the Rockefeller Foundation, organized and conducted a three-day meeting attended by participants from the film, video, and television industries of Africa, including South Africa. The meeting produced a program of action proposing nine specific activities:

- establish a cooperative regional financing system to produce high-quality entertainment films for theatrical and television release;
- dub the most popular Francophone films into English, increasing the variety of films available in English;
- conduct a regional study to find ways for television broadcasters to increase budgets available for local productions;
- develop a sound and mutually supportive business relationship among African producers, distributors, exhibitors, and television broadcasters;
- pressure African governments to enforce laws designed to eliminate copyright infringement;
- motivate governments to offer investment incentives for the refurbishment or building of new exhibition centers;
- strengthen existing information structures and develop information networks among producers, distributors, exhibitors, and broadcasters;
- hold annual workshops and consultative meetings to bring together distributors, broadcasters, exhibitors, and representatives of regional and overseas organizations with key

roles in the distribution of African films; and

- establish mechanisms for coordinating activities, exchange of information, and networking among the key regional and overseas organizations involved in the distribution of African films and videos.

It is encouraging to note that some of these activities have been initiated and have brought positive results. Most of the South African participating organizations have established business relationships with other African countries. A number of joint projects have been initiated. While these developments are encouraging signs, there is presently a need to consolidate them. The above program was left to participating individuals and organizations to implement as they saw fit. There is now a need to provide management and coordinate arrangements to advocate continuity and expansion. A good example of the kind of work required is what the National Video Resources (NVR) of New York did to promote the films made by independent producers in the United States. Obviously, this will require adaptation for the African situation.

NVR, a New York–based organization, was created in 1990 by the Rockefeller Foundation to address ways of overcoming market barriers to independently produced media—the work of artists, educators, and activists—and to assist in increasing public access to and awareness of these media. Advocacy and leadership on issues of importance to the field of independent media are also at the heart of their mission. NVR is not a distributor, but rather facilitates the distribution of independent works by providing information, training, and technical assistance to independent film and video distributors, and by supporting efforts that help programs reach audiences in new ways. The organization spent U.S.$3 million over the past four years on a wide variety of projects in the field of technical assistance, research and information dissemination, marketing initiatives, policy initiatives, rights projects, and international research and initiatives.[14]

CONCLUSION

Slavery and colonialism undermined the internal processes of African cultures to provide self-generated development and progress. While liberation movements delivered African people from colonial bondage, they did not address the long-entrenched system of marginalization and disempowerment of African cultures. Their priority lay in consolidating and maintaining political power. Unwittingly, they further marginalized African cultures. Postcolonial governments must raise the status of African cultures in their own countries. The new status must go beyond simply overglorifying African cultures. The struggle for nation building and development in Africa is about restoring the capacity of African cultures to be functional, dynamic, and equal to other cultures of the world.

Postcolonial African governments must bring the majority of people into the mainstream of development. They must recognize that development is not about transplanting ideas and technologies from rich or developed countries. This approach only serves to limit and perpetuate the marginalization of African cultures. Real development and progress evolve in cultures that enable individuals and communities to promote a consciousness of accurate self-awareness, which is the first step to creating a new destiny rooted in native cultures.

NOTES

1. Madubuko Diakite, *Film, Culture and the Black Filmmaker* (New York: Arno Press, 1980), 10.
2. FEPACI, Africa and *the Centenary of Cinema* (Dakar: Presence Africaine, 1995), 47.
3. Angeline S. Kamba, "Tolerance—Africa's Response to the Challenge of Pluralism and Diversity" (paper presented at the Conference on Democracy and Tolerance, Seoul, 1994), 6.
4. Costatinos Berne-Tesfu, "Priming the African State: Post–Cold War Political Transitions and Sovereignty," Addis Ababa, 1995, 7.
5. Shushi Hayashi, *Culture and Development* (Tokyo: University of Tokyo Press, 1988), 178.
6. FEPACI, *Africa and the Centenary of Cinema*, 63.
7. Diakite, *Film, Culture, and the Black Filmmaker*, 8.
8. Colin Fraser and Jonathan Villet, *Communication: A Key to Human Development* (Rome: United Nations Food Agricultural Organization, 1964), 6.
9. Atsen Ahua,"URTNA: The Programme Exchange Centre" (paper presented at the Film and Video Distribution Workshop, Victoria Falls, 1994).
10. FEPACI, *Africa and the Centenary of Cinema*, 100.

11. Ibid.
12. Ibid., 49.
13. Marlin Adams, "Film and Video Distribution" (paper presented at the Film and Video Distribution Workshop, Victoria Falls, 1994), 5.
14. Steve Smith, "The National Video Resources" (paper presented at the Film and Video Distribution Workshop, Victoria Falls, 1994), 5.

CHAPTER 5

Radio Stations in Africa: Issues of Democracy and Culture

Diana Senghor

INTRODUCTION

A certain democratic process has been taking shape in Africa since the beginning of the 1990s. It is most obvious in two regions of the continent: West Africa, especially in the Francophone countries, and Southern Africa. In Southern Africa, first in Namibia (in 1990), then in South Africa (in 1993), apartheid has been replaced by democratically elected governments that affirm their determination to be multiracial and multicultural. In West Africa, the progress of democracy has also been spectacular. Until 1989, twelve of the sixteen West African states were under military rule. By 1994, only six still had military governments. Even though the new civilian governments are not all democratic, a majority of them have held multiparty elections (nine countries between 1990 and 1992).

Yet democracy in Africa does not seem to go beyond the organization of elections and the recognition of political parties, which sometimes number in the dozens. A majority of the population, especially the underprivileged—such as rural people, women, and young people—do not feel that these parties represent them or reflect their aspirations and concerns. To them, the multiparty system appears to be little more than a redistribution of power among the traditional elite. This disappointment in the multiparty system has been reflected in low voter participation (in 1993, less than 25 percent in Mali and in Burkina Faso). Last but not least, citizens' opinions are ignored as soon as election results are in. Voters have little control—and even less influence—on the decisions made and carried out in their name by the various authorities, whether legislative, political, or administrative, even at the local level.

There is no culture of democracy: it remains to be developed. But who will do it and how? Some states—the possibly slightly more democratic ones—are trying (e.g., Mali and Senegal, for example, through policies of administrative decentralization), but they may not succeed; the objective of reducing the role of the government with the help of the government is a paradox.

By 1991, there was at least one independent newspaper in each Francophone West African state. The print media definitely played a decisive role in the development of multiparty systems in those countries, and continue to do so in the maintenance of these systems. They ensure the continuation of public debate. But do they contribute to the development of a democratic culture? Their pages are mostly devoted to politics in the narrow sense. More importantly, they target and reach only a small number of citizens: generally, the educated wage earners. Even though these newspapers are each read by ten people, on average, their press runs are relatively small, from 2,000 or 3,000 copies (*Anfani*, in Niger; *Les Echos*, in Mali) to 10,000 to 20,000 copies (*Sud* or *Walf Fadjiri*, in Senegal). At best, their readership ranges between 20,000 and 200,000 people. Their distribution is 80 percent urban for lack of appropriate distribution structures, and their price of 150 to 300 CFAF is equivalent to one or two meals.

In this context, radio is the only mass medium in Africa. Television often remains an urban luxury (even though half of all households have a set in Dakar or in Abidjan). Its presence in rural areas is almost nil not only for technical reasons, but also for cultural and economic ones. (Programs are in French and a set costs 300,000 CFAF in Dakar). In contrast, radios, often imported from Asia, on the black market and inexpensive (in Dakar, a set costs 1,500 CFAF or U.S.$3), have mushroomed over the last few years. In 1991, according to UNESCO figures, between 20 and 50 percent of the people owned a radio in Francophone countries[1] (4 million sets in Senegal for 7.7 million people; 2.3 million in Mali for 8 million people).

RADIO AND THE DEVELOPMENT OF A DEMOCRATIC CULTURE

There is no doubt that, starting in 1990, there was a liberalization in the field of radio in a number of African states: state radio is striv-

ing to become "public radio" or even "public service radio." Radio
has started to change its institutional, administrative, and financial statutes, as well as its programs and even its audience. New
legal and institutional frameworks have been adopted to ensure
pluralism on the airwaves. Last but not least, stations of a new
type have appeared: private, local, and broadcasting on the
FM band. Thus, through the profound changes that some countries are experiencing, radio seems to be both a *result* and a *sign* of
democracy. Judging by the role, impact, and mode of operation of
some of the new types of stations, radio may be more than just a
sign. It may be a *factor of democracy* inasmuch as it contributes to
the development of opinions and to their public expression among
listeners who did not have a say before or on topics that could not
be mentioned or discussed publicly for political security reasons
(the questioning of leaders) or out of social conformity (the relations between the sexes; authority, parental or otherwise).

Furthermore, some of these new stations have emerged as
among the most unexpected and innovative forces, not only socially, but also culturally and even economically. It may thus be
that, beyond their impact and the new developments they represent, radio stations are factors of social, democratic, and cultural
change. They are a factor of social change, first, because they manage to mobilize and represent the interests of excluded groups,
and also because they accomplish the amazing—and rather paradoxical—feat of uniting the rather disparate social interests of listeners, broadcasters, and radio developers. They are also a factor
of cultural change because they not only record, preserve, and file
traditions peculiar to the territory, land, or community in which
they broadcast, but also manage to create or encourage the creation of new and popular verbal or musical forms. By preserving
and creating local popular culture, radio stations succeed where
the state and the elitist civil society of experts and intellectuals seem
to have failed.

From an economic point of view, these stations sometimes
manage to tap local financial resources usually deemed nonexistent; to adopt and use modern communication technologies at a
low cost; and, finally, to mobilize energies and to provide jobs, if
not real incomes. In short, at a time when all (economic and human) development indicators are in the red—with a fall in incomes
per capita, a drop in investments, a decrease in school attendance,
a decline in public services, and the collapse of cultural identities
and productions—radio might in fact be one of the few areas ca-

pable of moderating widespread pessimism in Africa. This remains to be seen and a few questions deserve to be asked:

- The experiences of some private stations may seem exemplary. However, are those stations not isolated cases?
- What is the extent, if only geographically and geopolitically, of this liberalization of the airwaves?
- Has a critical mass capable of bringing about continentwide changes been reached? If not, can this be achieved and, if so, how?
- There is no shortage of statements of intent, and many new institutions and regulations—such as communications high commissions (*conseils superieurs de la communication*) or public radio statutes—are being adopted, even set up. How effective and efficient are they? Can their effectiveness and efficiency be insured or reinforced? If so, how?
- Supposing that some of these new stations are real *factors of democracy and culture*, might they not turn into the opposite and become lethal weapons against culture by stifling it through tribalism or simple conservatism, or by undermining it through standardization (some music stations foreshadow this risk)? But more dangerously, might they not represent so great a risk for democracy and peace that they destroy them? The specter of the Station of the 1,000 Hills (Radio des 1000 Collines), which called people to genocide in Rwanda, still looms. Can such dangers be averted? If so, how?
- Finally, are these experiments economically viable and can they be reproduced? If so, under what conditions?

There is no doubt that these questions warrant a closer examination. This is no easy task because the "radio scene" is changing rapidly and because the data are few (the only studies of private radio stations that I know of have been those conducted by the Panos Institute), geographically limited (mostly to West Africa), and difficult to collect (especially in the informal sector of private stations). Let us nevertheless venture onto this ever-changing scene.

STATE-RUN STATIONS

Is a new role being assigned to state-run radio? How is this new role expressed in the statutes, the programs, and the very audience of these stations?

Propaganda and Training

There is no doubt that radio was one of the most powerful tools of the authoritarianism, indeed totalitarianism, that characterized almost all African regimes until recently, and for a very good reason: a close examination of the objectives set by the leaders of newly independent states in 1960 reveals that they were the same as those they set for radio. At the time of independence it was stated that "African political systems . . . must face four fundamental problems: the building of a state, . . . of a nation, the participation of citizens in decision making, and the distribution of goods and services."[2] Thus, at the time, the democratic objective was present. In the regimes that claimed to be a part of the African socialist movement, like that of Senegal, it was even a priority and a strategic objective:

> Development is a collective undertaking, and citizens must be organized accordingly hence a "training and supervision of the masses" [*encadrement des masses*]. They must understand and accept the importance and the imperatives of development. . . . The goal of this training seems to have been to enable the communities affected to make decisions regarding their development freely and with full knowledge of the facts. That is probably what explains the importance given to rural organizations in Senegal, and to the one-party system in African countries in general.[3]

The same objectives were set for radio: the purpose of national radio "is to strengthen—even to create—the national identity of each State."[4] Moreover, radio was to "increase agricultural production and productivity through the development of skills; the organization of the dialogue between farmers and the authorities, and among farmers themselves; and the appreciation of the cultural heritage and of local knowledge."[5] Along the way, the priority given to democracy became blurred. It was even supplanted by the other objectives: institution building (the state and the nation) and economic development (production). Democracy even came to be seen as an obstacle to development. Thus, exit democracy.[6]

By the same token, radio stations also found themselves confined to the twin objectives of institution building and production. First, radio was assigned the role of educating farmers through advice and one-way instructions or directives (on the subjects of the popularization of farming techniques; health care for farmers, their children, and their livestock; and functional literacy). This education was but *training* in the military sense. Besides, it is clear that radio was not aimed at listeners as whole human beings, but as *farmers* (even though they also used public services), while listeners as *citizens* were totally ignored, as if they simply did not exist. Second, the goal of state and nation building soon became corrupted. The state and its builders, the decision makers (i.e., political leaders and civil servants) became one and the same. Radio was then used as an instrument of *political propaganda* and of mobilization for the party, which itself became indistinguishable from public service (civil servants were automatically party members). Radio statutes were shaped accordingly. National radio was simply a department within the ministry of information, which defined its daily editorial policy, enforced a tight and close censorship, and appointed the director and the people in charge. Journalists were civil servants on the one hand, and development agents specialized in communication on the other. Radio stations were funded by the public revenue department. They were thus statutorily part of the government.

Programs obviously reflected the dual role of radio. As far as propaganda was concerned, political news reflected the government perspective. As far as training was concerned, most national radio started producing specialized programming called "rural radio" in the mid-1960s. This programming was especially aimed at farmers and broadcast in the most widely spoken local languages, and its audience was sometimes gathered in villages (as in "radio clubs," in Niger or in Mali).

By the beginning of the 1990s, national radio was completely discredited, described as "the deaf speaking to the dumb." It has not even managed to achieve the—limited or questionable—objectives set for itself, for the following reasons:

- The potential audience is smaller than expected because national radio is technologically incapable of reaching the whole country in very large states (like Mali or Chad, where stations broadcast over 40 percent of the territory) or in hilly areas.
- As for the actual audience, it is limited by the language of broadcast. Complete and unabridged news bulletins are generally broadcast in English or French—which are spoken by less than one-third of the population in some cases, including in capital cities (in 1988, 42.4 percent of the people in Bamako, and in 1991, 35 percent of the people in Ouagadougou could not speak French)—even if abridged versions are broadcast in national

languages.[7] Moreover, the exclusive use, on national radio, of widely spoken local languages excludes linguistic minorities from the audience. In Senegal, where comparatively few languages are spoken, there are twelve local languages, but only six of them are used on the air. Imagine the situation in other African states, with their multitude of languages.

• Finally, the contents of programs do not appeal to the remainder of the listeners who are not affected by geographical or linguistic barriers. Even rural radio programs, which at first aroused some interest, have been abandoned by their listeners, who are put off by the artificial and schoolish nature of the broadcasts (for financial reasons, programs are produced by technocrats in studios in the capital city).

Independence and Civic Responsibility

"The SWABC was an instrument of propaganda intended . . . to carry out the objectives of Apartheid. No opinion that did not conform to these objectives could be broadcast. . . . The Terrorism Act and the Anti-Communism Act reinforced this position."[8] In 1993, SWABC became the Namibian Broadcasting Corporation (NBC)—a model of pluralism of sorts. Indeed, it is governed by rules and regulations that guarantee political diversity and pluralism at election times. None of the eight competing parties complained about the coverage of the December 1994 elections. In its daily operations, the NBC seems to have managed so far to reflect the country's multicultural nature thanks to its programming in various national languages, its ability to broadcast (via satellite) over a larger area, and, finally, its institution of an ongoing and open debate among citizens and between citizens and their leaders, through interactive programs that do not focus solely on political issues. "'Prime Minister's Question Time,' for example, is a weekly broadcast during which listeners can ask the prime minister questions on a variety of topics."[9] While Namibian public radio appears to be a spectacular success for the democratic process, it is also a beacon for public radio stations in the rest of Africa.

Changing Statutes

Over the past few years, the administrative and financial status of national radio across Africa has changed notably. Most national radio used to be run according to the administrative and institutional pattern that still governed the Radio Television du

Benin (RTB) in 1992: "[as] a State institution run according to a budget set-aside in the State budget. Payments are approved by the Ministry of Finance."[10] The status of national radio has evolved toward greater administrative and financial autonomy. Formerly simply departments in the ministry of information, most stations, as in Mali and Niger, have acquired the status of administrative public institutions (*etablissement public administratif*, or EPA), which gives them a greater administrative and financial autonomy. Boards of directors that replace the ministry of communication have been set up to guarantee administrative autonomy.

Financially, national radio now has the possibility of managing its own budgets and of seeking and raising its own funds. In Senegal, "the new statute specifies that the Radio Television du Senegal is responsible for all the commercial, industrial, property, and financial dealings required to carry out its mission."[11] This increasing autonomy (which did not start in the 1990s, by the way, but actually dates back to the 1980s—and even to the mid-1970s, in the case of Senegal) does not in fact result from "democratization" but from the economic crisis and the disengagement of the state that followed.

Administratively, this autonomy is relative. These EPAs remain under the direct supervision of ministries of communication. Boards of directors are hardly a guarantee of independence. Boards are made up, at best (as in Senegal, for example), of representatives of various public services (such as electricity and communication) and, at worst, of representatives of various ministries (such as finance or the interior). Few, if any, members are professionals (from associations and unions of journalists) or listeners (from consumer or legal associations, etc.).

Financially, autonomy mostly means restricted government subsidies. Overall, this autonomy has at least three negative consequences. The budget is essentially used to pay personnel salaries. (In Niger in 1992, 640 million CFAF out of a total budget of 825 million CFAF—or close to 80 percent—was spent on salaries.) The first consequence is the deterioration of technical equipment. In Nigeria, in 1992, 50 percent of transmitters were out of order. The second consequence is that the small size of the remaining portion of the budget allotted to the production of programs causes a decrease in or even an elimination of broadcasts recorded on location and a proportional increase in programs recorded in the studio in the capital and produced abroad by international stations (BBC, RFI, etc.). Local and national productions find themselves sacrificed on the altar of autonomy! Even worse, the search for their own funding leads stations either to give up public service programs for profits from advertising and underwriting, or to sell their services—often at the highest possible price—to various development agencies (local associations, nongovernmental organizations, and international aid agencies). Such commercial funds make up almost 25 percent of their total budget (or 380 million CFAF out of 1.774 million).[12]

Are the Programs More Democratic?

Political pluralism now seems welcome on the air, at least at election time. In most countries, decrees, committees, and even permanent bodies have been set up to ensure that political parties have an equitable access to state-run media (in January 1993, in Mali; in May 1991, in Senegal, with the creation of the High Council of Radio and Television). While the airwaves are no longer overrun by governmental rhetoric, and while debates, one-on-one and otherwise, are common, the airwaves are still dominated by the speeches and talk of politicians. In Cape Verde, for example, political programs take up 60 percent of airtime.

Access to radio by civil society organizations, and even more so by ordinary citizens, is guaranteed neither in regulations nor in fact. The few programs in which they can participate thus seem but merely a democratic façade. A look at programming schedules shows that less than one hour of airtime per day, on average, is allocated to such programs on each West African station. By contrast, music takes up eleven hours of airtime.

The National Radio Audience

Are audiences larger? Probably not. A major obstacle to the growth of national radio audiences is the language barrier. In countries where the majority of listeners (from 60 to 90 percent) do not speak the official language (French, English, or Portuguese), the majority of programs are still produced in those languages (in Cape Verde, 95 percent of programs are in Portuguese; in Ghana, 51 percent of programs are in English). Besides, as mentioned above, their programming contents are not really likely to attract large audiences.

The second aspect of the strategy devised by national radio to diversify and increase its audience is the decentralization of stations. Regional stations are appearing, and their numbers have steadily increased since the late 1980s (Senegal has four; Kenya and Chad, three; Mali, Ghana, Burkina Faso, and Guinea, two; Algeria, nine; and Niger, one). This decentralization is actually rather timid, and sometimes rather deceptive, because stations produce few, if any, of their own programs. They simply relay the national radio signal, which mostly broadcasts in the official language, barely understood and spoken in the countryside. Furthermore, in some cases, these "regional" stations only manage to broadcast locally, in the city where the transmitters are set up. (This is the case for all three regional stations in Chad.) Finally, this decentralization comes with ulterior political motives (whether concerning domestic or foreign policy). Algerian authorities, for example, bluntly admit that, when it comes to the establishment of new stations, they give priority to border regions, which are bombarded by broadcasts from neighboring countries.

Local FM state-run stations intended particularly for young people have multiplied in the capitals of some African countries such as Senegal, Mali, and Burkina Faso. These are precisely the countries in which private FM stations first appeared. Are we witnessing an underhanded and belated attempt by state-run stations to recover their diminishing audience and to contain the liberalization of the airwaves, as private stations maintain? Pluralism and democracy in state-run stations, brought about as a result of the double economic and political liberalization, thus seem to progress slowly and cautiously.

The consequences of the financial autonomy of radio stations are contradictory. Diminishing resources affect not only the functioning, maintenance, and replacement of technical equipment, but also the quality and diversity of programs. These consequences are also sometimes perverse. In the search for revenues, national radio gives greater importance to supply (advertising) than to demand (society). The consequences of decentralization are limited—sometimes to better reception or to the broadcasting, over a larger territory, of programs that only partially address the most urgent preoccupations of their listeners. However, one must acknowledge the progress represented by the appearance of political pluralism, public debate, and more interactive programs on the air. The new institutional framework may well be the strongest guarantor of a democratization of radio, provided pressure is applied, alternatives take shape, and a domino effect speeds up its evolution.

PRIVATE STATIONS

In September 1991, under the democratic transition government set up after the fall of Moussa Traore's military regime in Mali, Radio Bamakan started to broadcast without authorization. Radio Bamakan, started by an association, was most likely the first private station in Africa, but probably not the first local station. As early as 1986, local stations established and supported by the state appeared in Burkina Faso. In 1987, Radio Rurale in Kayes started broadcasting in Northern Mali, but it was initiated and run by an Italian nongovernmental organization. Also in 1987 Horizon FM appeared in Burkina Faso, but it is a commercial station, broadcasting in French, that mostly plays music.

Radio Bamakan immediately aroused the enthusiasm of the people of Bamako, and not through music either. It had them glued to their sets because it translated simultaneously in the local language (Bamanan) the debates of the democratically elected parliament, conducted in French, which less than 30 percent of the people in Bamako understood. It broadcast every week, also in Bamanan, a review of the—national and international—press with equal success: less than 13 percent of the people in Bamako could "express themselves well" in French. This success was surprising considering that voter turnout had been just 25 percent. In 1993, Radio Bamakan broadcast two hours of women's programs every morning, made its studio available to local associations every week, and broadcast news bulletins several times a day. Finally, according to its director, it allocated altogether 60 percent of its airtime to cultural programs.

Radio Bamakan does seem to have taken up, on a smaller scale, the place and the roles that state-run stations find it difficult to fill. Since 1991, private stations have mushroomed. Their format is sometimes very different from that inaugurated by Radio Bamakan. They have not appeared everywhere and not always at the fast pace at which independent newspapers blossomed in the print media. While these stations take up with a measure of success some of the roles public stations are expected to play in the democratic process, they constitute first and foremost sociocultural events, previously unheard of in Africa. Finally, as an alternative, but certainly not a replacement to state-run stations, they have a domino effect on the whole West African radio scene.

The Paucity of Stations

In West Africa, only eight of the sixteen states that make up the Economic Community of West African States (Commmunaute Economique des Etats d'Afrique de l'Ouest, or CEDEAO) had effectively authorized private stations to broadcast as of May 1995—Mali, Senegal, Niger, Burkina Faso, Gambia, Côte d'Ivoire, and Sierra Leone. In North Africa, private stations are illegal in spite of the existence of several projects (such as Radio 7, in Tunisia, for example) and of the pressure that developers put on their governments. Eastern and Central African states had not authorized the establishment by their own citizens of local private stations, either, with perhaps one or two exceptions. In Zaire, Radio CANDIP, which was authorized as early as 1976 and started by an Advanced Institute of Pedagogy, has set up several hundred radio clubs in the area.[13] Another example is that of a religious station in Kenya.

In contrast, private stations are beginning to grow in Southern Africa. In Namibia, a religious station, Channel 7, has been authorized since October 1993. In Zambia, also, there is a religious station, Christian Voice, which was inaugurated in December 1994. Finally, in South Africa, two private stations, Radio 702 and Capital Radio, have broadcast since 1980 and 1984, respectively. But in January 1995, 189 requests for broadcasting licenses were registered with the Independent Broadcasting Authority. Thus, the largest concentration of private stations is in West Africa, but their numbers vary greatly according to the country. Niger and Senegal have only two private stations each (Sud FM and Radio Dunya, in Senegal; Radio et Musique or REM and Anfani FM, in Niger). In January 1995, there were nine private stations in Burkina Faso and eighteen in Mali. Altogether, about fifty private stations operate in West Africa, and half a dozen in Southern, Central, and Eastern Africa. Almost all private stations are located in capital cities. There are exceptions in Burkina Faso (the four regional stations of Horizon FM and Radio Palabres, which broadcast from Koudougou), in Mali (nine stations out of eighteen), and in the Côte d'Ivoire (one).

Commercial, Local, and Religious Stations

It is no easy task to categorize or classify the various types of stations. Generally, the official regulations covering private stations (except maybe in Niger) do not differentiate between them. For a start, one might separate private stations according to their type of ownership and management, on the one hand, and to their purpose and mission on the other. Thus, "association radio" would be a station owned and run by an association; its mission would be social; and its status would be nonprofit (which, according to the French Act of 1901 in force in Francophone West African countries, does not preclude profits as long as they are not shared by the members of the association). In this sense, religious stations would be only one type of association radio.

A religious station would be run by a religious community or association, with the not necessarily exclusive purpose of spreading or at least testifying to the faith expressed by this community or association. Conversely, a commercial station would be owned by an individual or a group (*Groupement d'interet economique*, limited liability company, etc.); its purpose would be commercial and its profits would go to the owners. While association-owned stations, in the strict sense of the word, that is to say the nonreligious ones, are the majority in Mali (nine out of eighteen), they are certainly not in the rest of Africa, or even of West Africa. In fact, there is only one other station owned by an association. It is Radio Palabres in Burkina Faso, which means that only a dozen out of the fifty-odd private stations that currently broadcast in Africa are owned by associations.

Religious stations share the distinctive characteristic of being present in countries where no other private station has yet been authorized (i.e., Kenya, Namibia, and Cape Verde). Altogether, there are currently a dozen of them across Africa. Religious stations are essentially Christian—either Catholic or Evangelical. Catholic stations are mostly located in West Africa (Radio Espoir, in Côte d'Ivoire; Radio Nova, in Cape Verde; and Radio Maria, in Burkina Faso). A great many African dioceses are already applying—or are about to apply—for a frequency. Among the Protestant stations, Evangelical stations are the most numerous (in Burkina Faso and in Eastern and Southern Africa). There are currently only two Moslem stations. One is in Sierra Leone (Alkuraan Alqarem), broadcasting over shortwave throughout the region. The other is in Bamako (started in 1994), in Mali (La voix de l'Islam, with a transmitter located on the roof of a mosque).

Commercial stations are the most numerous of all (both stations in Niger; both stations in Senegal; the only nonreligious station in Sierra Leone; both stations in Gambia; five out of the nine stations in Burkina Faso; and seven out of the eighteen stations in Mali; as well as the only two private stations in South Africa). Altogether then, there are more than twenty private commercial stations in West Africa, and most of the pending applications are also for this type of station.

Studies conducted by the Panos Institute reveal that the difference between commercial stations and stations owned by associations is not always very significant.[14] The diversity within each category actually blurs the dividing line between the two. Taking into account initial investments; employee qualifications, salaries, and numbers; quality of equipment; as well as management (if not content and quality) of programs, similarities are much more significant between a so-called "commercial" station like Radio Badenya (in Sikasso, Mali) and a so-called "association" station like Radio Douentza (in Douentza, Mali), than between Radio Badenya and other commercial stations—such as Radio Kledu (in Bamako, Mali).

In certain association or commercial stations, which could be termed "amateur," initial investments hardly exceed 10 million CFAF (or U.S.$20,000). The equipment is often nonprofessional, or even secondhand. There are often many (twenty or more) underskilled employees who have been trained on-the-job, and the management is quite creative. In West Africa, almost all stations are in the same boat. In contrast, a few stations, so few in number that it is possible to mention all of them (Sud FM and Radio Dunya, in Dakar, and Radio Kledu, in Mali), have required considerable investments (over 50 million CFAF, or U.S.$100,000) partially borrowed from banks. The equipment of these modern stations is more professional and their offices more functional and spacious—even luxurious—than those of most state-run stations. Their employees are specialized, qualified, and paid according to the salary scales used in their respective trades.

One can see that there is no single model for West African private radio stations. It is even difficult to find a dominant format, except to say that the most numerous stations in West Africa today tend to be urban, commercial, and certainly amateur. However, these stations share a number of characteristics that make them, collectively, a unique sociocultural phenomenon.

Social, Economic, and Cultural Characteristics

The social impact of these private stations can be assessed through their listeners (target audience and degree of popularity) and through their programs (what meanings do they convey?) Who makes up the audience of private stations? While this is a difficult question to answer with precision, the study conducted by the Panos Institute in 1994 yielded some information. In the case of stations located in the capital cities, this potential audience amounts to the entire population of these capitals (over a million people in Dakar or in Bamako) that owns a set (the vast majority of households). Stations located in rural areas—or in cities other than the capital—have the technical capacity to reach between 100,000 and 300,000 people (this is the case, for example, in Sikasso and Douentza in Mali and in Kongoussi in Burkina Faso).

Their target audience varies partly, but not only, according to the location of the station. Some so-called "rural" stations actually reach urban populations living in secondary cities. By the same token, so-called "urban" stations located near cities actually reach a rural audience, especially because of large seasonal rural migrations. Furthermore, urban stations address the concerns of relatively marginalized populations through some of their programs (such as the programs about women, for example, on Radio Bamakan, or those intended for young people on Horizon FM in Ouagadougou, or on Sud FM in Dakar). By contrast, rural stations devote a seemingly disproportionate amount of airtime to the tastes of the local elite. (On Radio Douentza, located in a small town in Dogon country, hundreds of miles from Bamako, they play jazz every night.)

Even though it is difficult to measure under present conditions, these stations appear to enjoy considerable popularity. In any shop, in any taxicab in Dakar, Bamako, or Ouagadougou, radios are tuned to private stations. One study, conducted in Dakar a few months after Sud FM started to broadcast, revealed that 89 percent of the radio audience in the city listened to that private station (in contrast to 50 percent who listened to national radio).[15] The second survey, conducted in Douentza, Dogon, showed that five months after the creation of Radio Douentza (in July 1993), that station's audience had doubled. Another significant figure in that survey was that of radio sales: the number of people who owned radios had grown by 14 percent since the station started to broadcast. Yet another indicator of popularity is the amount of support given by listeners to their station in hard times—as in Sikasso, Mali, for example, when the station was sacked by the military. This is not the only example: in Kongoussi, Burkina Faso, listeners formed a club to save their station when it experienced financial difficulties.

Program Content

The combination of content and format accounts for both the popularity and the originality of private stations. The easiest programs to evaluate in terms of popularity are the interactive or retroactive programs. Listeners call in live. The switchboard sometimes has to shut down during these shows. But one might raise the objection that, even so, one still has to have a telephone to participate. That is not necessarily the case. Sometimes listeners go to the station in large numbers to engage in a debate, on the show if possible, or just among themselves late into the night. Radio then turns into a real local forum. Furthermore, listeners also participate through the mail. They themselves write or have others write for them. Radio Rurale in Kayes, Mali, receives dozens of letters every month, according to Fily Keita, one of its directors.[16]

Such programs take up a lot of airtime on private stations (ninety minutes every day, six days a week, on Radio Badenya, in Sikasso) both because they contribute to the success of the stations and because their production requires little equipment and few people (no editing or special journalistic skills are necessary). This highlights a difference between private and public stations, for public stations still fear improvisation and their listeners' uncontrollable spontaneity. However, goaded by competition, they are now trying their hand at it with varying degrees of boldness.

Finally, these programs are well liked by listeners, not only because they give them a say at last, but also because they are produced in their own language. In fact, private stations sometimes exhibit considerable multilingualism. On Sud FM, for example, it is common to hear a listener, as well as the host, switch languages in one and the same show. At the stations that have been studied, over 50 percent of programs are broadcast in local languages. However, it must be acknowledged that, when several languages are used (such as Bamanan, Soninke, and Peul, on Radio Bamakan), the dominant local language (that of the largest population group or that of the most powerful social group) tends to overshadow the other languages. In fact, in the study conducted in Douentza, Dogon, speakers expressed their indignation at what they saw as the monopoly of Peul and French at the station.

An examination of program schedules[17] showed that private stations clearly give priority to social issues. Depending on the station, these issues take up two, three, or four times more airtime than do political issues (news and debates), which are the most common on public stations. Programs devoted to social issues are regularly scheduled, frequent, and often long (three hours a day on average on Radio Badenya, in Sikasso), and interactive.

Social Issues. Social issues include relations between generations, and between the sexes, and between communities. Some special programs are devoted to migration, relations between neighbors, unemployment, polygamy, and other issues—in short, the very topics that are currently sensitive in West African societies. Private stations, by addressing them, accomplish two goals at once. On the one hand, the relative importance (measured in amount of airtime) they give to the various topics reflects that given by listeners, who, as mentioned above, care little for political and intellectual debates among the elite. The stations' perceptiveness in this respect is another reason for their success. They respond to the expectations and demands of the public. They address their listeners' priorities in their programs—something that neither public stations, nor independent or official newspapers, which overwhelmingly prefer politics—manage to do.

On the other hand, private stations accomplish another amazing feat. Conflicts and crises are announced and discussed on the air, that is to say publicly, by ordinary people (often young people and even, at last, women), sometimes with virulence and a complete lack of moderation. Through these debates, private stations have emerged as a new and innovative sociocultural force. They are contributing to the development of public opinions. Some observers have stated, not without a certain condescension, that, traditionally, public opinion did not exist in Africa—that, because African societies are based on consensus, only the final consensus is public; that all negotiations are conducted in whispers away from the public eye, and that debate is thus private and confidential; or, that debates are conducted and decisions made by an elite (in terms of age, sex, caste, or clan) so that public opinion traditionally results from consensus and special qualifications. Radio stations, however, make possible the public expression—maybe all the more openly because this occurs under cover of anonymity—of competing points of view, which could only be whispered among peers if they were not on the air. Credit does not go to the individual private stations—it goes to radio itself as a medium—but private stations were the first, and sometimes are still the only ones, to have encouraged public discussion.

In West Africa, radio seems to play the opposite role of that which it has been accused of playing in Western countries—especially since the 1930s, when it was used by Hitler, and later by commercial interests. According to some communication theorists (T. Adorno, J. Ellul), radio has become an instrument of (political or commercial) propaganda in the West because it reaches and affects isolated individuals. They claim that family, community, and territorial landmarks and roots, which were crucial, and even unchallenged, in the formation of an individual's opinions have been lost in industrial society. Because the individual is now alone, he/she has become easy for mass media to manipulate. Conversely, do private stations in Africa today not powerfully counterbalance the—family or social—influences openly experienced by the individual and precisely reinforced by public stations? Private stations in West Africa encourage what, according to Adorno, Western stations prevent: "the formation of autonomous independent individuals, capable of making informed judgments and decisions. These individuals are a prerequisite for a democratic society that can only survive and blossom through free human beings."[18]

Politics. While politics is not absent from private airwaves, it is addressed essentially through news bulletins and magazines and through public debate. Politics occupies without a doubt a more prominent place on urban stations than on rural stations (ninety minutes a day in one case, fifteen in the other). News programming on private stations bears witness to two noteworthy changes. For one, it is also broadcast in national languages. Furthermore, the news is more—and sometimes exclusively, as on Radio Liberté—local, at times by necessity. "For lack of technical and financial means, this bulletin is exclusively devoted to local news. Every morning, the station's three journalists go on location, in Bamako and its surrounding areas, looking for news which they analyze and broadcast at 2 pm."[19]

Debates (among politicians and between politicians and listeners) are a genre practiced by most urban private stations ("Explain Yourself on Radio Liberté," "The Hour of Truth," "Open Microphone for City Halls"—their titles speak for themselves). Finally, some (rare) stations broadcast educational programs that are less about day-to-day politics than about political and civic institutions (for example, "The Institutions of the Third Republic," on Radio Kayira). These programs tend to be hosted by intellectuals and experts.

In inaugurating this type of program, private stations have played a dual role. On the one hand, they play a civic role: they allow listeners to *question decision makers* and to force them to respond. They also force intellectuals to step down from their ivory towers and express themselves—not without difficulty—in everyday language. On the other hand, these innovations have had a domino effect on public stations, transforming them in turn into so many forums and multiplying the places where open debate about decisions is possible.

Culture. The place allotted to cultural programs, as well as the nature of these programs, varies greatly depending on the station. Two accusations have been leveled at cultural programs on private stations. Some stations have been suspected of being the Trojan horses of Anglo-Saxon culture and music and, thus, of hastening the disintegration of local cultures. At its beginnings in 1989, Horizon FM did in fact devote nearly all its music programs targeting the young people of Bamako to such cosmopolitan content. Programs included reggae, rock, or even pop music; they were hosted by a disc jockey who, wearing a baseball cap, spoke in a jargon of "franglais." The role played by these music programs, and thus by the private stations that devote a lot of airtime to them, is also an object of criticism. This entertainment is said to feed the apathy of citizens and to function in fact as nothing but a diversion that helps listeners temporarily forget their sense of resignation.

These criticisms, however, are somewhat suspect. Indeed, the success enjoyed by the mainly musical stations bears witness to a demand from listeners that state-run stations—preoccupied with training and indoctrination—did not know how to address, and that other institutions (like schools or even the family) have also not met: a need for entertainment and pleasure. A station that exercises a single function that attracts a very limited audience (generally young, urban, and unemployed), condemns itself to failure. Most stations, however, allot a relatively generous place to cultural programs—programs that actually *ensure* the collection, preservation, and survival of the local cultural heritage (music, stories, etc.). Every Wednesday, Radio Badenya, in Sikasso, Mali, for example, welcomes artisans who come to speak about their trade, their experiences, and their perspectives. Several stations broadcast programs about traditional medicine, history, or the origin of words and idiomatic expressions.

While not all stations are willing to play the role of banks of collective local memories, Radio Rurale, in Kayes, does. It has already built an impressive sound library—organized and filed—of 7,000 programs. Preserving the heritage is not enough, however; one also needs to keep it alive. When questions are asked on the air about the "deeper meaning" of some proverbs and sayings, radio can be said to have taken over the role of lost forms of initiation—or simply of education. Even keeping the heritage alive is not enough, however; one also needs to *enrich* it. Some local stations encourage the creation of new cultural forms. They sometimes succeed in catching the spontaneous creativity of author-actors, through more or less improvised skits. Sometimes radio stations succeed where other media and cultural institutions (such as books or the cinema) fail—they find an audience and produce programs at a reduced cost. Despite the risk of seeming ephemeral and overly facile, these stations appear to be opening up new paths for exploration.

Technical Resources

Aside from the three "modern" stations identified on the African radio scene, stations often have rudimentary equipment. Their offices are generally small (three or four rooms for production, administration, and reception) and located in overpopulated, working-class areas. High-frequency equipment (transmitters, antennae) is often low-powered (less than one kilowatt), with the transmitting power sometimes restricted by law. As for the low-frequency equipment (tape recorders, microphones, turntables), "they are not worth those of a good disco," according to an international expert. In the four stations at which the study was conducted, costs (before devaluation) ranged between 6 million CFAF and 20 million CFAF (when the equipment is solar powered).

Financial Resources

In the case of stations run by associations, Western or international aid agencies generally finance equipment costs for radio stations (e.g., in Mali through nongovernmental organizations like OXFAM and Terra Nova). To the best of our knowledge, bi- and multilateral institutions have never financed the setting up of private stations. The financing of stations referred to as commercial is generally more opaque. The three professional and modern stations seem to have turned to formal systems of credit.

In contrast, in the case of amateur commercial stations, the investors are individuals: a former radio host back from the United States, where he worked for a long time; a former emigrant worker back from France; a schoolteacher who took up business upon retirement; a wealthy businessman. Many of the owners are also the directors of the stations. The investors' motivations do not seem to have been primarily financial. Such ventures are hardly lucrative; some of the stations lose money and must be bailed out by the owners' other businesses. This is the case for FR3, in Bamako, for example, which only gets 20 percent of its annual budget from its own revenues and posted a deficit of over 5 million CFAF in 1994 (or U.S.$10,000). The other stations barely manage to support themselves and their owners, with a couple of exceptions. And even those owners who appear to earn their living from their stations do not display signs of dazzling wealth.

Other investment opportunities offer greater, quicker, and safer returns. The primary motivation of these investors seems to be social, if not philanthropic. Station directors are influential men, sought after, or in any case treated with consideration, by the people in power. They are well known in society. The main motivation appears to be gaining or preserving a certain social prestige. Thus, the wealthy businessman who invested in "Radio Badenya" felt compelled to finance a station dealing with the problems in his community (*badenya* means kinship). Coming from a traditionally important family, known for his wealth, could he resist the pressure without being socially discredited? He agreed to invest without seeking profit, but on the condition that he not lose any money. Is it going too far to say that this is an absolutely new method of starting up a business? One might conclude that this is a form of patronage totally unknown in Europe and more closely related to that of the great men of the Renaissance than to the ways of large corporations.

Human Resources

In the stations included in the study (commercial or association stations and all amateur ones), the human resources stand out by their large numbers, lack of appropriate qualifications, and low salaries. The personnel of most of these stations range in number from ten to thirty or forty people. Most frequently, the vast majority of employees are more or less full-time hosts (as many as twenty in some stations and often serving as free-lance journalists, as well). In contrast, the number of technicians is small (one, sometimes two), and only rarely does the position of administrator or manager exist. The director often assumes this function along with that of chief editor. Employees have very few qualifications. Technicians have been trained on-the-job (which would explain why half of the antennas in Bamako broke down in 1994). Very few stations have a full-time, professionally trained reporter (sometimes reporters from the national radio stations moonlight at the private stations). As for the hosts, they can be divided into two groups. Some are unemployed young people who may have a degree. The rest are local intellectuals (lawyers, teachers, medical doctors, and veterinarians) who host specialized programs. These "freelancers" are usually referred to as consultants.

Staff salaries are generally very low. The monthly salary of a full-time journalist is not much more than 25,000 CFAF (or U.S.$50) in Bamako, that of a full-time freelance person, 15,000 CFAF (or U.S.$30). These freelance employees are also usually referred to as "volunteers," which means that they only receive gratuities ranging from 10,000 to 1,500 CFAF (or between U.S.$20 and U.S.$3). Why would anyone agree to such low salaries, which do not even allow their recipients to make ends meet? One explanation may be that, more than looking for an income, these unemployed young people are looking for a job: something to do with their time. Why do they choose radio work? Maybe for the same reason that intellectuals and directors do it: for the prestige and fame such work confers. Finally, one may go so far as to say that the motivation might arise from a perspective that some have claimed is totally lacking in Africa: volunteerism.

Small salaries and low qualifications sometimes place these stations in a situation of illegality, or at least, of irregularity (e.g., with regard to regulations covering working conditions, collective bargaining agreements, and statutes for reporters). But the low salaries, the result of a desire both to contain costs and to distribute what few financial resources exist among a large number of people, may be a necessary condition of the operation and survival of the stations. As one can also see, these "radio ventures" operate along the lines of enterprises in what has been called the "informal sector" (marginality with respect to regulations, with a small amount of money divided among a large number of people, etc.). In this sense, private stations are a new economic force. They are informal cultural ventures. Up to now, African cultural ventures were "modern" (e.g., publishing, television), and the informal sector had largely not ventured into the cultural domain.

Risks and Obstacles

In the pursuit as well as in the expansion of its civic and cultural social role, radio nonetheless finds itself confronted by a number of risks and obstacles. Through the work of the Panos Institute, we have tried to point out the potential problems, while at the same time indicating some actions that may be undertaken to identify and overcome them. These risks and obstacles concern the content of the programs broadcast by radio stations, as well as these stations themselves, inasmuch as they are "means" (or media).

Tolerance and civic responsibility. Without a doubt, the deregulation of radio, as we have seen in the case of Rwanda—where the Radio of the 1,000 Hills ignited and fanned the flames of a conflict that resulted in hundreds of thousands of deaths—can have perverse and explosive effects on democracy and, above all, on peace. In this respect, two major potential risks exist in a majority of African countries (or West African countries, at least). These are the risks related to interethnic conflict and the rise of a certain religious intolerance. Does the exploitation of these dangerous and sensitive areas constitute a temptation for radio? What mechanisms have been put into place to ward off the possibly seductive aspects of such an exploitation?

Avoiding unethical deviations. In countries such as Mali and Niger, new private radio stations have demonstrated remarkable wisdom when faced with ethnic conflicts. This can be contrasted with the excesses to which certain representatives of the print media abandoned themselves in these same countries (notably in Mali), openly taking sides with the civil counterrebellion during the so-called "Northern" conflict and broadcasting, with impunity, messages calling for murder. However, two radio stations in Mali did call their listeners to violence during the 1993 antigovernment student protests, although these were the exceptions to an overall record of restraint on the airwaves.

The establishment of religious radio stations (which comprise one-fourth of the stations existing today) does not seem to have had—to date—any effect on the development of religious intolerance. When not devoting airtime to general development issues, these stations carry humanistic commentaries and exegeses of religious texts.[20] The previously mentioned study conducted by the Panos Institute shows how, out of four local radio stations, two devote no airtime to religious questions, while the other two divide their time equally between the three major religions (Fridays, Islamic; Saturdays and Sundays, Catholic and Protestant).[21] However, the danger of powerful religious groups taking hold of the airwaves cannot be ruled out. The directors of several radio stations in Mali report having been the objects of insistent solicitations from such groups and having been offered very attractive financial deals. Furthermore, the preaching of conversion—if not of fundamentalism—tends to insinuate itself surreptitiously into certain "lay" programs by means of (innocent?) listeners who divert interactive broadcasts to religious ends. Finally, in countries getting ready to liberalize the airwaves, the majority of candidates for frequencies are religious groups, which would seem to raise the question of whether the threat of a religious war on the airwaves might become more acute in the future? However, several initiatives have been taken in the face of such risks by the media, the professionals who work in them, and the organizations that represent them.

In January 1995, on the occasion of the inauguration of the first private Senegalese station, Sud FM, its director B. Toure declared: "I invite my colleagues to review the treatment of information relative to those conflicts [in the Valley of the River Senegal and between the Touaregs, the army, and the Black African population in Mali and Niger], so true is it that we have at our disposal instruments with a great capacity to emulate, but also to harm. Let us unceasingly question the legitimacy of this delegated power claimed in the name of a public opinion which we are as inclined to shape as to follow in its impulses, including its most negative ones." The press group of SUD-COM had already applied this attitude to itself, by imposing upon every reporter, at the time he/she signed his/her contract, adhesion to a charter of professional good conduct. Certain other stations, in Senegal and elsewhere, did not have to wait for such an appeal for professional ethics. The "mission" of various radio stations (Radio Kayira, in Mali, for example) publicly and expressly includes respect for human rights. For nearly ten years, the Association of Journalists of West Africa (Union des journalistes d'Afrique de l'ouest) and most of the national organizations that comprise it have adopted "codes of ethics." In 1995, the Association of Free Radio and Television Stations of Mali (Union des radios et televisions libres du Mali) decided to start a debate on the nature of an ethical practice of journalism. The Panos Institute also is interested in promoting such a debate on ethical problems and on the institutions and mechanisms capable of regulating them, but on a regional scale in West Africa. A study on breaches of ethics and on their perception by professional journalists is currently in the works. It was the focus of a regional conference scheduled for the end of 1995.

Without a doubt, the commitment of radio stations to a balanced reporting and the prevention of certain deviations in the nature and treatment of broadcast information are not the responsibility of professional organizations alone. Such tasks are also the responsibility of independent authorities who have been charged with regulating the audiovisual field as well as with setting up safeguards for radio stations.

Diversifying and defining program content. Failing a desire to use the "capacity to harm" denounced by B. Toure, radio can still neutralize the power at its disposal to implant in its listeners a culture of democracy, tolerance, and cultural, as well as ethnic, identity. While one may consider the amount of time allotted to music on certain stations still inordinately large, the time allotted to the news (fifteen to ninety minutes a day according to the cited survey) and to social issues (at least an hour and often several hours, according to the same survey) is not insignificant.

It remains to be seen which social issues are addressed in the schedule of programs announced by radio stations. In fact, according to a recent Panos Institute survey of thirty-one stations in seven West African countries, topics related to the theme of "peace and democracy" (human rights, civil and civic rights, minority rights, interethnic conflicts, and religious tolerance) take up less than 2.5 percent of airtime.[22] This finding certainly underestimates the real amount of time allotted to these topics in a more broadly defined form through more general programs. Nevertheless, this percentage acutely raises the question of the editorial priorities and vision of those in charge of stations.

Another remarkable finding of this study is that two themes that constitute two major stakes for the future of African societies—ethnic conflicts and religious tolerance—are not priorities for those in charge of the stations surveyed. The theme "interethnic conflicts" even seemed downright overlooked in the country that was most prey to it at the time of the survey. While the coverage of social crises, tensions, and conflicts in programming does constitute an innovation on the part of private radio stations, could this come at the expense of addressing the most serious and threatening forms of crisis?

Another question concerns how the topics addressed on the radio are treated. The findings of the two studies cited show that the treatment of these themes is poor. The preferred format is "the interview," which involves the lowest technical production costs: a microphone suffices. "Reports," which require trips and time, and above all "magazines," which presuppose more elaborate technical work (editing, sound mixing), are not the rule in radio programming.

Finally, these programs are generally directed by reporters at the station who are without formal technical training or background with regard to the themes they address. Moreover, collaboration with institutional sources of information—whether the state or nongovernmental and human rights organizations—is infrequent. The lack of technical and financial resources, the poor qualifications of reporters, and the difficulties of gaining access to qualified sources of information are factors that contribute to the often dull, repetitive, superficial, and incoherent treatment of subjects, which, in turn, may turn off the listeners. However, a variety of initiatives have been taken to overcome these obstacles through the training of reporters and providing assistance to stations in producing and broadcasting their programs.

Thus, the Panos Institute has organized two national conferences to educate journalists about the environment each year since 1992. These conferences are made up of three parts: thematic training provided by experts and local resource persons, retraining in journalistic techniques, and practical exercise in the field. Since 1994, these conferences have been multinational (Senegalese, Malian, and Mauritanian journalists, for example, were brought together in St. Louis, Senegal, around the theme "managing natural resources for a lasting peace" in the Valley of Senegal). Since 1993, this same institute has also awarded small grants to thirteen radio stations to encourage and help them to produce a two-hour monthly program on the environment and sustainable development. Starting in 1996, the funded theme will be "peace and democracy." Lastly, the Panos Institute set up a "Regional Audio Bank" in Bamako in 1995 to develop exchanges of programs between stations and to allow them to examine themes from a variety of perspectives.

Establishment and survival of private local stations. In order for radio stations to play the innovative role we have seen, or envisioned, it is necessary for them to exist in the first place. And once they exist, it is necessary for them to survive.

Setting up and strengthening the legal, institutional, and regulative framework of pluralism in radio is an important step. While pluralism is gaining ground in West Africa, the actual liberalization of the airwaves remains to be won in half of the countries in the region. Indeed, eight of the member states of the CEDEAO still have not authorized private radio stations to broadcast. Either no law or clause has been adopted to liberalize the airwaves, or, more frequently, the law is not being enforced, or the institutions in charge of enforcing it are not yet in place or operational (Benin, Guinea Bissau, Guinea, and Ghana). This is without a doubt the most underhanded, but also the most effective, way to slow down the demonopolization of the audiovisual field.

In Mali and Niger, the liberalization of the airwaves was attained in the wake of "national conferences." Three or four years later, the democratic process seems to have slowed down. Yet advances continue to be made, though more slowly and accompanied by reverses. In this area also, initiatives have been taken to ensure that the laws are enforced. In Guinea Bissau and in Ghana, conferences were organized in October and December 1994 by nonprofessional and professional organizations with the support of the Panos Institute. Perhaps as a result of the Bissau conference, the government authorized, a few months later and on a temporary and experimental basis, the country's first private station, Radio Pindjiguiti.

Furthermore, if democratic competition really exists among the countries of the region for the benefit of pluralism in radio, why not introduce it among the various regions of Africa, between West Africa and Southern Africa, for example? In countries where the liberalization of the airwaves is a reality, much remains to be done. It has become a question of creating a balance in the field of radio. Indeed, there is a geographical imbalance in the establishment of radio stations regionwide and within each country. Today, half of the private stations are in the capital cities. In five of the eight countries that have liberalized their airwaves, all the stations are in the capital. In addition, most of the stations established outside the capitals are not really in rural areas, but in large and economically active cities. What measures would compensate for this urban bias? Moreover, this bias is accompanied by another, in favor of radio stations of a commercial nature, which are currently the most common.

Another imbalance, which is at this time still only a risk, is that of the restoration of a monopoly, a private one this time, over the airwaves; a concentration of local stations under the aegis of a single group. Horizon FM, in Burkina Faso, operates four regional stations, while only one other private station currently broadcasts in the countryside.

Finally, a third imbalance concerns the guarantees for the pluralism of programs. What are the guarantees on the subject of ethics, of national and local production of programs, of the utilization of local languages, etc.? These areas still remain to be clarified. And yet mechanisms must be invented and put into place—essentially, incentives to facilitate the establishment of radio stations in economically disadvantaged areas or for minorities or marginalized social groups; and to encourage associations to produce local programs and promote local cultures. There must also be mechanisms of dissuasion, to prevent the restoration of monopolies—whether they are of a religious nature, or not—and to stem political, ethnic, or religious biases. Without a doubt, this task is the responsibility of regulative authorities—provided they have the political will and the means to carry it out and that professionals and their organizations do not ease up on their demands.

Financing and investing in stations. A final obstacle to the creation, proliferation, and survival of radio stations must be mentioned: it is financial. According to the study conducted in 1994, the cost of equipping a local station ranged from 10 to 40 million CFAF (from U.S.$20,000 to U.S.$80,000).[23] Without a doubt, costs have doubled today in Francophone countries now that the CFA Franc has been devalued. While the cost is not very high when viewed from the perspective of Paris or New York, it can be prohibitive for a small association or for an entrepreneur from the informal sector.

Three sources of financing have so far provided the funds necessary to equip and set up private stations. The most surprising of all these sources is that of businessmen from the informal sector. For them, the social motivation seems to have been a determining factor. Can this motivation, which has worked in Mali (Sikasso, Timbuktu), work in countries where traditions of solidarity are very weak? And can it have a lasting effect unless stations become financially self-supporting and gain additional prestige? Another source of financing is the modern economic sector, which partly financed Sud FM and Radio Kledu, in Mali.

But don't these cases constitute exceptions and risk remaining so unless station promoters have enough credibility, confidence, or power to sway institutional investors, and in particular convince them of the profitability of their projects?

The final source of financing is associations. The funds they use to finance stations come rarely from their own meager resources, but generally from outside. Securing such funds presupposes that international aid agencies, as well as the association itself, give priority to information and to the media, which is still far from being the case.

Can African states constitute a source for the financing of private stations, by reallocating their communication budgets, until now exclusively devoted to public media, in a manner more favorable to private media, for example? The economic crisis they are currently experiencing is not conducive to this, even in those countries that were open to the concept of supporting private media, like Senegal, which has set aside a fund for aid to the press. However, new mechanisms of economic support for private radio stations are taking shape. Most notable is the "multilateral fund for aid to the private press," for which the state would offer its support and its institutional guarantee. Investors would be assured of an equal and open management, which would simplify the process of choosing aid recipients.

Securing funds for operating costs. The operating budgets of small private stations can be extremely tight (from 5 to 15 million CFAF before the devaluation, or from U.S.$10,000 to U.S.$30,000).[24] Nevertheless, they are without doubt considerably larger in more "professional" stations. However, financing such budgets is still all but impossible in many cases (three out of four), as sources of financing are relatively limited.[25] Advertisements and announcements provide some stations with fairly considerable resources. Sud FM, in Dakar, announced revenues of 72 million CFAF (or more than U.S.$140,000) after a few months (close to 10 million CFAF per month or U.S.$20,000). However, such revenues presuppose that the station be located in a city—the capital—where the advertising market is large and where competing stations are few (there are a dozen of them in Bamako); and that, if the station is owned by an association, it have access to the advertising market (which is illegal in Niger, for example). Ultimately, such a means of financing stations seems workable only in the very narrow context of a market where the number of advertisers would remain high, while that of the stations likely to attract them would remain small.

Another source of financing for operating costs is contracts. These are agreements signed by stations with local or international development agencies. Some of them (UNICEF, the Malian Company of Textile Development, etc.) constitute regular sources of revenues for a few stations. However, these contracts are not very large, and they may condemn stations to advertising for the agencies and to editorial incoherence.

A final source of financing is the public itself. The Radio des Lacs derives most of its meager revenues (240,000 CFAF or

U.S.$500) from such subscriptions. The same study revealed that one subscription (less than 200 CFAF per listener or U.S.$0.40) would enable a small rural station to secure its annual budget. But are listeners prepared to consent to such an expense, no matter how low, if they are not fervent supporters of their station? It is then up to stations to maintain the enthusiasm they initially evoked.

NOTES

1. J. Barrat, *The Economic Geography of the Media* (ITEC, 1994), 397.
2. B. Kante, "Democracy in West African Political Regimes," *Annales Africaines* (1993):98.
3. Ibid., 92.
4. A. Tudesq, *Radio in Sub-Saharan Africa* (Paris, 1984), 36.
5. E. Aw, *Radio Craze* (Paris: Syros Publishers, 1993).
6. A. Tudesq, *Feuilles d'Afrique* (Bordeaux,1995), 219.
7. Ibid.
8. "Pluralism in Radio in Africa," working paper, Panos Institute, Dakar, 1995, 58.
9. Ibid.
10. *Pluralism in Radio in West Africa*, vol. 1 (Paris: Panos Institute, 1993), 23.
11. Ibid., 113.
12. Ibid., 118.
13. P. Berque, *Radio Craze* (Paris: Syros Publishers, 1993), 77–79.
14. *And Yet They Live!* (Dakar: Panos Institute and UNICEF, 1995).
15. B. Toure, "Official address for the inauguration of Sud FM," January 12, 1995.
16. Fily Keita, interview from the documentary *Ondes africaines en liberte*, Panos Institute, AITV, Rockefeller Foundation, 1994.
17. *And Yet They Live!*
18. T. Adorno, *Communication No. 3* (Paris, 1963).
19. *Pluralism in Radio in West Africa*, 29.
20. See special issue on religious radio stations in *Radio Actions* no. 3 (Dakar: Panos Institute, July 1995).
21. *And Yet They Live!*
22. *Media, Peace, and Democracy: Information for More Tolerance and Civic Responsibility* (Paris: Panos Institute, August 1995).
23. *And Yet They Live!*
24. Ibid.
25. Ibid.

CHAPTER 6

Storytelling: A Part of Our Heritage

Gcina Mhlophe

In the beginning was the word
The word gave birth to language
Language gave birth to stories
Through stories real fun began!

INTRODUCTION

I heard someone speak, maybe it was a voice in my head. Maybe my ears are shaped like cups, always ready to receive something. Maybe my whole being is always hopeful and ready to learn something new. *Umuntu ufunda aze afe*—a person learns until the day they die. This is an old African idiom and I really believe in it. I was born in a place called Hammarsdale, near the Valley of Thousand Hills on the East Coast of South Africa. I was brought up by my paternal grandmother and she was a great storyteller—her expressive face, her eyes, her voice, even the way she used her hands—these images are still very vivid in my mind. She deserves the praise for creating the storyteller I am today.

Storytelling must be the oldest art form on earth, as long as there have been people there have been stories. All the other art forms stem from them. There is an obvious universality to the art of storytelling. People have found that it is easier to explain certain concepts through stories or anecdotes. When people meet for the very first time they talk, yes, but until they reach a stage where they can share little stories about themselves, their observations, or news of the day, they don't really feel they have met. The types, sizes, and characters of stories always vary, and this is what creates the feeling that there is a sea of stories out there—new stories are born every minute, we will never run out, but the challenge is in how we choose to present or represent them. Some people might feel that storytelling is too ancient or old-fashioned to be of any use in the modern hi-tech world we live in. Stories may be old, yes, but so is water, air, fire, love, and the desire to live. All of these will never lose their importance to us.

Africa is one of the few places in the world where the oral tradition still survives and plays a role in people's everyday lives. Things are changing very quickly, though, so if we do not take note, in less than a decade we may be talking about it as we talk of the old extinct creatures of the past. Preserving the art of storytelling means preserving the great heritage left in our care. Stories have been passed down from generation to generation; they have survived this long for a reason. We need to sharpen our hearing and listen to the voices from the past as they speak through stories; what they have to say is like gold—ever shining and precious.

THE ROLE OF PERFORMING ARTS IN THE STRUGGLE

Following in the clear footsteps of our traditional praise singers who were always by the side of the chiefs and kings, we as South African artists have naturally found ourselves a part of the struggle for democracy. The praise singers of old knew how to guide their communities with constructive criticism and also gave praise where it was deserved. Their use of language was polished and very sharp. They had dignity and vision. These are the things we strived for in our work as playwrights, poets, singers, and fine artists. We tried to articulate the feelings of our people no matter what the consequences, hence many were jailed, detained without trial, tortured, and even killed. In the 60s, 70s, and 80s the situation continued to escalate politically and artists were in the forefront of the struggle, many times being the only ones voicing what banned leaders could not. Facing frequent police brutality, artists produced posters for political organizations in the middle of the night. They choreographed dances through which to share the experiences from different communities and felt stronger together.

At mass funerals we performed poetry that was born out of the pain that was our life in this country. We sang songs that were composed spontaneously, and somehow an invisible glue held us together in all kinds of weather. Artists soon realized that show business was in other countries; we were workers and fighters like any other oppressed people in our country. We had no facilities in the townships where we lived, but we always found places to perform our work and we never ran short of audiences.

This is an example of the kind of poetry I wrote:

THE DANCER
Mama,
They tell me you were a dancer
they tell me you had long beautiful legs
to carry your graceful body
they tell me you were a dancer
Mama,
they tell me you sang beautiful solos
they tell me you closed your eyes
always when the feeling of the song
was right, and lifted your face up to the sky
they tell me you were an enchanting dancer
Mama,
they tell me you were always so gentle
they talk of a willow tree
swaying lovingly over clear running water
in early spring when they talk of you
they tell me you were a slow dancer
Mama,
they tell me you were a wedding dancer!
they tell me you smiled and closed your eyes
your arms curving outward just a little
and your feet shuffling in the sand;
tshi tshi tshitshitshi tha, tshitshi tshitshitshi tha...
O hee! how I wish I was there to see you
they tell me you were a pleasure to watch
Mama,
they tell me I am a dancer too
but I don't know . . .
I don't know for sure what a wedding dancer is
there are so many funerals
where we sing and dance
running fast with the coffin
of a would-be bride or a would-be groom

strange smiles have replaced our tears
Our eyes are full of vengeance, Mama
Dear, dear Mama,
they tell me I am a funeral dancer.

HOW STORYTELLING HELPED IN THE YEARS OF STRUGGLE

Word of mouth is another form of storytelling. With all the banning orders we had to live with, we shared stories of the happenings around us to stay informed. In secret gatherings we told stories of what had been happening to comrades, family, friends, and sometimes to ourselves while in detention. Similar stories were also related at the Detainees Support Center, as people waited for the lawyers to help them trace their loved ones. At the time there was no organized storytelling group, but I often found myself referring to the old stories and idioms to try and interpret what was taking place around me.

The arrest of an 11-year-old child in Alexandra Township where I lived spurred me to go out and speak to his mother and find out the whole story. I wrote it down and published it in *Learn and Teach* magazine, where I knew many ordinary people would read it and feel stronger about coming forward with their own stories. I performed that story many times and I went on to look for more. When I shared them, at women's gatherings especially, I found that it opened up the channels of communication and enabled us to freely share ideas and advice.

When I decided to concentrate more on storytelling full time, I found that I could draw many different kinds of people who would not necessarily come if they thought I was telling strictly political stories. All these people came and enjoyed the stories of long ago and found their own meanings. Many told me how surprised they were at seeing the South Africa of the day in the stories. They also saw very vividly the similarities in character of some of the people around them. Many lively discussions were born out of something that was supposedly so harmless. The police certainly thought so anyway.

Communication across the invisible walls was possible, and I think that is what really drew me to look at storytelling as a profession. The art of storytelling was being practiced all over the country, but there was no infrastructure and people hardly knew about one another in different provinces. We needed to be in touch and try to build the art form in a more organized way so that we could improve and update the presentation or packaging to suit our varied audiences. Even today storytelling has the role of trying to make people use their imaginations. We look at idioms from different languages spoken in South Africa and we see that we will probably not live long enough to do all we need to do.

Zanendaba Storytellers holds an annual storytelling festival at the end of each year, and this is where we evaluate the flexibility of this art form by incorporating dance, painting, wall murals, environmental awareness, and so on. Our audiences feel free to go in and out of the real and imaginary world and we try to look for a deeper understanding of one another in such a fun-filled environment. Still, we need to learn more from artists here and in other countries; that is why we invite international storytellers to come and share with us their skills and experiences. Financial support is not always there for all the training we need, but we are always looking for new ways to make the road smoother for future storytellers.

STORYTELLING AND THE FUTURE

South Africans are increasingly aware of the fact that we belong together no matter what language we speak or what religion we belong to. The young people seem to be more flexible and more prepared to try to understand one another. Adults are finding that it is crucial for them to listen to their young—there is much for them to learn. As storytellers, we are approached to run workshops that try to bring young and old people together in an effort to communicate better. Storytelling is also playing an important role in raising awareness about environmental and health issues facing our country today.

There was a time when stories were told by old people at the end of the day around the fire. The young listened with so much enjoyment, but they were also made to understand that these stories carried many lessons to help them grow. There were no formal schools, and so these storytelling sessions taught children about their people and cultural values, the use of language, the difference between good and bad, active listening, and other lessons. Today these needs are coming back in a very strong way. We do have formal schools but modern children find it very hard to communicate and articulate exactly what they want to say—they are having major difficulties with the use of any one language. That is where storytelling comes in, encouraging people to take time to learn to improve their storytelling and as a result their communicating skills. In a country that has such a young democracy and a crucial need to avoid any unnecessary misunderstandings, we certainly need good communication to achieve harmonious relations.

In the name of development, cities and small towns are suffering from the effects of industrial waste and all sorts of pollution in this country. Our rivers and beaches are affected so badly we feel cheated and always fear for our health. Storytelling needs to play a role in educating people about the dangers they face and the fact that they as communities can play a role in correcting the situation. Small nongovernment organizations are trying to bring people together to work against these almost invisible threats to their health. Our storytellers need to join the fight. There are no trees in the townships where the majority of African people live; we need to tell stories that encourage people to see the value of planting their own trees and, more than that, to be aware that our indigenous trees are being neglected so we must identify and plant them in our townships.

Health is another issue that needs attention from all fronts. Some of the illnesses that affect poor people are illnesses that can be prevented. The government needs to play a role, but also education, or edu-tainment, as we say, is very important if some of the health problems facing us are to be curbed. The exciting part of this situation is that we find it really challenging to look for and write new stories to fit all these needs. This means that storytelling as an art form is never dull; it seems to turn to clay in our hands and let us mold and remold new ideas until we feel we cannot live long enough to do the things that need to be done.

South Africans are sometimes overwhelmed by their own problems, as can be expected. But we also know that we are part of the African continent, and there are many problems, contrasts, and opportunities that lie ahead of us as a continent. We have been through so much that some people might begin to lose hope for Africa, but we are not only storytellers, we are also dreamers and visionaries. We can see that the circle of life is affecting the whole world, we can see too that ancient ways of thinking and looking at life are needed to solve today's problems. Some of the most educated and respected experts in various fields are running out of ideas and looking to the old ways. Africa still has a very vivid memory and clear contact with the wisdom of the past. The ancestral connection is alive and well. Storytelling is at the forefront of this exciting turnaround.

TELEVISION AND OTHER MEDIA

There is a question that is frequently asked, "Is television a threat to the art of storytelling?" No, it is not. There are many opportunities to reach thousands or millions of people through this powerful medium. We tell stories on television and radio, and as the storyteller's face and voice reach so many people at the same time, there is also something that is very special about the way the individual listeners receive and interpret the story they hear. Mediums like television and radio should not be seen as a threat but as instruments for spreading the magic of stories.

I feel there will always be opportunities for storytellers to have that one-to-one contact with the listener in live performance. Television, radio, books, and tapes are all very important in today's world and we should not lose sight of that. But we know, too, that some things cannot be replaced. No matter how many kinds of drinks we may invent, water will always be nature's number one drink, and no matter how many types of candles and other powerful lighting devices we may invent, the sun will always be nature's number one source of light. It goes to show that oral storytelling, at home, at school, and everywhere, will always be the warmest and most special way of reaching out and touching one another.

CHAPTER 7

National Development and the Performing Arts of Africa

J. H. Kwabena Nketia

INTRODUCTION

The importance attached to the performing arts has assumed a new dimension in modern African states, for they have come to be valued not only for their traditional role as a source of aesthetic enjoyment and a medium of communication but also for their creative potential and the contemporary role they play in national development.

As became evident at the Inter-Governmental Conference on Cultural Policy held in Accra in 1975 under the auspices of UNESCO and the Organization of African Unity (OAU), many Africans believe that national development is multifaceted and includes any development intervention that may be deemed necessary on the national level for improving or enhancing the quality of any sphere of social and cultural life. In other words, as a process, development is applicable not only to technology and the material things of life but also to any aspect of a people's way of life. Accordingly, cultural development was viewed as a political priority soon after independence, for there was a general consensus among African leaders that Africa should renew its connection with its own past while it worked to make appropriate transformations of the legacy of the colonial epoch. This dual approach to culture in national development has guided individual initiative and development programs in the performing arts, for the social and cultural transformations that have taken place in Africa in the last hundred years have given rise to new communities of taste that cultivate their own contemporary genres of music, dance, and drama alongside historical or traditional forms that antedate the colonial period and that are handed down to posterity orally or by practice.

These two categories of art forms complement each other. The traditional arts are cultivated in contexts in which behavior is guided by ethnicity, kinship, and a common indigenous language, religion, and culture; contemporary arts are cultivated in contexts in which linkages beyond those of ethnicity form the basis of social life. Such linkages are established through membership in educational institutions; churches; industrial institutions; new social, political, and economic associations such as trade unions and market unions; and recreational associations such as soccer and sports clubs.

This chapter examines the factors that have defined the role and function of traditional and contemporary forms of the performing arts or contributed to their growth and development since independence, taking into account the context of creativity and performance, including the social network or community whose patronage and sensibility validate artistic processes, and development issues and needs related to the promotion of the arts as a dimension of culture in contemporary society.

THE TRADITIONAL ARTS

The rapid social changes taking place in Africa today tend to give the impression that the traditional arts will soon disappear and must be preserved before they are lost forever. In an article he wrote in 1904, Eric von Hornbostel, the father of comparative musicology, urged anthroplogists and missionaries, his primary field collectors, to bring back as many recordings as they could and raised the battle cry again in 1905, for he believed that

> the danger is great that the rapid dissemination of European culture will destroy the remaining traces of ethnic singing and saying. We must save whatever can be saved before the airship is added to the automobile and the electric express train, and before we hear "tararabumdieh" in all of Africa and in the South Seas that quaint song about little Kohn.[1]

When Hugh Tracey, who devoted his life to the recording and documentation of African music, embarked on this project in the 1930s, he used this notion to support his application for field research grants. After getting acquainted with the field, he changed his plea but justified his efforts in terms of the need for making the rich heritage of Africa accessible through the medium of the radio and the gramophone record to people in Africa and the world at large. Everywhere he went, he came across musicians and performing groups for whom music making still constituted part of their way of life. Those of us who have had the privilege of doing field work can testify that the traditional arts are "living" arts and not "relics" of the past or "folk arts" that survive only in the memory of a few. In many regions the arts are cultivated not only in rural areas but also in urban areas where traditional institutions such as chieftaincy and communities that observe traditional customs, ceremonies, and festivals exist. This is particularly true where indigenous communities invariably form the nucleus of urban populations.

It appears also that traditional methods of enculturation in the arts have not ceased, even though severe interruptions were caused in some quarters by colonial intervention and conversion to the Christian religion. In countries where colonial education did not lead to the total rejection of African cultures by the literate community, one can also find literate members of contemporary society who have learned to perform traditional music and dance through this process rather than through formal institutions, and who participate voluntarily in community events either for fun or because they belong to royal households or lineages that have responsibility for preserving particular traditions. This is the arrangement by which traditional states, particularly those with centralized political systems, ensured continuity of tradition in the past, especially where knowledge was specialized. Some households were responsible not only for particular musical types and instruments but also for arts and crafts and recitals of a specific corpus of oral literature, by word of mouth or by drums and other instruments that can function as speech surrogates. There are also artists who straddle the traditional and the contemporary and who play the music appropriate for each context when they are invited to social events.

Nature and Scope of Traditional Arts

The resilience of traditional performing arts, a quality attested by African survivals in the Caribbean and the Americas, can be attributed partly to their community orientation, which makes them a dimension of life, and partly to certain structural characteristics and features that pervade their organization and practice.[2] Among these characteristics are certain tonal, rhythmic, and expressive features that set African musical expressions apart as a major stylistic family.[3] While ethnic groups maintain their own preferences in the matter of tuning because they do not have to make music with those outside their own communities, the total number of distinct or significant tones they utilize within an octave may be five, six, seven, or as few as four. Melodic organization tends to follow common principles, while distinctive polyphonic forms are used in both instrumental and vocal music.[4] The formation of rhythm patterns follows similar procedures while rhythmic progressions and phrasing are controlled by defined time spans. Polyrhythmic textures are favored, especially in the music of drums and other percussion. In addition, particular use is made of the attributes of speech and the potential of instrumental speech surrogates as precompositional materials and sources of expression in performance.

African dance forms are similarly quite distinct in conception. The human body is not approached merely as a plastic material for creating meaningful shapes and designs but as an instrument that can respond to multiple musical stimuli through the polyrhythmic coordination of different parts of the body. This is evident even in the set of movements that members of a community learn through social experience to use for responding to music. In some societies this limited vocabulary lays emphasis on movements of the upper part of the body—often in the form of contraction and release of the shoulder blade, upward and downward shrugging of the shoulders, or forward and backward movement of the trunk or ripples of the belly. Others emphasize movement of the pelvis and the torso, intricate footwork, stamping, or upward elevation of the whole body in stylized jumps.

The actual presentation of dances takes several forms. It may take the form of solo dances in which individuals enter the dancing ring one at a time, or as a mass dance in which any number of individuals dance at once, each person going along in his own way. There are also dances done in twos and threes, and team dances in which participation is limited to a small group of people who perform identical movements. In the latter case the formation may be designed linearly in one single file or in rows or columns. It may also be organized in a circular or serpentine formation.

There is a great deal of emphasis on singing and dancing: first, because these allow for group participation in musical, ritual, and social events; and second, because of the scope they provide for the communication of individual and group sentiments. Creative artists express not only their own personal thoughts and feelings but also address themselves to the needs and concerns of individuals and groups as well as those of the community and its leaders. Like proverbs, forensic oratory, folk tales, and other narratives, song texts embody allusions to history, legends, and myths, references to common situations, familiar incidents, and characters as well as social and moral values, interpersonal relations, and relations with the unseen.

Singing also allows for exploration of verbal sources of play in song texts. Assonance, alliteration, repetition of words, phrases, interpolation of interjections, use of nonsense syllables, or phonaesthetics may be stimulated by play. So may the interpolation of expressions of wit, humor, and sarcasm or words of insult, flattery, or obscenity. A remarkable though somewhat exaggerated description of the manner in which singing could be a vehicle of communication and play is given by Brodie Cruickshank, a nineteenth-century writer who lived in Ghana for eighteen years. Writing in 1853 about the songs of the inhabitants of the coast of Ghana, he makes the following points:

> They are very expert in adapting the subjects of these songs to current events, and indulge in mocking ridicule, in biting sarcasm, in flattery, or in just praise of men and things, according as circumstances seem to demand. The bravery of a chief, the beauty of a young girl, the liberality of a friend, the avarice of a miser, the poltroonery of a coward, the affection of a mother, and the disappointments of a lover form indiscriminately the themes of these extemporaneous effusions. If a White man were to pass these songsters, while thus employed, they would quickly seize upon some peculiarity of his character, whether good or bad, and celebrate it aloud, amidst the unrestrained merriment of the bystanders. Even a passing stranger whom they had never seen before, would come in for a share of their notice, and some eccentricity of look or gait, or of apparel is quickly fastened upon as worthy of praise or of ridicule. This

habit of publishing the praise or shame of individuals in spontaneous songs exercises no little influence on conduct, for the African is most sensitive to public opinion and dreads being held up in ridicule, while the incense of flattery incites him to actions which will gain for him the admiration of his countrymen. In this way these singing men and women become the organs of public opinion and supply the place of our journals.[5]

Communication and play are of course not confined to singing. They are explored in dance and drama, symbolic or representational use of musical sounds in ritual contexts, miming, and impersonation in special dances and storytelling.

Instrumental Resources

The importance attached to singing and dancing has not precluded the development and use of instrumental resources, for instruments can be used not only independently as substitutes for the singing or speaking voice but also as accompaniment to singing and dancing as well as for a variety of other functions.[6]

The most common sound sources are percussion instruments. They provide the basic rhythms that unify the components of a performance; define, articulate, and reinforce the feeling of propulsion and the energy levels that the rhythms of African music generate; and heighten the mood and atmosphere of ritual and ceremonial contexts. They include nonmelodic idiophones (that is, objects that produce sounds by themselves without the addition of a stretched membrane or string) such as: container rattles, beaded rattles, rod rattles, concussion rattles, percussion sticks, percussion beams, bells with and without clappers, scraped and friction sticks, stamping sticks, stamping tubes, and slit drums. To these, one may add body percussion, the most common being handclapping and stamping, and rattling devices attached to the wrists of instrumentalists or strapped to the wrists, waists, knees, legs, or ankles of dancers.

Two instruments in the class of idiophones are particularly worthy of note because they perform both melodic and rhythmic functions and have wide distribution in Africa. They are: lamellaphones, referred to in the literature as hand pianos, thumb pianos, finger pianos, or by their African names such as mbira, likembe and so on; and xylophones, known by a variety of names such as timbila, balafon, gyilli, and so on. There are frame xylophones with gourd or animal horn resonators and xylophones whose slabs are laid across a pit, a box, or two pieces of banana stalks.

Membranophones (drums with parchment heads) abound in Africa. They have enormous potential because they can be played in the signal, speech, and dance modes.[7] They can be played singly, in pairs, or in larger ensembles, and can be played alone or used to accompany other instruments or a chorus of singers. They include hourglass tension drums, goblet drums, kettle drums, cylindrical, and semi-cylindrical or barrel-shaped drums. Some of them are single headed and open, while others are closed or double headed. They are played with sticks, bare hands, or stick and hand, while a few are activated by friction.

Aerophones (wind instruments) are used principally as melodic instruments. Some of them are also used in ceremonial and ritual contexts as speech surrogates or as signals or sounds played intermittently to heighten the mood of an occasion. They include flutes made of bamboo, the husk of cane, millet, reed, the tips of gourds and animal horns, or carved out of solid wood. Ocarinas and pan-pipes occur in a few places, while horns made out of the tusks of elephants or animal horns and trumpets carved out of wood or made from sections of gourd or even metal tubes appear to be widespread. Single-reed instruments occur in the savanna belt of West Africa, while double-reed instruments are found in some parts of East and West Africa, among those who have adopted Islam and other aspects of Arabic culture.

Chordophones (stringed instruments) also abound in Africa. There are musical bows of various types, zithers in the form of a flat bar, a bow, a trough or a raft, bowed and plucked lutes, harp lutes, bow lutes, arched harps, and lyres. Instruments in this group are played solo or in small ensembles for self-delectation or in restricted public contexts as vehicles of praise singing and narratives or as the mainstay of dance, special rituals and games. All these instruments are of course not found everywhere. There are societies that play drums and other percussion instruments but who have no chordophones, and a few that do not possess drums or have only recently adopted them. Similarly, some societies place their instrumental focus on aerophones and aerophone ensembles, while others focus on xylophones, mbira, or bowed and plucked lutes.

Within each society or its constituent communities, various restrictions on the use of instruments may also apply. While some instruments are in the public domain, others are restricted to the royal court or the chief's palace, or to the worship of particular deities. Instruments in the public domain may similarly be restricted by use. For example, in many places women may play rattles, bells, and other nonmelodic idiophones but not drums or stringed instruments, flutes and trumpets, while a few societies encourage their women to play drums, musical bows, and bowed lutes as a general practice or in specific situations related to their ritual or celebratory domains and contexts of creativity. Performance roles and functions are determined not only by musical competence but also by the manner in which traditional societies structure their social and cultural life.

Performance Organization

Performances of music, dance, and drama take place on formal and informal occasions, for as John Chernoff aptly puts it, "Africans rely on music to maintain the happiness and vitality of their social worlds."[8] Domestic life provides avenues for singing cradle songs or play songs for entertaining or interacting with small children as well as songs that can be combined with sound-generating activities such as threshing, pounding, grinding grain, or beating the mud floor of a new house. The latter become fun rather than chores when the sounds they generate are ordered in regular beats or recurring patterns and even more so when a number of people participate in them. Accordingly, in some societies such activities are habitually organized as group activities.

Similarly, it is not uncommon to find some music making on a market day in areas where such days are regarded as important social occasions, or performances during celebrations and other activities of occupational groups such as hunters, fishermen, or craft guilds. Some form of music making and dancing also takes place whenever people in kinship or associative relationships come together for fun or celebration, for the expression of shared grief and concern, praise, and criticism, or for the affirmation of their sense of tradition or their bonds with the unseen. That is why Francis Bebey describes African music as:

> music borne out of a meeting of individuals whose collective aim is to integrate it with the life of their community, so that against the general background of life, it plays a coordinating, regulating role, using rhythm as its tool.[9]

African communities do not of course play any rhythms or sing any songs that come to mind at such "meetings of individuals." Recognizing the differences in the expressive requirements of the various performance situations and their participants, individuals and performing groups draw on repertoires developed by previous generations for each occasion and enriched with their own creative additions. This heritage, which needs to be recorded, documented, and disseminated is quite large and includes children's games and songs, women's songs and play activities as well as those for men, mixed groups, lineages, age sets and age grades, secret societies, hunters, warriors, craft guilds, kings, and deities and their corresponding instrumental and dance forms.

Taking into account differences in depth of knowledge and performance competence, African communities allow for differential participation in the design of performance types and the distribution of performance roles. There are music and dance types that can be performed by all and sundry because of the simplicity of their structures and directness of communication. This is the basic level of organization and is applied to cradle songs, children's songs, work songs, processional songs, some interludes in folk tales, and songs intended to be sung by entire ritual assemblies.

There is a second and higher level of organization, in which items intended for group performance are designed in such a way as to allow for the leadership of persons with more than average command of knowledge and skills, who take up the complex or variable sections or provide instrumental support or leadership, while others perform the straightforward response section. In some societies such performance types, particularly those intended for recreation or performance in other recurring contexts, such as funerals, tend to be the focus of specialization. Interested members of a community constitute themselves into an organized performing group that learns and rehearses the repertoire of a performance type of their choice or expands it in their own way for performance whenever the opportunity arises. Occupational, religious, and voluntary associations similarly constitute themselves into performing groups when they have their own distinctive repertoires.

The third level of organization is the specialist level, where persons with distinct competence in some area of vocal and instrumental music or dance forms perform on their own in community contexts for their patrons or for general enjoyment. As in the second level of organization, the internal structure of the performance types usually provides for a hierarchy of performing roles and functions. In a West African drum ensemble, there are complex master drum parts and simpler supporting parts, instruments that provide the time line and others that enrich the texture or heighten the intensity level of the music. All these call for close collaboration and the willingness to specialize or perform in any capacity required by changing performance contexts.

As the variety of expressions practiced in community life enhance levels of consciousness of group identity, patronage and spontaneous participation in certain defined ways are usually expected of members of the community irrespective of who the performers are or where the event takes place, except in very special cases in which rites are performed outside the view of the general public. Performing groups, therefore, perform in the presence of an active rather than a passive or contemplative audience. Hence performance types designed for the second or third level may allow individual members of an audience to join in chorus responses, take a turn in the dancing ring, shout words of encouragement, or respond in other ways to moments in the performance.

Interrelations of the Arts

Although each of the arts makes its own aesthetic impact on the senses through its formal characteristics and modes of expression, it is customary to present them together as components of a performance event and not in isolation. This is done in order to widen the areas of aesthetic focus and the basis of interaction between artists, audiences, and spectators. What seems for a moment static in the music may be relieved by the text or the dynamic quality of the movements that accompany it. Similarly, the appearance of a masked dancer in a performing arena may reinforce the essence and intention of the occasion and give added meaning to the musical and dance forms. Naturally, very intense moments arise in performance when the high points of the arts converge.

An event of this nature may be a festival, a ritual, a ceremony, or an artistic event such as a "play" or music-and-dance event performed in a recreational context. For example, in southern Nigeria, there are little plays intended to amuse spectators that may be performed by marionettes, and traditional sacred "plays" presented by various religious societies that may be performed by masked actors who assume the personality of supernatural beings.

The interrelation of the arts is manifested not only in performance events but also in the creative process. Some fundamental features of style or expression, such as rhythmic progressions, cadences, or breaks, and some features of articulation may be shared. Musical instruments provide some of the ideas for works of art in bronze, brass, or gold. Gold drums and gold harps form part of the ensemble of objects that accompany the golden stool of the Ashanti of Ghana. There are gold weights of musical instruments. A similar relationship between art and oral literature is evident in the artistic symbolization of proverbs or scenes from traditional stories, and in the use of art objects to aid one's memory. In some parts of Tanzania, figurines are created for didactic purpose during puberty ceremonies. Particular objects are assigned to songs and verses so that they could be used to recall them after they have been memorized.[10] Appliqué works on the fabrics of the Fon of Benin are said to constitute a virtual handwriting that can render a complete text in pictorial images, making use, where necessary, of a riddle.[11] Many of them are prepared on the occasion of a death by the intimate friends of the deceased, who compose a song as a tribute to him and decorate a fabric with designs that bring out the text. Each person chants the praises of the deceased during the funeral ceremony, with the fabric hanging beside him as he sings.

Art and oral literature are also linked in the area of metaphor or imagery. When the poet uses the lion and the buffalo as symbols of power, authority, and might, the artist may see in these the attributes of kings, gods, and spirits, which can be portrayed through the symbolic use of images of those objects.

The unity of the arts may be seen in the breadth of knowledge expected of artists and other exponents of traditional culture as well as in the roles that certain individuals are called upon to assume. Among the Akan of Ghana, for example, the Okyeame (the official spokesman of a chief) is expected to be not only a good speaker but also someone with a wide knowledge of proverbs, maxims, precepts, oral traditions, and history. He is expected to understand the language of drums and to be able to interpret symbolic gestures in the dancing ring. Similarly the musician is expected to be versatile. He may be a praise singer or a drummer whose duty it is to recount genealogies or act as a chronicler. A good singer may also be a poet of some sort, someone with the knack for creating appropriate verse in spontaneous situations.

In addition to spontaneous variations, creative additions to repertoire, reinterpretation of forms that have lost their freshness or vigor, the creation of new dances and other art forms, or the revival of old forms as well as adaptations of ideas, materials, and forms borrowed from neighbors or through external contact occur in the practice of traditional arts. Evidence of these abound in oral tradition and other sources. What seems important is that these contribute to the practice of the arts in community life as vital areas of shared experience and orally transmitted knowledge, for in community life, musical performances and cognate events are valued for the opportunity they provide for the renewal of experience.

Although much emphasis is laid on the arts as vehicles of communication, it is also widely recognized that they are an important means of enriching this experience. Hence, in some contexts the relationship of the arts may be epiphenomenal rather than integral. The annual odwira or great adae festival of the Akan of Ghana, for example, includes a traditional art exhibition. Art objects that form part of the regalia of a chief's palace are removed from storage and carried in a procession accompanied by music so that the public might see them as objects to admire and as evidence of the contribution of successive chiefs to the heirloom of the state.

On the same basis, the exterior of drums, resonators, and tuning pegs of instruments and resonators provide avenues for creating artistic designs and symbols that carry their own message, in much the same way as utility objects such as combs, chewing sticks, and household stools may be treated as a focus of artistic expression. Similarly, there are instances where the design concept of an instrument with a shell such as a drum, a gourd rattle, or resonator, or a flute includes encasing it completely or partially in leather or leather thongs, fabric, or ornamental sheets of brass or decorating it with brass tacks.

Apart from basic aesthetic considerations, some instruments are made imposing or spectacular by attaching symbolic or ritual objects to them, or by decorating them with anthropomorphic and zoomorphic figures and emblems or abstractions of the human face, the eyes, the limbs, or even figures of birds, trees, and other objects where the source of the elaboration is a proverb, a folk tale, an episode from history, some myth or legend, a deity, or spirit. Another way of achieving this effect is by transforming the regular form of an instrument. For example, instead of a simple calabash rattle, one or two spherical container rattles may be threaded together by a vertical piece of decorated or sculptured stick handle. The handle of an iron bell can be transformed or extended by inserting it into a sculptured figure.[12]

PERFORMANCE IN CONTEMPORARY CONTEXTS

The Context of Nation Building

The main provenance of the traditional performing arts discussed above has continued to be traditional communities, defined by ethnicity. However, as these arts constitute the most visible and dynamic testimony of the achievements of the African past, they were made to assume a dual status on the attainment of independence from colonial rule as community arts cultivated and practiced on the basis of ethnicity and as national arts that could be performed on national occasions as well as in other contemporary contexts. The freedom to drum, sing, and dance in the traditional way in contemporary contexts from which such activities were excluded in the colonial period constituted a symbolic affirmation of the declaration of independence, while the reconceptualization of the arts as national arts enabled them to be used in fostering national consciousness. Not only was independence celebrated with music and dancing, but also its subsequent anniversaries have been occasions for the renewal of this experience.

It was also believed that the integrative role played by the arts in traditional society, where they foster a sense of community, could be transferred to contemporary contexts. They could make a contribution to nation building, in particular, the process of creating and maintaining new institutional frameworks and loyalties that transcend the boundaries of ethnicity. Accordingly, everywhere, upon the achievement of political independence, national arts festivals were instituted as a strategy for promoting unity in diversity by getting performers and audiences from different regions to interact and share cultural experiences. In some countries these festivals took place annually and were organized on a number of different levels:

First, on the district level, performing groups and individual artists from different towns and villages noted for their excellence in particular types of music and dance were invited to perform in the district capital or some other convenient venue. Special guests were invited to join the local community. Second, on the regional level, a selection of the best and representative groups from the districts were invited to perform in the regional capital for a scheduled number of days. And third, on the national level, performers from the regions were again reassembled in the national capital (or a selected regional capital) so that city dwellers, who are the most out of touch with traditional musical life, could see performing groups from different parts of the country. Thus, besides their political objectives, such programs also served aesthetic and educational objectives. The coverage provided by national radio and television organizations enabled many people who were unable to attend to share in the programs, both during the actual event and later when the recordings were replayed.

In addition to festivals, elements of traditional arts were incorporated by some countries into state ceremonies because of the distinctive character they brought to such events. Presentations were also made at official parties and political rallies by selected groups or, in the rare case of a highly politicized state, by animators or cultural activists, who performed wherever the head of state or his representative made a public appearance. Occasional performances were also arranged for the entertainment of official visitors, just as in traditional society music and dance are offered as a homage to dignitaries or a tribute to individuals who formed the focus of public ceremonies. All these arrangements for performances of traditional arts in contemporary contexts have persisted in different forms in various African countries. Anniversary celebrations of independence are still occasions for the performance of traditional music in contemporary contexts, while some countries, such as Kenya, now have special centers for tourists and city dwellers who may otherwise not get the opportunity of seeing music and dance in their rural setting.

Performances in contemporary contexts naturally impose a number of constraints on the duration, scope, and content of the elements of traditional arts that are presented, and even on their quality and modes of presentation, especially where they are performed for audiences who may not always understand the symbolism of the dances or the message, humor, wit, or sarcasm in the songs. However, this does not discourage traditional performing groups. Because of the interactive structures that bind them together, they always constitute their own inner audience. Performers also learn over time to make contextual adaptations, including substitutions and the elimination of specific situational references.

Pan African and Global Perspectives

In addition to the process of nation building, which has encouraged the instrumental use of the performing arts in contemporary contexts for advancing national unity, larger questions of African unity and the philosophical issue of the African presence in the world of the arts—including pressures from the international theater world, trade, fairs, and similar events for African participation—have also engaged the attention of some African leaders. It seems that here also the performing arts can play a vital role in affirming the unity and diversity of African cultures as well as in projecting a fuller cultural image of Africa than the outside world has yet known.

Leopold Sedhar Senghor, the first president of Senegal and a strong advocate of the philosophy of Negritude, took the first significant step to provide such a rich, panoramic view of the arts of sub-Saharan Africa and the Black world at the first World Festival of Negro Arts, held in Dakar in 1966. Participants included a number of traditional performing groups as well as new groups whose art preserves some link with the historic traditions of Africa. Arab North Africa was deliberately excluded.

The initiative taken by Senghor was followed by two major festivals: the Algiers Festival of Arts, held in 1972 under the auspices of the Organization of African Unity (OAU), which emphasized the political dimension of the arts by including Arab North Africa, which had been excluded from Senghor's Festival of Negro Arts; and FESTAC—a festival of much greater proportion held in Lagos from January 15 to February 12, 1977 in collaboration with all the governments of Africa, and which extended the coverage of the two previous festivals in order to give scope to both the African Diaspora and the worldwide concept of Black culture that was beginning to be espoused. Participants in this festival included performers from Australia. The festival brochure lists the principal objectives as follows: to ensure the revival, resurgence, propagation, and promotion of Black and African Culture and Black and African cultural values and civilization; to present Black and African culture in its highest and widest conception; to promote Black and African artists, performers, and writers and facilitate their world acceptance and their access to world outlets; to bring to light the diverse contributions of Black and African peoples to the universal current of thought and arts; and to promote better international and interracial understanding among men.

The enormous problems involved in organizing inter-African arts festivals of such magnitude and the economic decline faced by many African countries have held this program in abeyance for nearly two decades, as no country seems willing to make the capital outlay for developing the necessary facilities and resources. National festivals of the arts on the postindependence scale also seem to have declined for similar reasons. But perhaps it is just as well, for it seems that postindependence euphoria, which focused on festivals and was necessary at that time for asserting a consciousness of identity, must now be superseded by strategies for intraterritorial and interregional African exchanges able to stimulate much-needed development and cultural cooperation in a number of mutually beneficial areas.

Outcome of Cultural Policy

Four significant consequences of governmental intervention in the status of traditional music and dance and the approach to culture have emerged. The first is the creation of institutional support in the form of ministries and departments of culture, arts councils, and national commissions on culture, for the promotion of the arts, which did not exist in the colonial period. Another aspect of this is the emergence of a new cadre of directors of cultural programs, cultural officers, managers, and promoters, many of them with no previous experience in arts management. This situation has lingered on in some countries and needs to be addressed through systematic training programs conducted in Africa itself, since such programs should include background knowledge and an understanding of the traditional arts and their contextual problems.

The second is the increased mobility of traditional performers, particularly those in the professional class of griots, who have increased their range of patrons and venues to include contemporary contexts. The urban nexus between migrant labor and migrant musicians has expanded. The third is the incipient eclecticism that has followed the reconceptualization of arts practiced as "ethnic" arts or as "national" arts, and their presentation in contemporary contexts. Instead of limiting themselves to one music and dance type as has been the custom, some traditional performing groups with aspirations for performance in wider contexts now try to be competent in the presentation of more than one traditional form in their community. As we shall see later, a different type of eclecticism has been generated by this process among contemporary artists.

The fourth noteworthy consequence is the presentation of traditional performing arts in contemporary contexts as "staged" performances, an innovation comparable to the orientation that makes ceremonial and ritual objects the focus of aesthetic contemplation in museums. The underlying assumption of this innovation is that whatever their contextual meanings, unlike the spoken language, the impact of the arts transcend ethnic barriers. While some contextual meanings may be lost to those who do not have the requisite background, there may yet be other areas, however small, to which they can relate, especially when the presentation combines music and dance or music, dance, and drama.

The presentation of traditional arts as "staged" performances (which began as a matter of expediency) and the recontextualization of tradition in contemporary contexts have become artistic procedures in contemporary music and dance presentations.

CONTEMPORARY ARTS

Unlike traditional arts, which are closely integrated because of their community orientation, contemporary arts are evolving separately in a milieu of change, in which the focus is on individual creativity that takes the arts beyond the historic forms and modes of expression established in traditional communities. Individual artists endeavor not only to work out their own styles as they create new works, but also to explore other formal possibilities that are not yet in vogue, for it appears that change and innovation have come to be valued as ends in themselves.

In some countries, a new impetus for this development was given through the launching of a national theater movement. In Ghana it was spearheaded by the Interim Committee for an Arts Council set up by the government in July 1955, later becoming a statutory body. This came almost at the same time as strategies for the restoration of traditional performing arts in contemporary contexts were being implemented, for it was felt that it was not enough to reproduce the traditional arts on national occasions and in the other usual contemporary contexts. The development of contemporary arts that maintain a link with tradition had to be part of the national cultural policy.

Creative Orientation

A number of stylistic and procedural features distinguish the approach of contemporary artists from their traditional counterparts. Conscious of the fact that knowledge and experience of other cultures form part of their background, many artists bring the totality of their individual knowledge and experience (which includes

African and Western or, in some cases, Arabic forms as well) into their creativity. Accordingly, while traditional artists draw their creative models from their own culture and that of their neighbors, their contemporary counterparts may also use external models as a springboard. This is evident, for example, in the early use of Caribbean, African American, and Latin American models as a starting point in the development of African popular music and the continued fascination that later forms have had for some artists as a framework for developing their own personal styles.[13]

Artists in traditional society employ the spoken medium, instrumental speech surrogates, and song as avenues for their verbal art, using their own languages to communicate because they inevitably address themselves to their own communities. Their contemporary counterparts, on the other hand, write their lyrics, poems, short stories, and novels in the adopted language of a former imperial power that serves as a lingua franca for all ethnic groups in their subregion and elsewhere who belong to the same imperial linguistic zone. They may, to a lesser extent, also use African languages when writing for members of their ethnic groups.

Traditional musicians generally stick to the instruments of their societies or those of their neighbors and, in some cases, a few adopted instruments of foreign origin such as the guitar, the one-string fiddle, and the double- reed aerophone (oboe), integrated into traditional musical cultures of the pre-European period. Their contemporary counterparts generally adopt the Western instruments they learned to play at school, in the church, or in urban centers, as well as the electronic instruments and synthesizers now at their disposal.

Similar differentiations occur in other arts. For example, while traditional artists may paint murals and excel in body arts, sculptural forms, and various crafts, their contemporary counterparts paint on canvas and may take advantage of the rich legacy of sculptural forms, in their own work or use African objects, scenes from cultural life, and other themes as the basis of their work.

All these trends in contemporary arts arise not only because of the intercultural background of the artists of today, but also because they do not have to relate their art to royal courts, traditional events, celebrations, and recreational life in traditional communities. The venues for their arts are clubs, cafes, ballrooms, cinema houses, theaters, churches, educational institutions, and galleries in museums and elsewhere, and of course radio and television. Some of these venues are increasingly becoming a part of the rural environment, while economic pressures force some contemporary artists to reach out to such communities where the forms they practice are readily accessible to audiences because of the artistic medium used.

Another reason is that contemporary artists relate their creativity to external genres like popular music, jazz, art music, the novel, the short story, and scripted plays, all of which carry their own conventions and performance practices that do not always correspond in certain essential details to the roughly equivalent forms in traditional practice. Since these genres are part of the legacy of acculturation, those who have passed through this process are also able to relate to them. Situating their creativity in any of them enables artists to reach both local and wider audiences. African popular music, for example, continually diffuses from particular countries to other African territories and beyond, even though the lyrics are in local languages, for stylistic innovations and new sonorities are greatly appreciated. Although this has not happened to the same extent with other arts, it is perhaps only a matter of time.

While many accept the intercultural approach to music, dance, drama, literature, and art as the natural consequence of a long period of acculturation followed by cultural awakening that tries to integrate the old and the new, indigenous and foreign, some artists and critics assert that vestiges of the colonial past must be eradicated as creative elements in the arts of independent Africa because they compromise their cultural identity. Accordingly, the latter veer toward a monocultural approach that permits them to concentrate solely on indigenous African materials. However, it appears from what they do in practice that while averse to borrowing tangible aspects of other cultures, they are not opposed to using processes and procedures found in other cultures. Neither are they opposed to intercultural forms when these are derived from different African and diasporan sources, for like other artists, they do not see themselves as returning to traditional communities to join traditional artists but as continuing from where the latter seem to have left off. In other words, the task they set themselves is to create new art based entirely on indigenous resources.

Thus, in music the creative artist may restrict himself to indigenous African instruments and organize them in ensembles, or form a Pan-African orchestra out of them, by re-tuning them to a standard pitch, employing various techniques of orchestration to create new sonorities and textures beyond those evident in traditional multipart structures. Or he may take the music of one traditional drum or xylophone ensemble and elaborate it or create new music for it.

In drama and theater one may opt for nonscripted plays or use the structure of traditional rituals, ceremonies, pageants, and festivals as the framework for developing contemporary forms of African theater. In other words, one may fall back on the methods of oral cultures rather than on those of literate cultures.

On the same basis, the contemporary African dance theater is seen to be better off reproducing and re-working Africa's rich heritage of traditional dances than importing external concepts of posture and movement sequences. In any case it seems much easier and more logical to establish a contemporary dance theater simply by rearranging or elaborating traditional dance forms, until such time as new dances based on the vocabularies evident in traditional dances are created by choreographers who have had time to do the required research into and analysis of African dance forms.

With the exception of dance, the monocultural approach has not yet gained a large following because much of what has come out of it is still "experimental," as its protagonists describe it, for it is difficult to set the clock back after a prolonged period of intense acculturation, particularly when the public reception of intercultural forms has made them the norm rather than the exception. It seems that as long as the strong features of African artistic idioms are present, few question the hymn-like harmonies of pop music, for example, and other contemporary genres because they sing and hear such harmonies all the time in church and school. But this is not a strong enough reason for not opening up the monocultural approach for development, particularly in areas where it is likely to make a unique contribution.

There is something to be said for both approaches to contemporary creativity, for they have common meeting grounds. Both attempt to explore traditional resources, one in combination with other resources and the other without any external materials on the surface. Both are open to different external processes and procedures as they respond to the challenge for innovation and change. The need to maintain an African identity in contemporary creativity is acknowledged in both approaches, except that it is unmistakable in a monocultural approach and not always as well defined in the intercultural approach. Both approaches have in fact been used by a few individuals and should continue as options available to contemporary artists.

Contemporary Relevance

Although maintaining a link with the past is accepted, it is held that African identity is not established only by reference to the past. It can be established through conventions operative in the present. While situating their creativity in the global genres they have adopted, contemporary African artists should seek to develop their own conventions both through transformations of traditional forms and through their own innovative practices, which crystallize into procedures and performance practices. There is evidence that this institutionalization process is already taking place informally, for although they work as individuals, they learn from one another through the constant regrouping of bands and other performing groups and, in some countries, also the formation of various arts associations and unions that bring them together.

Another concern of contemporary artists is the kind of critical relationship they establish through their art between themselves and their society. Going beyond traditional arts also means responding in creative terms to contemporary issues and concerns in all spheres of life. Hence, in addition to the foibles of human nature that are of interest to artists, it is maintained that, like their counterparts in literature, contemporary song writers and playwrights should show keen sensitivity to the aftermath of colonialism, the need for affirmation of consciousness of identity, the sense of history rooted in the African past, the impact of social and cultural change on the lives of individuals in cities, and the plight of the peasantry, particularly those who used to have right to the land of their birth but are now a landless class because of capitalist displacement. They should be concerned about institutionalized social injustices, power structures, and the vicissitudes of contemporary politics as well as the many ambiguities of contemporary social and cultural life.

Some of these contemporary themes and concerns are echoed in the texts of popular songs, for now and then song writers go beyond their preoccupation with love themes and moral issues and become either critics who create songs of protest or sycophants who play the role of praise singers. Other themes, such as religious themes, patriotism, national unity, the virtues of hard work, and the attributes of civil society occur in songs in other styles.

Creative Output and Patronage

The productivity that the search for new creative orientations has generated since the era of political independence is remarkable when compared with the colonial period. This is particularly noticeable in African popular music, which occupies a dominant position in contemporary African culture because of the accessibility of its idioms and modes of communication as well as its participatory nature, linking it closely to the traditional African approach to music and thus enabling it to foster a new sense of community among those who patronize it. Almost every African country now has its cadre of band leaders and songwriters who have made it to the top of their local charts as well as others who have now become part of the international popular music scene. As a result of this growth, popular music is no longer confined to its traditional venues. In some countries, such as Zaire and Congo, it has gained state recognition and may be performed at official state functions. Like traditional music, it may be performed at funerals and other ceremonies as well as at private parties, for the themes of its repertoire of songs are wide-ranging and allow for appropriate selection and contextual adaptation. Availability of commercial recordings of popular music through the growing cassette and video culture as well as radio and television extends the contemporary musical environment to homes, streets, shops, and public places.

The impact of contemporary creativity on musical practice in the bastions of colonial culture has been far-reaching, for there are practically no significant areas of performance in contemporary contexts in which contemporary forms have been disregarded. This is true even of conservative colonial institutions such as the military and the police, who treasure their legacy of Western ceremonials. Arrangements of African tunes are increasingly being incorporated into their repertoire as additions or alternatives to some of the standard Western military marches.

The Christian church, noted for its early opposition to African music and culture, is now also an important venue for contemporary developments in music. Several choral groups that specialize in new African church music have emerged. The formation of national and district choral unions based in churches is now a feature of contemporary musical life, while quasi-popular music ensembles that create and perform their own brand of "gospel" music in churches carry their art to contemporary entertainment venues. As this music is the artistic outgrowth of a new wave of spirituality, the new cassette industry is also fully exploited by artists in this area who arrange to release their new recordings in churches, cinema halls, and other public venues.

Because choral groups also function as voluntary associations, there is a growing interest in the formation of such groups outside the church. In Ghana, where there is a large repertoire of choral music in the African idiom written by Ghanaian composers, a tradition that goes back to the late 1920s, municipal and industrial establishments and other organizations establish and maintain their own choral groups for the entertainment of their workers and also to give them visibility on national occasions and at festivals.

New African art music designed for concert venues rather than the church and social areas has also emerged, except that it does not yet have the same following, even though all those who pass through formal education are exposed to such performances in schools. Establishing it as a dimension of culture that the literate community and others can patronize has been a slow process, for the idea of performances presented outside social areas and events in community life has not been the practice in traditional African societies. Performing artists take their art to where people assemble or are likely to be drawn to it by the proximity of the sound, and not the other way around.

Another reason for the limited patronage given to new African art music is, of course, the kind of musical idiom it presents and the nonparticipatory nature of the stimulus it generates. It seems, however, that this becomes less and less of a barrier when the African characteristics of the music become evident. An annotated catalog of African composers and their works compiled by Akin Euba, the Nigerian art music composer, shows that the productivity in this lesser-known area of contemporary African creativity is growing.[14] In spite of the limited patronage it commands, it may also establish itself in the world of art music, for not only are Western composers using African materials in a similar manner but Western performers have also begun to show interest in presenting African compositions to Western audiences. A festival of new African chamber music comprising thirty-five compositions by twenty composers was presented by the Hochschule für Musik Würzburg from May 20 to 28, 1995 in Würzburg and later in two other cities in Germany—Bremen and Dresden.

Drama and theater face similar problems of patronage, since in traditional society, these are generally an integral part of special events such as storytelling, public rituals, and festivals. In West Africa, popular musicians who were already well established in their social areas of music took the bold step of adapting and popularizing the drama they had been exposed to in schools. They created their own varieties of popular drama, combining popular music and dance as well as songs and dialogue in the languages of their own communities, which they took on the road. This activity, which began in the colonial period, was greatly intensified soon after independence as popular drama groups called "concert parties" proliferated. Theatrical presentations of music and dance in South Africa, culminating in variety shows in the 1950s, similarly gave artists the opportunity of reaching out to audiences in their communities.[15]

Alongside popular drama and musicals, the so-called legitimate theater and holistic theater, combining music, dance, and drama—such as Mikanza's *Lianja Epic*, produced in Kinshasha—have also had their exponents via schools and departments of theater established at African universities, or drama and theater units established by ministries of culture. Contemporary African playwrights, producers, and drama groups have emerged in many countries. The availability of published plays by African playwrights in different countries is encouraging the development of Pan-African perspectives in the programs presented at some national theaters. This trend and the growing popularity of amateur drama groups, who are promoted by radio and television as well as the film industry, have eclipsed the concert party tradition in some countries.

Interest in community drama, based on nonscripted plays produced in local languages, with the members of a local group as coproducers and actors, has also emerged. The primary objective is to restore the role of drama in traditional social life, while using it to advance social change or the communication of development issues and other matters of common concern.

Another significant area of performance in the contemporary context is dance theater. Although the concept of dance as "spectacle" or theater exists in traditional society alongside dance as a spontaneous participatory activity, its contemporary adoption as a theatrical form was not widely considered until shortly after independence, when colonial—and missionary—generated prejudice against African drumming and dancing was gradually broken. Even then, the paucity of African choreographers made it difficult for the theatrical possibilities of traditional dances to be meaningfully explored everywhere. The need to create national dance companies that would highlight the traditional cultural heritage on national occasions, or by going on tours locally and abroad, compelled many African countries to establish a framework for developing such troupes.

Three approaches emerged. First, there is the ad hoc approach adopted by many countries when they first embark on the creation of standing performing groups. Selected traditional groups and individual artists who are good exponents of particular forms of music and dance are brought together to form one composite group. Each subgroup performs items from the music and dance repertoire of its ethnic group at appropriate points within a program schedule. Because such a national troupe is usually an amorphous group, for theatrical purposes performers of the spectacular and the sensational—such as acrobats, fire-eaters, and stilt dancers—are included to make up for what the troupe lacks in artistic coherence. Second, there is the workshop approach. Here the members of the national troupe similarly drawn from different ethnic groups are selected on the basis of elaborate local and regional auditions and competitions and brought together not only to demonstrate what they can do but also to undergo theater training through workshops set up for the purpose, so that all or some of them can assume new theater roles when their contributions are recreated in the form of dance, drama, or presented with a story line, new spatial design, decor, and mime. This approach, which inspired the national Dance Company of Guinea (popularly known as Guinea Ballet), a pioneer in this field, can also be seen in other countries—such as Mali, Senegal, Zaire, and Tanzania.

The workshop approach assumes that artists already accomplished in the tradition of the area can always be found and that additional training in theater, given through workshops, would be adequate to hold them together. Thus, this approach tends to leave the basic training in music and dance to the normal process of enculturation—the process by which the individual acquires knowledge of his culture through social experiences or exposure to social situations. The third approach developed in Ghana is the institutional approach. It takes advantage of the workshop approach but does not leave training in the basic skills of music and dance to chance. It provides for the acquisition of these skills in a practical but systematic teaching program, supplemented by workshops for specific productions. Naturally, it is a slower process of building a performing group than the approach that picks up ready-

made artists. But it has the advantage of giving individuals training in a wider range of skills, as well as in a variety of idioms of the
national heritage, than do the other approaches. It provides a more
lasting basis for the integration of the arts and also encourages a
greater degree of mutual tolerance and respect among artists.

Another advantage of the institutional approach is that it provides a basis for the teaching of the basic skills of music and dance
in educational institutions, thus ensuring continuity of tradition
among the literate community. It also makes it possible to extend
the range of knowledge to the forms prevalent in other countries.
The existence of national dance companies has encouraged the formation of similar companies by enterprising individuals who see
them as avenues for their own creative endeavors, and sometimes
also by promoters, who see them as possible sources of income,
since such companies can perform in hotels for tourists or in night
clubs and similar venues inappropriate for national troupes. Some
of these private groups also seek their fortunes abroad.

The new focus on dance as theater has encouraged the substantial incorporation of dance into other events, such as drama
and performances of popular musicians and their associates, who
create their own floor shows or choreograph dances to back up
their music videos. Similarly, popular dance competitions held from
time to time now inspire transformations of spontaneous participatory dances into forms which combine structured and improvi-
satory movements.

BRIDGING THE OLD AND THE NEW

A great deal is going on in the performing arts, as individuals respond to the pressures and challenges of their cultural environment as well as those from the wider world with which they interact. However, there is no doubt that much more could be achieved
in certain directions, if development goals and strategies went beyond those of the postindependence era, which were concerned
primarily with the political and philosophical dimensions of the
arts. While restoration of the past continues to be a political imperative, I believe that the challenge facing the performing arts
today is not just restoration but building bridges between the old
and the new. There is, therefore, an urgent need to take a new look
at the creative, institutional, technological, social, and economic
dimensions of the arts from this perspective as we consolidate the

conceptual and material gains of the postindependence period and plan new development initiatives.

Since both the monocultural and intercultural approaches aim at creating new works that show some continuity with the past, development initiatives in the creative area should include: workshops that examine different ways of bridging the old and the new; the organization of a regular composers' forum for the presentation of new works to critical but appreciative audiences; and residencies that enable artists to try out their ideas. Our experience at the International Center for African Music and Dance at the University of Ghana shows that providing such opportunities for contemporary African composers, choreographers, and performers (who have hitherto worked largely in isolation) to interact and share ideas and techniques can yield fruitful results.

To facilitate the process of building bridges between the old and the new, opportunities should be created for traditional and contemporary artists to interact at some of the workshops. The possibility of inviting traditional composers and performers to workshops for literate composers as instructors or demonstrators of traditional techniques (for example, techniques of text construction) should be explored. Similarly, the possibility of using the performing arts to advance social and cultural change could be explored with traditional composers and creative performers who serve Africa's rural populations. In addition to the traditional themes on which they focus, they could also deal with development issues that affect their own communities through the medium of the song if they are sensitized.

In this connection it must be noted that new Christian evangelical strategies are already exploring this approach. The composition of new Christian songs by traditional nonliterate or newly literate musicians is encouraged at workshops where they are urged to compose songs based on selected scriptural texts—such as psalms translated into the local language. These compositions, learned by the members of the congregation who attend the workshops, are later rehearsed, recorded on cassette, and reproduced for distribution in the community so that the texts may be stored in the memory of those who listen to them. Involving traditional musicians in the communication of development issues in their communities or the meaning and implications of new concepts like democracy and the values of civil society along similar lines might be more effective than entrusting this to contemporary musicians who write in new idioms.

Another important initiative that must be considered as an ancillary to the creative dimension is the development of archives in Africa for reference and study. This must be tackled with vigor, for it has lagged behind in spite of the testimony of Alan Lomax that "Africa is the best recorded of continents."[16] Except in South Africa, where Hugh Tracey's international Library of African Music is housed, the bulk of the recordings made in the colonial period can be found only in archives in the Western hemisphere. There is nevertheless a growing accumulation of field recordings in Africa itself that could form the nucleus of archives in individual African countries. They include private collections; recordings at broadcasting and television stations; ministries of tourism, culture and information; museums; and academic institutions.

There is at present very little information about what is held in these collections, and whether they are managed as archives with properly documented card catalogs and so on. The first step might be to collate this information, create a general consciousness of the need for proper archiving, follow this up with seminars on archival management, and identify training needs—so that common policies regarding acquisitions, use, exchanges, etc., can be worked out. The creation of national policies on audiovisual archives might facilitate the grouping of these materials for developing private, institutional, and public archives. Private archives are archives not normally open to the general public, such as the archives of corporations (for example, those belonging to broadcasting, television, and film corporations). Institutional archives are archives administered as units within research institutions, arts centers, and museums, which may grow out of the work of a scholar or a collector associated with the institution and the contributions of other archives and field collectors who share a collective vision. Public archives are archives that emerge through an administrative mechanism for bringing together scattered collections in private custody that are donated or acquired, holdings in ministries and departments, as well as other public institutions.

Every effort should be made, therefore, to disseminate materials from such archives in a form of value to artists—composers, choreographers, dramatists, and performers—and educators in Africa, for unlike scholars whose work habits frequently take them to repositories, many artists tend to build their own small collections of available materials that attract their attention or excite their creative imagination so that they can refer to them at their leisure or even work with them. To facilitate such noncommercial dissemination, a network of composers, educators, and other interested people identified in each country could be compiled in order to determine the size of the initial distribution and other modalities that such a project would require. In this connection, collaboration between music institutions, museums, radio and television, and film industries in Africa would be highly desirable, for there is a very important role that the media can play, not only in the recording and dissemination of the arts, but also in their promotion.

The task of recording, documenting, and archiving should of course not stop with the collation of existing materials. Effort should be made not only to fill in the gaps that become evident, but also to document the changes that are continually taking place, as traditional performers adjust themselves to the challenges of their time. Further, if the goal is to build bridges between the old and the new, the task of recording, documenting, and disseminating should not be confined to traditional materials. It should be extended to contemporary forms not available through the regular commercial channels but judged to be significant in terms of their artistic merit or innovative dimension.

Performing arts institutions in Africa should be strengthened so that they can also build bridges between the old and the new in their course offerings and practical training programs, and generally act as spearheads in culture and development in their areas of specialization. This could mean in some cases a reformulation of the mission of an institution or of its goals and objectives. Further, because of the fact that many of these institutions are (unfortunately) modeled after Western university departments, conservatories, and institutes of fine arts, or staffed mainly by Africans who are themselves products of such institutions, it may be necessary to provide opportunities for some of their faculty to enlarge their background knowledge and skills in African performing arts through field studies and/or graduate studies in an African institution with such facilities. Such opportunities for study can be achieved through the award of scholarships or the institution of fellowship programs in the performing arts. In addition, one must ensure that the personnel of such institutions includes, for the time being, carefully selected preliterate traditional experts for instruction on certain levels or as field assistants, for they have much to give in terms of knowledge, skills, and experience.

Where prevailing conditions make all these steps impracticable, or where a country does not yet have a performing arts institution, much can be achieved through the creation of a small research-and-development unit, which can initiate and implement programs in conjunction with relevant departments and cultural organizations. Such a unit could be an integral part of an existing performing arts institution. In the absence of such an institution, it could be established in a cognate department or institute such as an institute of African studies or a cultural studies center. It was such an arrangement at the University of Ghana in 1952 that enabled me not only to do extensive fieldwork but also to participate actively in the development of cultural programs, as I laid the foundations for a school of music, dance, and drama. Although it may not work in the same way in every country, I mention it for what it is worth.

Another area in which bridges could be built between the old and the new is the development of musical instrument technology. Collecting African musical instruments as ethnographic specimens and keeping the large overflow in the vaults of museums was the outsider's approach, as he had no other use for them besides exhibiting some of them periodically. We must go beyond that. Making these instruments available in reasonable quantities for new creative and educational purposes requires studies of the technical aspects of their production in traditional societies, the application of appropriate technology to their manufacture, and the establishment of musical instrument workshops.[17]

The task of bridging the old and the new must not be confined to the technical and institutional aspects of the performing arts. Consideration should be given to the social and economic dimensions, for the boundaries of the traditional and the contemporary in national life are beginning to intersect. In many parts of West Africa, for example, traditional rulers play customary roles in their provinces and new roles in national politics. Traditional farmers, artisans, and craftsmen are increasingly identifying themselves with both traditional and contemporary societies, as they participate in the new market economy and its related associations, while professional people such as doctors, lawyers, and teachers now and then elect to be traditional rulers because they belong to royal lineages. Some of them also accept nomination as leaders of traditional organizations because it enables them to identify with their own people, while giving them the rare opportunity of playing a significant role in traditional contexts. Such change in status often carries with it the obligation to be familiar with the arts associated with the particular role.

Cultural programs in the performing arts have not yet caught up with this. Many members of traditional communities still go to contemporary events as passive participants except when they are given the opportunity to perform or exhibit their own art. Similarly those brought up on contemporary arts become passive participants at traditional events simply because they do not have the requisite knowledge and skills. Building bridges between the old and the new through appropriate institutional and outreach programs will provide those in contemporary society access to traditional arts that form a part of their heritage and increase the opportunities for those in the traditional community to share in contemporary forms. This might, in turn, promote greater interaction and the versatility that artists need to relate to all sections of their societies. The old and the new must now be regarded as a continuum and not as a duality.

Audience development has become critical in some areas of contemporary performing arts, not because audiences never existed in traditional societies but because new factors have entered into the picture. Of course, venues with captive audiences exist in contemporary society, such as the clientele of social areas like hotels and night clubs, congregations at church services, or those who go to parties and contemporary life-cycle events—naming ceremonies, weddings, and funerals. New situations have arisen in which the relationship between performers and their audiences is no longer defined solely by events or community ties as we find in traditional society, but by the art form itself and, sometimes, also by the particular exponent of it (i.e., the artist or performer him/ herself). Unlike the custom in traditional society, one goes to a musical concert, a dance concert, or a theater. This is not just a matter of attitudinal change. It is also a question of who can afford it, thus turning what used to be regarded as a regular dimension of life into a luxury. Alongside this is the commodification of the performing arts and artistic services, which assumes large proportions as one looks at the new crop of owners, managers, and promoters of popular bands and the music industry as a whole. There is certainly a correlation between the performing arts and development in other fields, not to mention the impact of global commercialization of music and cognate arts.

As problems such as the foregoing are common to all African countries, our strategies for dealing with culture and development in the performing arts must allow for inter-African cooperation, both in the search for realistic solutions and in the planning and implementation of procedures for dealing with them. While the development intervention assumed by governments soon after independence was inevitable, the time has come to adopt other approaches that will enable imaginative individuals, various arts associations and institutions, as well as nongovernmental organizations to contribute in their own way to the growth and development of the performing arts of Africa. An International Center for African Music and Dance could play a coordinating role in such initiatives.

NOTES

1. Klaus P. Wachsmann, Dieter Christensen, and Hans-Peter Reinecke, *Hornbostel Opera Omnia* (The Hague: Martinus Nijhoff, 1975), 270.
2. Portia Maultsby, "Africanisms in African-American Music," in *Africanisms in American Culture*, ed. Joseph E. Holloway (Bloomington: Indiana University Press, 1990).
3. J. H. Kwabena Nketia, *The Music of Africa* (New York: W. W. Norton, 1974), 116–74.
4. Simha Arom, *Polyphony and Polyrhythm in Central African Music* (Cambridge: Cambridge University Press, 1990).
5. Brodie Cruickshank, *Eighteen Years on the Gold Coast of Africa, Including an Account of the Native Tribes, and their Intercourse with Europeans*, 2 vols. (London: Hurst and Blackett, 1853), 266.
6. Nketia, *Music of Africa*, 69–115.
7. J. H. Kwabena Nketia, *Drumming in Akan Communities of Ghana* (London: Thomas Nelson & Sons, 1963).
8. John Chernoff, *African Rhythm and African Sensibility* (Chicago: University of Chicago Press, 1979), 167.
9. Francis Bebey, *African Music: A People's Art* (New York: Lawrence Hill and Company, 1975), 119–20.
10. Hans Corey, *African Figurines: Their Ceremonial Use in Puberty Rites in Tanganyika* (London: Faber & Faber, 1956).
11. Melville J. Herskovits, *Dahomey: An Ancient West African Kingdom* (Evanston, Ill.: Northwestern University Press, 1967), 328–43.
12. J. H. Kwabena Nketia, "The Aesthetic Dimensions of African Musical Instruments," in *Sounding Form: African Musical Instruments*, ed. Marie-Therese Brincard (New York: American Foundation of Arts, 1989).

13. John Collins, *African Pop Roots* (London: Foulsham, 1985); Graeme Ewens, *Africa O–Ye! A Celebration of African Music* (New York: Da Capo Press, 1992).

14. Akin Euba, *Modern African Music: A Collection of Selected Archival Materials at Iwalewa–House* (Bayreuth, Germany: University of Bayreuth, 1993).

15. Ewens, *Africa O–Ye!* 187; David Coplan, *In Township Tonight* (New York: Longman, 1985); Veit Erlmann, *African Stars: Studies in Black South African Performance* (Chicago: University of Chicago Press, 1991).

16. Alan Lomax, *Folk Song Style and Culture* (Washington, D.C.: American Association for the Advancement of Science, 1975), viii.

17. Craig Woodson, "Appropriate Technology in the Construction of Traditional African Musical Instruments in Ghana," in *Selected Reports in Ethnomusicology*, vol. 5, *Studies in African Music*, ed. J. H. Kwabena Nketia and Jacqueline C. DjeDje (Los Angeles: Program of Ethnomusicology, Department of Music, University of California, Los Angeles, 1984).

CHAPTER 8

Publishing in Africa:
Culture and Development

Walter Bgoya

INTRODUCTION

Some years ago in Dar es Salaam, Mrs. Shirley Du Bois, wife W. E.
B. Du Bois, the great African American philosopher and architect
of the Pan-African movement, told an anecdote that I would like
to share with you. After the coup that toppled Dr. Kwame Nkrumah
of Ghana, a group of soldiers went to her house and demanded to
make a thorough search of it. As they were about to enter her late
husband's library, she stepped in front of them and challenged any
one of the soldiers who was not afraid of the old man's spirit, which
resided in his books and papers, to dare touch his things. The soldiers, who had come with much force and determination, looked
at the impressive array of books and papers, thought about the
matter, discussed it in their mother tongue, and decided it was too
risky a business. They excused themselves and left Mrs. Du Bois
and her books alone. Taking no more chances, she had the library
transported to Cairo, where she also went to live soon after. If the
metaphor of the book as the house of spirits is extended, the publisher could be the builder of the house of spirits, with the author
as its feeder. This metaphor is, of course, not so far-fetched; the
concept of the union of the living and the dead is present in all
sub-Saharan African cultures. It is what explains the practice of
pouring libation before drinking and placing food and drink in
specially constructed huts outside the main house for the departed
elders, to whom individuals with problems pray for intercession

with God.[1]

By its weakness more than its strength, African publishing, which even at its best serves a minority of every African country's population, is cast in a special position of privilege and disadvantage. The privilege lies in its function of producing one of education's most important tools—the book—and the nobleness that function confers on the role of publishing in a country's cultural development. The disadvantage lies in its lack of a mass base for reasons of penury in financial, material, and technical resources on the side of production, and weak purchasing power of the majority of the population on the consumer side. Situation analyses of publishing in Africa appear periodically after major conferences on publishing.[2] In addition, the World Bank has commissioned book-sector studies, which have provided the Bank with the basis for its decisions on loans to African countries, with regard to programs aimed at "placing books on the desks of the children." The book-sector studies contain much useful information on the status quo in the country under study. However, the conclusions from those studies have been received with mixed feelings by African and other Third World publishers, who think that such studies have tended to emphasize the weaknesses rather than the strengths of the indigenous publishers, including state and parastatal ones. Indeed, a significant number of them hold the opinion that the book-sector studies usually pave the way for British and other multinational publishers, who follow in the footsteps of the consultants doing the studies. That opinion is reinforced by the fact that the authors of these studies, with Mr. Anthony Read at the head, are a British consulting firm with strong links to British publishing. Of course, the cultural context of those reports may have more to do with their conclusions than with any inclinations on the part of the authors in favor of British publishers.[3] To the best of my knowledge, these studies have not yet been published in book form and are, therefore, not readily available, although they are not restricted in circulation either. In the 1970s, UNESCO sponsored studies on books and reading in a number of African and other Third World countries that were rich sources of information on publishing in those countries.[4]

PUBLISHING IN AFRICA—A BRIEF OVERVIEW

Although there are marked differences in publishing output in different African countries, the situation is generally one of extreme underdevelopment. Descriptions of the situation invariably refer to the continent as "book starved," "bookless," or as suffering from "book famine." The general crisis that the continent has been undergoing is nowhere more manifest than in book publishing. An indication of this is given in UNESCO's yearbook for 1988. The statistics show that the number of books produced in Africa rose from 1,600 titles in 1955 to 10,000 in 1986, representing a growth from 0.6 percent to 1.2 percent, respectively, of worldwide total book production over thirty-one years.[5] "Africans had substantially lower likelihood of having access to locally published material than citizens of any other region of the world,"[6] and the situation has not improved. On the contrary, for most countries it has deteriorated.

There are four models of publishing in Africa: state publishing, where the government owns and runs publishing houses; parastatal publishing, where states own (often majority) shares in publishing companies but do not deal with their day-to-day management; multinational publishing, where foreign publishing companies dominate (Longman, Macmillan, Oxford University Press, Heinemann, Evans Brothers, and Nelsons—for the ex-British colonies; and Hachette—for the ex-French/Belgian colonies); and private indigenous publishing. Of the four models, the really successful one is the multinational. In a few countries—Zimbabwe, Kenya, and Nigeria—a certain level of development has been attained but even in those countries, the ratio of material produced by indigenous publishers to that produced by multinationals or imported is still heavily tilted in favor of the latter. In 1985/86, Longman Zimbabwe and College Press, for example, accounted for 80 to 90 percent of Zimbabwe's publishing output, and in some countries the percentage dominated by the multinationals is even higher.[7]

Those four models operate in countries at three levels of publishing development. The first group comprises "adequate capacity" countries that have attained efficient infrastructures of publishing—where private-sector printing, publishing, and distribution operate efficiently and where quality books are available at reasonable prices. This includes Zimbabwe, Kenya, and South Africa.[8] Countries in the second category, and Nigeria is the only example, have basically the same well-developed infrastructure but due mostly to political reasons are unable to meet their book needs. This is defined as "adequate capacity, raw material constrained." In countries in the third category, of "low capacity," only rudimentary infrastructures exist and books are expensive, poor in quality, and erratically produced. Tanzania, Zambia, Ghana, Ethiopia, Sudan, Mozambique, and Angola, among others, fall into this category.[9] These countries happen, incidentally, to have also been the ones that adopted the centralized state and parastatal publishing models soon after independence.

The situation described above refers to the Anglophone countries (whatever "Anglophone" or its opposite, "Francophone" may mean in countries in which barely 5 percent of the people are literate in English or French.) In Francophone countries, French publishers dominate the situation, although *Nouvelles éditions africaines* (NÉA)—which is owned by the governments of Senegal, Côte d'Ivoire, and Togo (60 percent), and the French metropolitan companies Edicef, Istra-Hachette, Armand Colin, Nathan, Presence africaine, and Le Seuil—publishes a significant portion of the textbooks.[10] The situation in Lusophone Africa until recently was dominated by the state-owned Istituto national do livros e discos in Mozambique and Angola. Uniao do escritores angolano (Union of Angolan Writers) is supported to such an extent by the state that it is hard to think of it in terms other than "state."

TEXTBOOK PUBLISHING

Textbook publishing is the most lucrative field of publishing in Africa. Schools and/or ministries of education provide the only reliable market for publishers. With profits made from textbook publishing, publishers can invest in producing other books—fiction, higher education, and general trade books. Without textbooks, and in the absence of other sources of finance, publishing cannot take off. In many countries in Africa during the colonial period and after independence, publishing was done either by transnationals or state publishing corporations. In the case of the former, decisions about what to publish, when, how, and at what prices, were made outside the African countries in which these firms operated. In a few countries, transnational publishers have evolved through buyouts into successful indigenous publishing companies,[11] and the value of their presence in Africa, it is often argued, can be demonstrated by how well the successor companies are doing in contrast to the wholly indigenous companies, whose fortunes tend to be uncertain.

That is not, however, the only legacy of transnational publishers in Africa. The debacle of the joint ventures set up after 1965 by Macmillan publishers of the United Kingdom and a number of states—Tanzania, Uganda, Ghana, Northern Nigeria, and Zambia—argues strongly against that model of association between African publishers and transnational corporations. The African partners not only got raw deals in terms of profit sharing; more harmful were the opportunities denied the African partners to develop independent editorial policies and capacities and to decide on what to publish, particularly in the field of fiction, and especially in African languages. For the transnational publishing companies, the only real interest in Africa was and remains textbook publishing. As Per Gedin notes, "the textbook market for the transnational publishers after the de-colonization of Africa was in the beginning the most lucrative market in the world. Profits were made not only through insufficient editing and overpricing books but also by dumping books that were obsolete in their own countries."[12]

In the absence of a "national" educational philosophy—that is, where there was no difference in form and content between colonial and postcolonial education in a given country, there was obviously no impetus for curricular reform and/or developing new textbooks. In addition, as there were lucrative deals to be made through commissions and kickbacks by the comprador capitalist class, importing books was clearly more profitable than venturing into indigenous publishing.

Although the main thrust of this chapter will be that fiction and journal publishing are the real promoters of literary culture, it would be incorrect to ignore the issue of the quality of general education, which can be facilitated greatly by textbooks that are good and relevant in content (i.e., appropriateness of material for the intended level), depth and organization, language, and design (including illustrations, layout, and overall presentation). It is no exaggeration to say that textbooks in many African countries (certainly in Tanzania) are generally drab-looking objects that leave a great deal to be desired. The reason for this is the lack of appreciation of the art of book design. Books do not inspire pupils to learn, and even where the subject matter is adequately covered, very often language and presentation do not receive adequate attention. Illustrations are not attractive and are often even misleading. Problems of curriculum development and insufficiently trained curriculum developers, the tendency in the last twenty years to ignore language training (whether the language is national or for-

eign), poor working conditions, and, especially, inadequate remuneration (static wages) in conditions of inflation and devaluation
all go into making the textbook a less effective educational tool
than it ought to be.

One area in which textbooks are especially lacking is gender
issues. It has been observed that teaching materials continue to
portray men and women in stereotypical roles, and the real contribution of women in such areas as the economy and history are not
included in texts.[13] The lower performance of girls compared to
that of boys at the end of primary school, in combination with other
factors, reduces the chances for girls to pursue secondary and
higher education and leads to a dead end as far as employment
and a decent future are concerned. The field of gender education
is new and there is a need to mobilize educators to grasp its basic
elements, particularly as they relate to traditional philosophies of
initiation, notions such as the "future of a woman is marriage,"
and the fear among educated men of educated women.

Gender biases are perhaps the most easily noticeable, but others with particularly insidious import for race abound in many
textbooks published by transnational publishers. Naturally, those
being published today are more sophisticated and less blatant than
those published before independence. But that does not mean that
the problem no longer exists—far from it. On careful examination
there exists, in varying degrees, even in books that are written and
published in Africa by African authors and publishers, evidence
of the prejudices of European colonial and class cultures. This
should not cause surprise; the present generation of textbook writers came up just before independence and soon after. They were
brought up on English, French, and Portuguese intellectual menus
and have not wholly lost their taste for those diets. Indeed, the
important question of relevance of curricula in use in African
schools is given such scant attention that one would have to be
blind and dumb not to see the link between African education and
the colonial models on which it hangs.

The situation has been further complicated in recent years. In
addition to the identification of African intellectuals with Western
intellectual traditions, there are the added attractions and even
"blackmail" in the form of large fees from consultancies offered by
organizations such as the World Bank and the threat of losing them
in the case of "departures" from conventional ideological prisms.
In conditions of low wages, inflation, and devaluation—products
of Structural Adjustment Programs—the casualty rate of indepen-

dent thinkers becomes very high. In her forthcoming book, Birgit Brock-Utne makes two observations concerning attitudes of some university professors, whose private opinions of the World Bank policy study, *Education in Sub-Saharan Africa: Policies for Adjustment, Revitalization and Expansion,* are very critical but who publicly support it. As one party official commented, concerning the public statements of such professors, "it is our people but the thoughts are World Bank's." She concludes that "it is not easy for an African intellectual who is unable to live from his regular university wage to write from an African perspective if this perspective is not what the donors want."[14]

Educational publishing is based on curricula, and the syllabus is the author's and publisher's blueprint for manuscript development and textbook publishing. Analyzing "the tensions between external standards and internal cultures," Angela Little asks

if international standards which in many instances means "external standards" produced in the West begin to take precedence over national and sub-national standards what are implications for nationally and culturally prescribed curricula? Will an internationalized education assessment technology begin to drive an internationalized curricula reform? How much wider will become the gap between the culture of those who control education and who design international tests and curricula, (i.e., the "supra national educators") and the culture of the child whose learning is the goal?[15]

It is no wonder that in the end the curricula developers, being themselves products of colonial-type education, need not be externally based to espouse the same values and tastes and to construct the same models of achievement. For publishing houses wishing to publish books different from the run-of-the-mill, it is difficult to find editors who have escaped from the international (Western) cultural mold that locks uncritical intellectuals into an adoration of Western educational and cultural values and a denigration of those that are African.

LIBERATION HISTORY AS A SPECIAL PUBLISHING PROJECT

If to "become like the West" is asserted as the modern objective of all development theory, its antecedent and underlying colonial, missionary worldview was that Africa had no history or culture. Since it was in that denial of African history that colonialism and imperialism executed their assault on all other African values, it must be in the reconstruction of that history that the process of rediscovery and validation should be undertaken:

> For several centuries Africa has had to suffer under the conception of the African past formed by Europe. As long as this was so, that European conception was "true," that is to say, effective. But the present and the future on the other hand will be determined by the conception that African intelligence forms of the African past. Neo-African Culture appears as an unbroken extension, as the legitimate heir of tradition. Only where man feels himself to be heir and successor to the past has he the strength for a new beginning.[16]

Frantz Fanon summed it up well when he stated that "while politicians situate their action in actual present-day events, men of culture take their stand in the field of history" and that "the passion with which the native intellectuals defend the existence of their national culture may be a source of amazement, but those who condemn this exaggerated passion are strangely apt to forget that their own psyche and their own selves are conveniently sheltered behind a French or German culture which has given full proof of its existence and which is uncontested."[17]

   Culture is about reliving our past—reworking material from the past while facing the present. In Africa at the present, the major cultural thrust appears to be mostly the reconceptualization of culture following Western trends. To be valid "internationally," it is not sufficient that music and literature are African; they must also be "universal," and if they are not, they are vilified in language that does not hide the deep prejudices of the critics as agents of the colonial legacy or the discomfort of African critics as apologetic victims of the latter. Chinua Achebe's response to Eldridge Jones on Wole Soyinka's *The Interpreters* is worth noting. Jones comments:

> This is the confrontation which *The Interpreters* presents. It is not an "African" problem. Events all over the world have shown in the new generation a similar dissatisfaction . . . Thus Soyinka, using a Nigerian setting, has portrayed a universal problem. This is what makes both this novel and the whole corpus of Soyinka's work universally valid.

And Chinua Achebe asks, with piquant sarcasm:

> For supposing "events all over the world" have not shown "in the new generation a similar dissatisfaction . . . ," would it truly be invalid for a Nigerian writer seeing dissatisfaction in his society to write about it? Am I being told, for Christ's sake, that before I write about a problem I must first verify whether they have it too in New York and London and Paris?[18]

And so on . . . unless African music is "reggaefied," unless *Tatunane*, a Tanzania musical group, wins some prize in Paris and their music is given "universal" appeal through international instrumentation, arrangement, and synthesis, it is not good enough. It is not good enough that it is African; it must be international—i.e., Western. But the opposite is not the case. To be international, Western music does not have to be Africanized, although I understand the great Moscow Bolshoi Ballet is being pressured to include some "break dance" routines into its repertory in order to appeal to American tourists and those that are resident in Moscow. No doubt all this can be easily explained as "exigencies of the market."

CURRICULA, PRINT RUNS, AND AFRICAN UNITY

One of the contradictions in the drive toward African unity is that the more evident the ways of promoting unity are, the less attention they are given. The dominant definition of Africa and Africans has never been the definition that Africans themselves have shaped, but the one that was shaped for them by colonialism. In that sense, the Organization of African Unity (OAU) is a continuation of the Berlin Conference. African economies have more in common that is the outcome of the general imposition of Structural Adjustment Programs (SAP) today than anything Africans have set up before. Highway vendors of cheap imports weaving in and out of cars in bumper-to-bumper traffic jams that I saw in Lagos ten years ago have taken over Dar es Salaam, as it begins to look more and more like Lagos: gold chains and gold rings are on every finger, the kind of ostentation that *Ujamaa* had frowned on. Expensive weddings, christening ceremonies, and prominent newspaper advertisements of funerals and death anniversaries are recent discoveries of a small minority class. These are the values that have accompanied SAP, and are to be seen everywhere one goes in structurally adjusted Africa.

One way that Africa can begin to find its own identity, which I take to be a precondition for development, is first to educate its young in the histories, geographies, and the cultures of its peoples. The answer to the question of who educates the educators must and can be found in new debates about education and development in light of the evident failure of past and present education theories and philosophies. Africa-centered education would demand curricula that ensure that students in every African region learn about other African regions. American universities make the study of Western civilization a compulsory course for all students including those that are not American. Shouldn't a common African history course be developed for all OAU member states? Shouldn't a set of the best books in history (UNESCO's *General History of Africa*, for example) be adopted for use in such courses?

A few years ago, while investigating the possibility of setting up a SADCC (Southern African Development Coordination Conference) University Press, it became clear that as long as the universities in SADCC countries did not have common and compulsory courses based on a SADCC curriculum, there was very little chance of books published in one country finding markets in the other SADCC countries. For example, since students at the University of Dar es Salaam are not obliged to know anything about the geography, history, or other aspects of countries in their region, they can never feel an affinity for these countries. If, on the other hand, universities in the region offered common courses in subjects of common interest, it would be natural for authors, publishers, and book distributors to think more in terms of the region than focusing only on their own countries. Inevitably, as universities and secondary school curricula reflected interests and aspirations of the region, the closer the countries and peoples would become, and the greater the chances would be for regional unity as a precursor to unity or at least to very close cooperation on a continental scale. This is obviously focusing on a limited and narrow area. But it happens to be the most important area because it would root the countries in a common consciousness of their past as well as their future. It would redress the colonial educational legacy of Africans, who were taught everything about the "greatness" of the colonizing power—history, geography, economy, culture, and what have you—but nothing or little (itself distorted) of their own countries. The impact of common curricula for countries in the same region in at least the key subjects of history, literature, and geography (especially its environmental dimension) would not be lim-

ited to the ideological benefits. By the same token, early specialization, with very few general culture courses, limits the breadth
and depth of knowledge and the possibility of the broadest participation in politics, science, and culture that is desirable among
educated citizens. In the regional context, this limits understanding and identification of each people with others in the region.

Publishing, particularly for university and tertiary levels,
would benefit by the large numbers of users. At present, numbers
of university students in each country are too small when disag-
gregated for different disciplines to provide a large enough internal market. That would change if the books were published for a
region and not for a country. It is common today to see that even
where books would be relevant for a region, the practice is to give
them narrow titles to reflect "nationalistic" sentiments. Multinational publishers encourage and exploit this by packaging books
basically to create a multitude of markets for themselves. A book
of geography for East Africa will be packaged in three books; one
for Kenya, one for Tanzania, and one for Uganda—as if there were
different geographies for those countries.

While recognizing the limitations that are inherent in the absence of common African languages for this project, one must also
recognize the potential even to deal with this question that would
be made possible by regional educational integration. African regional languages would have a much better chance to develop and
spread than they have in the present situation, where each country
grapples with its languages or opts for the easy way out with English and French, or Portuguese and Spanish.

MAJOR ISSUES OF AFRICAN PUBLISHING

Inter-African Cooperation

There are a number of obstacles facing inter-African cooperation in publishing. In the preceding section, the absence of common curricula was identified as a major obstacle, especially for
institutions of higher learning. There are, nevertheless, ways of cir-
cumventing the problems. One of them would be to take advantage of the differing levels of publishing in Africa—the fact that
some countries (South Africa, Nigeria, Kenya, and Zimbabwe) are
ahead of many other countries, both quantitatively and qualita-
tively. While it is inevitable and understandable that every country should seek some level of autonomy in publishing, there are

many advantages to be derived from joint publishing activities. Some benefits entail sharing of print runs, licensing, adaptations, or sharing in origination costs; this is possible thanks to the existence, in some African countries, of developed publishing industries.

There have been some noteworthy achievements in inter-African cooperation in publishing—such as the establishment of the African Books Collective (ABC) in Oxford in 1989, and the African Publishers' Network (APNET) in 1992. ABC, an initiative of African publishers, has received financial support from international donor organizations, and is responsible for marketing and distributing books of member publishers in Europe and North America. It aims to return to the African publishers in hard currency proportionately more than they would obtain from conventional distributors in those countries. ABC is making a major contribution to African book publishing by making African books known to all major public libraries and by exhibiting at important conferences such as those of the African Studies Association, the American Library Association, and at book fairs in London and elsewhere. ABC has also increased African publishers' revenues from export sales to an unprecedented high.

In addition to the financial advantage, there have been other benefits of ABC's trade for member publishers. Introduction and exposure to a wide market will attract African authors, particularly those who in the past could argue that publishing in Africa limited their chances of international recognition. Having one or two sourcing centers for the continent's publishing output will make it easy for librarians and booksellers outside Africa to keep up-to-date with intellectual trends in Africa, thus facilitating cultural exchange. Another advantage of ABC not foreseen in the beginning is the role it has been playing in facilitating the inter-African book trade. Through such programs as the Inter-African Book Service, books from one part of Africa are, almost for the first time, going to other parts of Africa. The irony of books from Nigeria having to go to Oxford first before they can go to Kenya, or even to nearby Ghana, cannot be missed. Still, if that is presently the only way available, there is every reason to support it. But clearly, as books from African publishers circulate in libraries in Africa, there will finally develop a desire to order books directly from publishers in Africa.

APNET was a child of the Bellagio Conference on Publishing and Development in the Third World, which was held in Bellagio,

Italy in 1991. Ever since its establishment, APNET has been the focal point for African publishers and their friends to exchange ideas, make plans, and consult. The project and activities report for 1993 and 1994 shows how extensive APNET's international contacts are, along with an impressive list of activities that were accomplished during that year. Significant events to note are development of close working relations with the Association for the Development of African Education (DAE) Working Group on Textbooks and Libraries, the Bellagio Group, ABC, UNESCO, the Canadian Organisation for Development through Education, and the World Bank. As a result of contacts with the DAE, a major study on the economics of textbook publishing in Africa will be undertaken involving at least eight countries. APNET receives and distributes information to members on all World Bank education and textbook projects, which will allow members to participate in international competitive bidding for supply of textbooks internationally.

APNET and Publishers Associations as Cultural Institutions

It is gratifying that APNET has been active in promoting not only trade-related activities but also others that are cultural in scope. Publication of the *African Publishing Review* in the three languages of APNET's membership—English, French, and Portuguese—opens up an important venue for publishers to exchange experiences and hopefully to develop a consciousness of themselves and their place in their societies and in Africa in general. Experiences such as the moving lecture given by Kenyan publisher Henry Chakava on "Publishing Ngugi: The Challenge, the Risk and the Reward," which was reproduced in *African Publishing Review*,[19] provides inspiration that is especially needed by young editors and publishers and those who think publishing lacks excitement.

One envisages publishing houses and publishing personalities competing and cooperating: writers, editors, and designers developing through publishing houses; making their debuts and their exits, staying on for years, or changing employment and changing publishers according to fortunes made and lost; or seeking ideological compatibility. One envisages critics gaining fame because their criticism has helped shape literary trends and traditions, resisting censorship and bad taste so that publishing flourishes and literature blooms. National publishers associations, writers unions, booksellers associations, and graphic artists associations are all necessary links in the field of literary culture, and an African umbrella organization such as APNET can act as a catalyst for publishers' efforts at the national level.

Book Fairs

Closely linked to cooperation in publishing are trade fairs, which provide authors, publishers, book distributors, and librarians the opportunity to meet and establish contact, to see the productions of the antecedent period, and to learn in advance about books planned for the coming period. A number of book fairs are organized on the African continent. So far, the Zimbabwe International Book Fair (ZIBF) has established itself as Africa's premier book fair. There are other fairs, modest but with potential for growth. The annual Pan-African Children's Book Fair in May, in Nairobi, is attracting more and more exhibitors and visitors and could in time become Africa's "Bologna." The Cairo International Book Fair is more for the Arab region than it is for the rest of Africa, primarily because of language. Dakar, Senegal, is the venue of another successful book fair mainly for Francophone Africa.

Apart from these four international events, book weeks or book festivals are organized at the country level in Nigeria, Tanzania, Zambia, and South Africa. In the case of South Africa, which has by far the most-developed publishing industry, there is no doubt that it is because of the abhorrent policy of apartheid that an international book fair was never contemplated there before. Now that apartheid has been defeated, there are no reasons to stop the organization of a major book fair. On the other hand, because of the proximity of South Africa to Zimbabwe, and because the ZIBF has already established itself, it could be argued that a South African Book Fair would be an unnecessary duplication of effort in the region. However, organizing book fairs, like book publishing in general, is competitive, and the venue that provides the best cost-benefit advantage will attract more exhibitors. It is in reality a question of participation cost; air fare, hotels, transport, and business potential; whether publishers can sell books through the fair and whether attendance at the fair is large enough to make rights deals possible. That, in turn, would depend on the sophistication of the markets—whether there was a large enough mainstream reading public to make translations of international bestsellers possible and profitable.

The ZIBF serves, first, the African publishers, which are able to see books produced by their counterparts in other countries. It also attracts foreign publishers (from outside Africa) with an interest in African books looking for opportunities to discover new writing. Clearly, these are publishers that are interested not only in the big names but in the less well known, since for the big names they would not need to come to Africa. They would more likely pick up new titles from the big writers at the Frankfurt Book Fair than from ZIBF.

The role of book fairs cannot be overemphasized. Advocating the widest planning and sharing of the benefits of educational and cultural integration in Africa includes also recognizing the necessity of regular venues for encountering, sharing, and reviewing efforts undertaken on a regional and continental scale. Issues already raised in respect to "educating the educators," new directions in interpretation of historical and cultural events, as well as linking researchers, can be addressed at book fairs as well as at cultural festivals.

Copyright Issues

Most, if not all, African countries are signatories to the Berne Convention. It is evident, however, that the issues involved in copyright are not understood, even generally, by the so-called educated elite of our countries. Neither the benefits of membership in the Berne Convention nor the disadvantages of not signing have ever been seriously addressed let alone debated. Furthermore, whereas protection may be advantageous to some of the intellectual producers, it is not certain that the advantages are obvious to others. The question of an individual creator's benefit as opposed to societal benefits have not been debated enough. One would have thought that this would be of primary importance, considering the fact that in traditional African societies the practice of art was treated as belonging to the social realm rather than to the individual creator, as was also the artist's remuneration. If the issue of copyright remains problematic, it is in part because there is a lack of consensus over it.[20]

Copyright law, as it is understood by most nonspecialists, aims to protect the works of authors and to ensure that they are able to enjoy financial and other advantages from the sale of their works. Copyright is presented as a norm of all "civilized" nations, and its philosophical underpinning is supposed to be self-evident. It seems, however, that what is taken as self-evident is not in fact so self-evident. It is particularly not so when those crusading advocates of today were the bold pirates of yesterday. The United States, in particular, is a case that merits more than casual reference. For more than 100 years, the United States violated—better still, did not recognize—the then existing copyright law for all "civilized" nations of Europe. Works, mainly from English presses, were pirated as a matter of routine, and it was not unusual for a novel to appear simultaneously in England and America, suggesting that typeset matter was actually stolen before publication. American sources recognize and admit that thanks to this practice, American publishing and printing developed rapidly. Until today, a work is not copyrighted in the United States unless within a specified period of five years it is also printed in the United States. The following quotation from an American authority on copyright says it all:

> In the 19th century, the United States—then a fledgling nation—was the biggest book pirate in the world, freely reprinting European (primarily English) works without either requesting permission or making payment. This activity was clearly piracy in the eyes of the Europeans, but it was completely legal under U.S. copyright laws at that time. The U.S. government chose to enable its citizens to obtain copyrighted works (and the information they contained) at low cost to encourage the growth of domestic printing and publishing industries by enabling them to produce books that were proven sellers in England, or elsewhere in Europe, without payment to copyright holders, thus greatly enhancing their chances of making a profit on their output.[21]

Further on in the essay, this writer states that even after the Berne Convention was passed in 1886, the United States still paid no attention to it to "avoid suppression of domestic interest that would have been involved in adhering to Berne," and also that, "actually through a loophole in Berne, the United States was able from 1928 onwards to obtain protection of its authors under the convention without adhering to it, by publishing editions simultaneously in the United States and Canada." When, based on the foundation that piracy provided, the U.S. publishing industry developed and American books became popular in England, piracy was reversed and American authors and publishers were paid in kind by the victims of their past practices. At that point the United States did acquire a willingness to respect copyright.

The following observations and questions come to mind: first, it is correct that nonobservance of copyright harmed U.S. authors. Did it also harm the overall interests of literary culture, and the material interests of the larger segment of creators—publishers, printers, and booksellers? Second, if, as it appears, all countries that have made great strides in promoting reading and publishing—Japan, India, Soviet Union, China, Cuba, Korea, Taiwan, and a number of other Southeast Asian countries—passed through the same stage (some are still not quite out of it), is it wrong to conclude that copyright law is an obstacle to developing publishing and for effecting a general education revolution?

Third, Africa has been the net loser in movements of cultural treasures worldwide. Major museums in Europe and the United States were built from profits that were directly linked to slavery and colonial plunder. These museums and private collections contain more African art treasures (including heads of African chiefs chopped off and taken to Europe during the heyday of colonialism) than there are in Africa. Most of these treasures were acquired freely at best, or they were taken by threat in the violent environment of colonialism. The voices from Africa asking for the return of these objects have fallen on deaf ears. Even worse, the issue is not recognized as a subject of serious discussion prior to negotiations of modalities of total or partial return. Under these circumstances, the question must be posed: Is cultural integrity a demand that only Western countries have the right to make?

Fourth, at the present time, when the copyright issue has become something of a crusade in Africa, a process of pirating of plant genetic resources from Africa and other Third World countries is going on at a furious pace. Gene banks in the United States and other countries, set up with the help of peoples of the South, are not freely accessible to the South. In other words, patents and copyrights being established on plant genetic materials that originate in areas far away from the collectors should provide that all materials are the common property of all humankind, with first right of access to the people of countries from which these plants originated.

But this will not be so, and patents, the industrial version of literary copyright, are being established on materials that do not belong exclusively to those who collect them. It was extremely generous of the Chinese, in their recent conflict with the United States over piracy of American goods, not to raise the question of Chinese treasures that were shipped out in enormous quantities to the United States from China throughout the years before liberation in 1949. But are such questions invalid because the United States will not hear them? As if that were not enough, a project in the United States has launched a campaign to

> take blood, tissue and hair samples from hundreds of so-called "endangered" and unique human communities scattered over the globe. The project is supported by the U.S. government's National Institute of Health and linked to the multinational, multi-billion dollar initiative to map the human genetic structure known as HUGO—the Human Genome Organization—and further . . . the material itself may be patentable even without further research. Will profits be made from the genes of poor people whose physical survival is in question? Who will have access to stored genetic material, and where will these collections be located? What benefits, if any, will accrue to the indigenous peoples from whom DNA samples will be taken?[22]

Finally, fifth, with the exception of a just a few individuals, African authors are very poorly remunerated, copyright notwithstanding. That is because print runs of their books are low, and prices of books are low, from the point of view of the author's income, and high from that of book buyers. Therefore, when considering support to authors, the focus must be on how to supplement authors' incomes from royalties rather than on reinforcement of copyright alone.

This essay does not suggest doing away with copyright and instituting piracy on a grand scale. It merely wishes to point out that prevailing systems of exchanges of cultural wealth and values are discriminatory when it comes to who gets what and through what means. On paper there are ways by which "developing" countries can, theoretically, access copyrighted material for a small fee. There are also mechanisms for compulsory licensing of books. But these do not work, in practice, as they are meant to. A plan to allow a twenty- to twenty-five-year moratorium, during which countries in disadvantaged situations would have the right to reprint all the books they needed without hindrance, would be the easiest to implement. Twenty-five years also seems to be the span of time that local publishing industries take to develop their own books. Once governments decide to make education the keystone of development, the demand for books will increase tremendously. Besides, a twenty-five-year moratorium would create a much bigger market for books than ever before, and would in the long run benefit all publishers, local and international. The door would be open permanently, thereafter, for a healthy book trade in which there would be exports to and imports from both sides in a dynamic and fair market.

Admittedly, in the contemporary world copyright is more a matter of software, CD-ROM, and other electronic information storage, retrieval, and transfer technologies; books are a small part of it. This does complicate matters, no doubt, although on the other hand, Northern copyright holders should at least be able to cede rights on the less extensively used of the technologies—the book——without as much loss of income.

PUBLISHING AFRICAN LITERATURE

In this section of the essay,[23] we discuss prospects of publishing African literature in view of the uncertainties of economics in this field of publishing. This topic will be discussed under the following headings: the general decline of publishing fiction in the decade of 1985–1995; the language question; journal publishing; and women in publishing and women and publishing.

The Decline of Fiction Publishing

The UNESCO *Statistical Yearbook* is, unfortunately, unreliable as a source of correct information on subjects such as this one. This is the fault not of UNESCO, but rather of its members, who either do not report, or report incorrectly, or give false reports to justify perceived notions of success and international recognition. According to the last four editions of *African Books in Print* (1975, 1978, 1983, and 1993), the observation of a sharp decline in fiction publishing in Africa (drama and poetry included) over the last six to ten years is correct.

There are, however, regional and country differences. The decline is most acute in West Africa and to some extent in East Africa, with the demise of East African Literature Bureau in 1977 and of the East African Publishing House in 1988. Neither the Kenya Literature Bureau nor the Eastern Africa Publications that took over activities of the defunct East African Literature Bureau in Nairobi and Arusha (Tanzania) was able to carry on publishing at the level that had been reached by the former company. East African Educational Publishers and Longhorn (ex-Longman) in Nairobi are the two publishers actively publishing fiction. In Uganda, Malawi,

Zambia, and Tanzania there is very little fiction publishing. Some works of fiction by writers from some of these countries have appeared under foreign imprints—Malawian Jack Mapanje's poetry and Tiyambe Zeleza's novels, under Heineman U.K.; and Tanzanian novelist Abdulrazak Gurnah's *Dottie, Pilgrim's Way* (Hamish Hamilton) and *Paradise* (Penguin), which was short-listed for the Booker Prize in 1994.

One country in which output has increased quite dramatically is Zimbabwe, with a number of works winning such international awards as the Commonwealth Writers' Prize, Africa Region, and the Noma Award for Publishing. However, the print runs for works of fiction are quite low, rarely ever above 2,000 copies, with some publishers printing as few as 750 to 1,000 copies.[24] Clearly, such print runs do not offer a chance for the development of national literature, which will remain bleak as long as only a few people have access to these works.

In Francophone West Africa there was a whole broadside of new fiction publishing by Nouvelles éditions africaines (NÉA) in Senegal in the early 1980s. But with the different branches of NÉA now going their own separate ways, the output has dropped sharply over the last three to four years. There are also fewer literary titles coming from CÉDA (Centre de l'édition et diffusion africaine) in Abidjan, and virtually nothing nowadays from Édition CLE in Cameroun. A number of smaller Camerounian publishers have all gone out of business. However, a number of new autonomous publishers have recently emerged in Côte d'Ivoire and Senegal (e.g., Mical-Drehi Lorougnon's Éditions du livre sud in Abidjan, or Aminata Sow Fall's Éditions Khoudia in Dakar, with active, albeit still fairly small fiction lists—interestingly, both are women publishers). Although the publishing output of fiction has probably declined overall in English-speaking West Africa, it certainly has not stopped altogether, and there are several independent new imprints publishing creative writing (for example, Malthouse Press in Lagos or Woeli Publishing Services in Accra). Other publishers with still quite sizable lists of African writing include Heinemann Nigeria, Spectrum Books, Fourth Dimension, Saros International, and University Press Ltd.

Support for Publishing African Literature

At the 1991 Bellagio Conference on Publishing and Development in the Third World, many recommendations on supporting

African publishing were made. They covered a range of macro- and microsubjects, one of which was support for dissemination of minority literature. In the context of present realities, minority literature would rightly include all literature in African languages— because of scant production—in addition to the more conventional understanding of minority literature.

A possible model of support for this field of publishing is the buy-back model—already successfully established and in operation in Tanzania—for children's books. Integrated into library support programs, this model would ensure that a part of the publisher's print run would be bought (guaranteeing partial or even full coverage of the printing costs) and libraries that are now mostly empty would be stocked with interesting works of fiction, produced in Africa and in African languages. The Norwegian model, where the state purchases copies of every work of fiction published in Norway for the library system, may have to be modified so as to establish selection criteria. Other support should go to publishing of translations of fiction from and into African languages as a part of international cultural exchanges.

The Language Question in African Publishing

The language question[25] in African literature—specifically the debate over whether African writers should write in their mother tongue or in national languages—is not likely to be resolved one way or another. I hope no one advocates that the debate should stop, because it is necessary. It keeps an important issue of African life alive, while accepting as given the fact that writers will continue to write in foreign languages if those are the languages they know best, or if for any other reason they are so inclined. Chinua Achebe makes the following comment on this issue:

> On language we are given equally simplistic prescriptions. Abolish the use of English! But after its abolition we remain seriously divided on what to put in its place. One proffered solution gives up Nigeria with its 200-odd languages as a bad case and travels all the way to East Africa to borrow Swahili; just as in the past a kingdom caught in a succession bind sometimes solved its problem by going to another kingdom to hire an unemployed prince![26]

The question of language is so complex that not everyone can agree on all of the issues it raises. For example, one may not agree that retaining one's own language is a basic human right. However, most people in the world share the perception that it *is*. Evidence of this is the passions that are evoked when there is a threat of imposition on a people of a language they do not consider their own. A policy, for example, that is unspoken in Tanzania but is there all the same would sacrifice all languages in favor of Swahili. This is an unacceptable policy that cannot be defended, precisely because no argument, no matter how dressed up—national, progressive, or revolutionary—can justify the loss of any language. Language not only serves the communication function, although that may be its most important role. Language carries with it visions of the society that speaks it; language is a corpus of knowledge, of sensibilities and identities, all of which will be lost if the language is not retained.

One crisis facing urban families consists in part of a confusion of identities when, for example, a single family can have three languages—the mother's, the father's, and a third for the whole family, with possibly an "I only hear" from the children with regard to the languages of the parents. Language is a vehicle for acculturation, and it is safe to assume that in the urban families referred to, the children are in some ways culturally shortchanged. Results of a number of studies that were carried out in Tanzania on the use of English as a medium of instruction in secondary schools show incontestably that the majority of the students cannot follow instruction in English. Therefore, they do not pass examinations that are set in English, although when translated into Swahili, they are able to give correct answers.[27] The arguments for using mother tongue/national languages at all levels of education lead one to conclude that resistance can only reflect a deep-seated rejection of the ability of African languages to instruct, in spite of the fact that nearly all production that sustains Africa, all mechanical, electrical, and other engineering occupations are accomplished by people using these languages.

In 1975, the Union of African Writers was formed in Acra. That was the decade when the language debate was at its sharpest. The Writers Union decided that Swahili should be adopted as the all-African language and, furthermore, that its future publications should not only be produced in the three European languages but also and simultaneously in Swahili.[28] Unfortunately, the Writers Union has not been very active. The output of African-language publishing has fared no better either, as *African Books in Print* shows over the last five to six years.[29] More children's books in Swahili have been published in the last five years in Tanzania alone, with more than seventy titles so far published under the Children's Book Project. If productions outside that project in Tanzania and books in Swahili from Kenya are considered, then there is no doubt that there is at least one area of publishing in an African language that is developing steadily. Outside East Africa, no one advocates publishing in Swahili; learning it, yes. In Tanzania, on the other hand, it is the only language that makes publishing possible. Swahili itself seems to be moving all over Southern Africa and winning adherents for itself rather effortlessly. It is interesting that within the ANC (the African National Congress) and PAC (the Pan Africanist Congress) in South Africa, FRELIMO (Frente de Libertação de Moçambique) in Mozambique, and SWAPO (Southwest Africa People's Organization) in Namibia, we are told that when officials and politicians in high places want to converse in private, they use Swahili. In Malawi, the expansion of Swahili is also reported as being phenomenal.

The question of writing and publishing in African languages will surface every time discussions take place about literature and its role in culture and development. It cannot be avoided as long as the majority of the African people do not speak the foreign languages in which some authors write. Admittedly, for publishers, there is the question of economic and financial feasibility, given that the authorities in power—educationists and cultural policymakers—will do nothing or very little to support local language publishing, and publishers do not have sufficient resources to invest in an area that will take too long to become profitable. Whether the future will continue to favor the foreign languages that have also become "African" as some people assert (Adewale Maja-Pierce), or whether the present crisis in all areas of African life will lead to a return to sources are matters that remain to be seen. Some people will work for the entrenchment of the foreign languages, and some will work for giving African languages a chance. At some point, Africa will have to decide.

Journal Publishing

One of the main problems for fiction publishing in recent years has been the decline of literary periodicals and "little magazines." From the mid-1960s to the late 1970s, there were a plethora of literary magazines, some of the highest quality—*Abbia, Asemka, Black Orpheus, Busara, Joliso, Kiabara, Marang, New Culture, Okike, Oyeame, Zuka*, the famous *Transition (later Ch'indaba, which was a political/*

current affairs magazine), and many more. Although one or two have resurfaced again from time to time (e.g., *Black Orpheus* and *Transition*, the latter now published from New York but bearing little resemblance to the earlier *Transition*), they all ceased publication a long time ago.

New literary or cultural magazines launched recently are either of poor quality, or have generally not survived beyond volume 1, no. 1. For example, the second edition, published in 1980, of *The African Book World & Press: A Directory (ABWP)*, which includes extensive magazine listings, listed thirty-one active literary and cultural magazines (published outside South Africa). Although some of these journals had updated entries in the third or fourth edition of *ABWP*, many had become dormant, published only sporadically, or had ceased publication altogether. Today, I do not know of a single significant African literary or cultural magazine (sub-Saharan and again, excluding South Africa) that is published regularly, although there are a few recently launched magazines such as *Egerton Journal* (Kenya), *Wasi Writer* (Malawi), *Les Cahiers du CAEC* (Senegal), *Zimbabwe Women Writing*, or the *Zimbabwe Review*; but none of these is a journal of the stature of a *Black Orpheus* or *Okike*.

The demise of literary journals, which has resulted in a dearth of publishing outlets for writers in general and for young and as yet unknown or inexperienced writers in particular, has probably also led to a stifling of creative writing. Much of the early work of the now "big" names in African literature was first published in a number of then flourishing literary magazines, but today there are fewer and fewer publishing facilities of this sort. This is, of course, a lamentable state of affairs. The demise of the journals that provided the outlets for young talent as well as opportunities for dialogue and debate has its origin in the crises in the African economies that began in the early 1980s. But that is certainly not the only reason. The problem also stems from political causes, intolerance, and the estrangement of African intellectuals from the ruling parties, individual leaders and heads of state, and government. Unfortunately, neither the ruling parties nor the leaders at the highest level, who could provide the protection and patronage, were interested in maintaining the vehicles through which debate and creative writing were carried out.

There are encouraging signs that another period of intellectual renaissance is at hand, thanks in part to the liberation of South Africa—the last part of the continent to be free—and quite honestly because things had fallen so low they can only improve now. New technologies, especially desktop publishing, are making it possible to reduce costs and to do a great deal in-house that was not possible until recently. Nevertheless, it is doubtful that a journal of the caliber of the ones pointed out above could survive in the prevailing economic situation unless it were underwritten by a committed donor or group of donors.

What has been said with respect to literary journals applies to scholarly journals as well. The publication of these journals has suffered the same fate: lack of adequate financial resources, decline of motivation for scholarly work that accompanied political and social instability, the deterioration of infrastructures of printing, and lack of foreign currency to purchase paper and spare parts for repairing the broken-down machinery. In brief, the university environment in Africa in the 1970s and 1980s deteriorated to such an extent that a general destabilization of scholars and academics occurred and turned them into nomads within and outside the continent, leaving little room for scholarly publishing.

Scholarly journals are an important vehicle for interuniversity exchanges and for keeping alive discussion and debate. Ideas are first tested and developed in scholarly journals, and the influence of ideas can be gauged in references to and citation of articles in those journals. The fact that journals take a shorter time to produce and ideally should be less expensive than books makes their influence even greater than that of books. Thanks to the development of new technologies, in particular desktop publishing and sophisticated photocopying machines, it is presently possible to produce journals fairly quickly and of acceptable quality. But those facilities alone are not enough. The most important input will be the ability of the universities to provide the necessary material conditions for academics and scholars that will enable them to pursue knowledge exclusively in an atmosphere of openness and security—something that has been missing for the last twenty years at most university campuses.

Women in Publishing and Women and Publishing

The ABC Research and Dissemination Unit has prepared a provisional listing of women in publishing and book development in Africa that shows how very small their number is relative to the number of men in the industry. Even in Nigeria, where one would have expected more women to be involved in this field, bearing in mind the intellectual muscle of that country in all fields, there are only two women who are in publishing after the regrettable death of Flora Nwapa in 1993. South Africa and Zimbabwe have the largest number of women in publishing, reflecting the relatively privileged position that women in the white section of Zimbabwean society enjoyed in preliberation days. In Zimbabwe, the number of black women in editorial positions of responsibility has been growing, and that is also true in other countries. In five to ten years, it is likely that the situation will change greatly in all countries in favor of women in high management positions.

Every oppressed class or gender must take the responsibility for pleading its own causes. It is imperative that women take up publishing books that will develop an ever-increasing awareness of gender issues. At the same time, one can ill afford to subscribe to the idea that a women's press should publish exclusively on gender issues. Although this might be possible where there is a large population of women with considerable purchasing power (as in the case of Kali for Women, in India), it seems unlikely that a commercially viable press that is exclusively for women is possible today in most African countries. It is, however, possible and even advisable in the first instance to specialize in publishing women's journals. This has been tried and shows great potential, although in order to survive and possibly to make a profit, one may have to compromise with those who demand light reading matter and who are not prepared for serious journals.

CONCLUSION

This essay has attempted to show the necessity of indigenous publishing in Africa for the development effort. In particular, it has sought to show that the colonial legacy in Africa is at the root of the problem of culture and, therefore, of development. For, whereas, "the simple fact . . . that man must eat, drink, have shelter and clothing, before he can pursue politics, science, art, religion, etc."[30] still remains valid, in ex-colonial societies, where the vestiges of colonial culture are still very much alive, politics, art and religion cannot come after food, drink, and shelter. Indeed, politics and culture may be the prerequisite to food, drink, and shelter.

Publishing in Africa has recently been enjoying support from the international donor community, particularly in the field of training. Emphasis has been on textbook publishing, reflecting the preoccupation with education and its problems. Culture and development are naturally not favorite areas of donor aid because, unlike buildings, dams, bridges, and, lately, election monitoring, culture is not always visible or tangible. Besides, both in the donor countries and in the recipient countries, cultural activists tend to be marginalized by bureaucrats whose understanding of culture is "entertainment" and for whom, therefore, culture is not a serious subject.

Systemization of the balance between work and relaxation, reality and imagination, concreteness and fancifulness are all necessary elements for a healthy mind and body, without which there can be no perfection in any endeavor. It is for this reason that cultural publishing deserves just as much attention as educational publishing. It is also for this reason that publishing in African languages should be given first priority, so that as many people as possible may encounter the adventures of living that are found in fiction, poetry, and drama. The more that people are touched by deeply moving cultural messages, the better placed they will be to draw from those messages the necessary energies for all of life's occupations. Development is the ability to harness the energies within for tasks outside oneself.

NOTES

1. Janheinz Jahn, *Muntu: An Outline of Neo-African Culture* (London: Faber & Faber, 1961).
2. Some examples of such events are: Ile Ife, Nigeria, 1973—Publishing in the Seventies; Arusha, Tanzania, 1984—Dag Hammarskjold Foundation Seminar on Building Autonomous Publishing Capacities in Africa; and Bellagio, 1991—Publishing and Development in the Third World.
3. For comments on the book sector concept, see Amanda Buchan, "Book Development in the Third World: The British Experience," in *Publishing and Development in the Third World*, ed. Philip G. Altbach (London: Hans Zell Publishers, 1992), 361.
4. Walter Bgoya, *Books and Reading in Tanzania*, no. 25 (Paris: UNESCO, n.d.).
5. *1988 UNESCO Yearbook* (Paris: UNESCO, 1989).
6. Eva M. Rathgeber, "African Book Publishing: Lessons From the

Eighties," in *Publishing and Development in the Third World*, 79.

7. Ibid., 87. Longman Zimbabwe is fully British-owned while College Press is 60 percent locally owned and 40 percent owned by Macmillan.

8. The South African situation is a special one in that it has both advanced and underdeveloped publishing industries, reflecting the effects of apartheid on publishing. New realities are in the process of emerging, but for the moment the dominant mode of publishing is through British multinationals and a few South African publishing houses.

9. Walter Bgoya, "Book Marketing and Distribution in Africa: Towards Creating the Missing Link in the Publishing Chain" (introductory paper for the Bellagio Network Roundtable on Book Marketing and Distribution in Africa, Dar es Salaam, November 28, 1994).

10. For a fuller treatment of the Francophone book situation, see Jerry Prillaman, "Books in Francophone Africa," in *Publishing and Development in the Third World*, 199.

11. Heinemann (Kenya) Ltd. was bought out by Kenyan investors, headed by its managing director, and the company was given a new name—East African Educational Publishers. Longmans was similarly bought out and was renamed Longhorn.

12. Per I. Gedin, "Cultural Pride: The Necessity of Indigenous Publishing," in *Publishing and Development in the Third World*, 45; and Walter Bgoya, "The Challenge of Publishing in Tanzania," in *Publishing and Development in the Third World*, 169.

13. Marjorie Mbilinyi and Patricia Mbughuni, eds., *Education in Tanzania with a Gender Perspective* (Stockholm: Swedish International Development Authority, 1991), 2.

14. Birgit Brock-Utne, *Education Policies for Sub-Saharan Africa as Viewed by the World Bank: A Critical Analysis of a World Bank Report* (forthcoming).

15. Angela Little, *"Education and Development: Macro Relationships and Micro Cultures,"* Silver Jubilee, Paper no. 4. IDS, Sussex, 1992.

16. Jahn, *Muntu*, 27–28.

17. Frantz Fanon, *The Wretched of the Earth* (London: Penguin Books, 1967), 168.

18. Chinua Achebe, "The Writer and His Community," in *Hopes and Impediments, Selected Essays* (New York: Doubleday, 1989), 96.

19. Henry Chakava, "Publishing Ngugi: The Challenge, the Risk and the Reward," *African Publishing Review* 3, 4 (July/August 1994).
20. Tanzania, which was not a signatory, finally succumbed and signed in 1994. There was no explanation of why there had been a change of mind. In fact, to date, the change of mind has not been made known to the people. The President of PATA (Publishers Association of Tanzania) learned of the signing of the convention at a meeting overseas to which he was trying to explain the rationale for nonsigning.
21. Paul Gleason, "Copyright, Licensing and Piracy," in *Guide to Book Publishing,* Datus Smith, Jr. (Lagos: University of Lagos Press, 1990), 251.
22. RAFI (Rural Advancement Foundation International) Communique, Ottawa, May 1993.
23. I wish to gratefully acknowledge the assistance of Hans Zell in researching material in this section and that on journal publishing.
24. Rathgeber, "African Book Publishing," 89.
25. I wish to acknowledge a stimulating and informative discussion with Professor Wamba dia Wamba, historian, University of Dar es Salaam, on this point.
26. Achebe, *Hopes and Impediments*, 60.
27. Z. M. Roy-Campbell and M. P. Qorro, *The Language Crisis in the Tanzania Education System: Reflections from a Reading Survey* (Dar es Salaam: Mkuki na Nyota Publishers, forthcoming).
28. See Hans Zell, "Interview with Dr. Kole Omotoso," *The African Book Publishing Record*, 2, no. 1 (1976).
29. Communication from Hans Zell, editor, *African Book Publishing Record*, March 1995.
30. Frederick Engels, "Speech at Graveside of Karl Marx," in *Karl Marx and Frederick Engels, Selected Works* (Moscow: Progress Publishers, 1975), 429.

CHAPTER 9

Culture, Museums, and Development in Africa

Claude Daniel Ardouin

LESSONS FROM THE PAST

The notion that culture is a strategic issue for policymaking in Africa was around before the contemporary debates within and among development institutions. It goes back to the beginning of the colonial period, although at different times the context and the concepts have changed. For instance, during the period of colonial expansion, justification for the invasion of Africa was based on cultural differences (e.g., "civilized" versus "savage"). Once established, colonial power and the subsequent exploitation of the colonies were expected to be maintained through policies aimed either at transforming the culture of the colonized peoples,[1] or at using their cultural values and sociopolitical organization in ruling their countries. The very complex relationship between political issues and interpretations of culture and of history was reflected in colonial ideologies and policies, as well as in the ideologies of the anticolonialist struggle. An example of this complex legacy is provided by the controversies and stories that have persisted for decades regarding the archaeological ruins of the Great Zimbabwe, which, as Henrika Kuklick observes, "have served to rationalize either colonial rule or African autonomy."[2] Kuklick also notes that "sound archaeological evidence can document the legitimacy of political regimes as effectively as can fanciful accounts."[3]

However, in terms of policymaking, the link between culture and socioeconomic development was recognized in the late phase of the colonial era. In that period, the issues of modernization and economic development of the newly independent nations, which were also underdeveloped, began to receive attention. What constituted development, as opposed to culture, became a matter of debate. This issue remained a theoretical exercise during a process that established the domination of non-African cultural (in a broad sense) standards—mainly Western—as part *and* instrument of a more global supremacy and influence. The main concern then became the social implications of the introduction into African societies of factors originated externally—technology, skills, concepts, and organization—that were identified as technical progress, and as necessary and unavoidable.[4]

In the context of the Cold War, development was defined as the evolution of underdeveloped countries along the lines of either Western capitalist or Soviet or Chinese socialist models and ways of life. Since the independence of African countries, and during the subsequent decades of dependent economic "development," the debate over culture and development remained largely an intellectual exercise without practical application. Priority was given in development policymaking to material development and to "economic growth," understood as replication of models from, or imposed by, the leading developed countries. Cultural issues were marginalized by governments and development specialists, not to mention bilateral and major multilateral economic agencies, be they from the West or the East. Culture was used—and abused—in various equivocal ways, but was never integrated organically into development policies. Those development policies are now generally considered to have ended in failure—in most cases, with tragic results for the people who were subjected to them.

The failure of these policies can be interpreted in different ways: first, as a clear indication of the need to reconsider the standard concepts and philosophies of development, most of which were—and often remain so—tied to ambiguous notions of modernization and progress. These concepts are themselves highly culturally and politically determined and informed by the values, standards, and often the interests of the parties embracing the concepts. Modernization describes something that is supposed to be "archaic" or "obsolete," and holds up a model—abstract or concrete—of what is considered to be "up-to-date" or "modern." Progress supposes a movement forward, from inferior to superior stages. In both cases, this logic, based on the linear evolution of all societies, has strong ties to ethnocentrism and the presumption of the universality of Western values and patterns.[5]

The failure of development in Africa has likewise revealed three important factors. First, the problems and crises faced by African societies are not exclusively economic issues but have critical cultural connotations as well. For example, experience has shown that industrialization and infrastructure equipment—which, for years, were considered key issues in development—must be looked at cautiously—in relation to other fundamental social and cultural variables and with a recognition that they have significant cultural consequences. Today there is no doubt that such basic problems as poverty, public health, education, production, consumption, urbanization, social instability, political change, and the degradation of the environment and of natural resources do not exist in isolation from one another, but are complex issues with vital cultural aspects.

Second, the replication of economic, technological, and cultural models from "developed" countries, without taking into consideration the social and cultural environment into which they are being imported, creates new problems without solving the old ones. Third, limiting the concept of development to such a replication has often led—in terms of official policies and doctrines—to programs to industrialize, build infrastructure, organize medical systems, expand public education, and so on, according to imported models. In the process, the considerable local knowledge, social memory, indigenous social mechanisms, technology, and know-how are ignored or rejected—that is, the whole rich complex of local cultural resources, developed in their particular environments by societies over time.

TOWARD A COMPLEX APPROACH

The failures of development policies have clearly demonstrated the need to pay particular attention to cultural parameters and processes. The diverse interpretations of culture and development support divergent, if not confusing, views of the relationship between the two concepts. One of the predominant notions of a well-established and widespread approach, at least within the international "hard development" establishment, draws a line separating development and culture into two completely different fields. Culture is viewed as the environment, or the soil,[6] which under specific conditions is able to react to change, whereas development seems to be viewed mainly in relation to action and economic change that are promoted, or brought about by and operated from the outside through policy intervention. The critical issue becomes how to take culture into account in policy interventions in order to find the keys to successful developmental activities: "culture does matter, in the sense that policies, management practices, and educational techniques interact with various cultural features of local populations."[7] For Aaron Wildavsky, "neoclassical economics has served economic development well. But not everywhere and not well enough. By looking more closely at culture, at the institutionally generated motivations that work for and against economic growth, we hope to create cultural instruments for doing better."[8]

Such a duality suggests first that development is still expected to come mainly from the developed world or the outside "developer"—governments and bilateral or multilateral agencies—which is in line with the failed, traditional approach to development. In addition, a restrictive definition of both culture and development establishes an order of priority and an operational hierarchy that excludes cultural processes and cultural life as development issues. As observed by Robert Klitgaard,

> as many will no doubt note, there is a play on words and a potential confusion here, between "culture" as art, music, literature, and architecture and "culture" as a learned body of symbols, beliefs, and ways of life. Without delving into this fascinating and important class of concerns, I simply note it as analytically separable from the other ways mentioned above of "taking culture into account."[9]

This perspective was justified, to some extent, in relation to development issues as perceived in past decades, but now deserves to be enhanced. One might wonder, whether the goal today is still to find the cultural "keys" or "instruments" to ensure economic growth, which is supposed to remain the absolute strategy for development, even if that strategy has proved to be invalid. Another consideration is whether attention should *also* be paid to changing global perspectives on the evolution of African societies. New approaches would need to take into consideration aspects such as domestic resources and potentials—strongly determined by the social and cultural history and environment—and the complex and changing interaction, at various levels, of social, cultural, political, and economic forces and factors.[10]

Cultural Identities

There is a growing understanding that cultural identities represent an important and complex social issue for development. This is being recognized not only within the traditional cultural disciplines, but also within development agencies themselves. Thus, as Ismaïl Serageldin of the World Bank points out,

> the clarity of that cultural identity and its evolving continuity are essential to create an *integrated* and *integrating* cultural framework. . . . Such a cultural framework is, I believe, a *sine qua non* to have relevant, effective institutions rooted in authenticity and tradition yet open to modernity and change. Without such institutions no real development can take place. Indeed, the lessons of failure in Africa frequently can be traced to the absence of such institutions.[11]

However, the concept of cultural identity needs to be investigated in more depth, for the apparent conceptual simplicity of cultural identity may lead to misinterpreting it as a rigid system of identification. This might well be combined, as far as Africa is concerned, with a romantic representation, on the one hand, of tradition—a precolonial, static past with a set of codified cultural traits and socioethnic groups—versus colonial change on the other. These interpretations ignore both the historical flexibility of social identification in Africa, and the history of social and cultural change at various periods, including the colonial and postcolonial eras.[12] Cultural identities are not generally static, clear categories but are profoundly embedded in history, in the concrete ways of life and systems of ideas and beliefs, in the relationships among various social, cultural, religious, economic, and political entities and forces locally, nationally, and worldwide. This ever-evolving complexity and flexibility produces and supports a great diversity of variations. In addition, each individual will develop different identities in the course of a lifetime, combining at the same time a number of different identities, according to environment, education, activities, interests, status, and other factors.[13]

One dimension that merits particular attention is the relationship between cultural identities and social stability or instability and cohesion or division. The participants of workshops run by the International Council of Museums (ICOM) in Lomé, Togo, stressed that cultural identities are "a reference point and criteria for the different individuals and communities for their self-identity on the basis of their history and environment. . . [and] an important factor which ensures individual and social equilibrium."[14] In African societies presently undergoing rapid change and crisis, and subject to powerful external influences, that equilibrium is frequently destroyed or damaged. We still know very little about the nature of these relations and their mechanisms. The issues surrounding cultural identity have worldwide dimensions, although they are particularly relevant in the African context. Despite their several contradictory aspects, these issues deal with some of the basic conditions for sustainable development.[15]

Another dimension to be considered is the link between cultural identities and social and political relationships. Having to do with the ways in which the self-affirmation and self-representation of social entities in their diversity are perceived, constructed, and expressed, cultural identities are closely connected to issues of power, status, freedom, independence, and dependence. Consequently, cultural identities have multiple ties with the social and political relationships and processes within each country and internationally.

On the basis of these two dimensions of cultural identity, several questions can be raised: For a society, a community, or an individual, what does it mean to lose sight of the guidelines that reveal the paths back into history, to be deprived of the legacy of cultural specificities and achievements developed over time by people who share a common history? At the same time, one should be concerned about the potential effects or repercussions of any approach aimed at rigidifying cultural practices and overemphasising cultural characteristics and differences. What do such approaches have to do with the ideologies of exclusion and hate, with political demagogy, and with marginalization vis-à-vis other cultures? What are the links between cultural identities, the social mechanisms of stability, and economic and political systems? Which identities and cultural and historical references will be the dominant ones among citizens of African countries in the future?

These issues have strong links with the social, economic, and political evolution of each country, both internally[16] and internationally, in relation to the world's predominant economic, political, and cultural forces. The question is not merely what the external makeup of African societies will be in the future, but how closely their internal systems of references will be tied to their history and cultures. This will reflect the extent to which the various local cultures and identities will find expression, whether they will be marginalized or eliminated, and how they will interact among each other and with regard to foreign influences.

Cultural Heritage

Emphasizing cultural issues leads to new ways of envisioning the place of cultural heritage in development. The concept of cultural heritage is a controversial one and is still in need of more investigation. However, it is a complex and dynamic category that refers to both material and nonmaterial cultural achievements and patterns, in their historical forms as well as in their present evolution. It reflects the diversity, creative skills, knowledge, traditions, history and interrelationships of the various social groups and networks over time, their specific and common features, and their interactions with their natural environment. From this, two implications can be drawn.

One implication is that cultural heritage contains the civilization resources historically developed in the form of a people's past and present social experiences, social mechanisms, knowledge, skills, and communication systems. Those resources should be used to address contemporary development issues, and they constitute an important potential that has often been neglected. Drawing on these resources may help in the search for appropriate strategies and alternatives in various areas such as medicine, rural and urban architecture and planning, education, the organization of administration, and economics.[17] The second implication is the potential for cultural heritage to become an important link between the past and the present for the purpose of revealing, channeling, or constructing cultural identities. At the same time, cultural heritage may provide insight into the features that are common to societies sharing the same threads of history.

Consequently, an important change must occur in the perception and the practical application of the concept of *cultural heritage*. Rather than being a mere "sprinkling" of traditional dress, song, and dance, it must be seen as a complex category of civilization resources and internal potential, an important source of knowledge and experience that can help solve crucial present-day development problems,[18] as well as form the basis for cultural identities. Cultural heritage becomes a vital element in the ongoing development and future of African societies. "To envisage a development policy without giving priority to the protection of the cultural and natural heritage would be to condemn the population of

Southern countries to live in amnesia and irreversibly sign away their future."[19]

Access to Worldwide Culture and Information

If cultural heritage and cultural identities are central for development, another crucial issue is Africa's relation to the enormous international flow of cultural and scientific information. The imbalance between the amount and the quality of cultural and scientific information coming to Africa and what is accessible in developed countries is not only very significant, but is also rapidly increasing with the development of the new communications media.[20] To this must be added the disparity between the information flows coming from developed countries to Africa and what is going out from Africa. This raises several issues—first, equal access for African citizens to the cultural achievements of other peoples and to the enormous body of international cultural and scientific information; and second, equal contribution by Africans to the world's cultural and scientific information. This cultural and scientific imbalance needs to be viewed in relation to the weakness of institutional cultural, research, education, and communication capacities, channels, and media in Africa. The potential consequences of this situation for Africa must be considered very seriously in terms of education, the creation of sustainable development capacities based on local resources and potentials, the risk of dependence on foreign partners, and, more generally, with regard to the future place of African societies in the world.

Seeking to integrate culture and cultural heritage into a global vision of development necessarily involves addressing how to define and actually achieve this integration. The question of having an articulated cultural policy—with subsequent central government cultural administration—can be answered in various ways, depending on the political doctrines prevailing in each country. However, the integration of culture must—at least for some time—be translated into global philosophies that will influence sectorial dynamics at various levels, policy interventions, and the allocation of resources to programs.

MUSEUMS AND DEVELOPMENT

Another implication of a more "cultural" vision is that institutions concerned with culture have a critical role to play in development.

Their contribution to improve society should no longer be seen as marginal, or less significant, or separate from the main development areas. Cultural institutions are able to play an active role in preserving and promoting cultural resources and heritage, serving as channels for education and communication, interacting with people in various sectors of the society, and providing advice in policy interventions.

As institutions replicating Western models inherited from the colonial period, contemporary African museums were and are rarely perceived or used as dynamic development tools.[21] Discussions on their role in development have taken place on several occasions during the last thirty years, and demonstrate the great complexity of the issue. This is due in part to the historical roots of most of the institutions, and to their ambiguous relations with Western ethnography, which still has a strong influence on their intellectual and professional approaches. Another aspect is the difficulty African museums have in escaping from imported cultural paradigms and old institutional models, and developing a system relevant to their own specific cultural contexts. They often remain marginal institutions of little significance to national communities and cultural life.

However, for some years, new approaches have been attempted to redefine the role of museums. At the 1991 meeting of African museum professionals held by ICOM in Lomé, Togo, the museum was seen as a "tool for cultural pluralism, national development, democracy," and for "public education."[22] In addition to safeguarding the traditional cultural heritage, museums should "incorporate urban and contemporary culture" in order to be more closely connected to the lives of their potential publics and communities. Museums are invited to "have a more global approach to the cultural *as well as* the natural heritage" and to address areas such as "problems of health, physical survival, galloping urbanization, environment degradation and political evolution."[23] In another illustration of the growing expectations that museums should make a strong contribution to public life, the West African Museums Program (WAMP) has launched a series of workshops for museum curators and researchers, on various topics covering archaeology, history, urban culture, contemporary arts, and the environment. The Southern Africa Development Community, Association of Museums and Monuments (SADCAMM) has initiated a collaborative museum education program.

Museums in Africa are traditionally associated with ethnography and/or with the fine arts and art history. This notion reflects a misunderstanding of the nature of museums. In reality they deal with the material evidence and products as well as related visual, written, and oral information in all possible fields of human activity and of the natural environment. The relevance of museums must be considered along with the development issues already raised regarding culture. In addition, another important perspective deals with the natural environment, and its preservation and management, which are vital for the development of African societies.

The potential impact of museums on public life and development is indicated in the various approaches and experiences developed by museum institutions and professionals in Africa, both at the national level and in connection with activities initiated by international professional organizations—such as ICOM, WAMP, SADCAMM, SAMP, etc.[24] The potential impact of museums can be realized in a number of areas: cultural heritage, education, scientific research, and general cultural information.

Preserving the cultural heritage is one of the main ways by which a society may establish a link between its past and present. Cultural heritage consists of a wide range of historical products that reflect the life, activities, creativity and the relationships of various groups and individuals *in the past and in the present*; it is an important component of memory and constitutes a major aspect of the historical background. Museums are among those institutions that help in the study and preservation of the material products of people's culture and the related visual, written, and oral information. They also act as channels to broad national audiences, through material culture and audio and visual media, providing views of past and present cultural achievements, patterns, values, and processes; and present various perspectives on people's relationship to the environment. This involves studying and preserving the cultural heritage—archaeological, historical, family, and community heritage—in all parts of each country. It also necessitates that citizens in each country must have access to their cultural heritage.

The concept of cultural heritage can be debated. Likewise, the relevance of the attempts to preserve material and nonmaterial products of culture can be questioned from various points of view, including that of the links with nationalism.[25] However, it is a fact that material and/or nonmaterial products of cultural systems help people to understand or interpret those systems from different perspectives—historical, sociological, and artistic. In that sense, these cultural products are important and deserve to be studied and, in some cases, preserved and used for public outreach. It frequently happens that a people or a social group selects certain cultural objects as important and seeks to preserve them. This is a process that has relevance for group cohesion. An example is provided in Burkina Faso by the collection belonging to Mr. Pacere Titinga, a lawyer who established a private museum in his home village. Hundreds of elders brought him ritual objects—mainly masks—for safekeeping because they feared that, after their deaths, the objects would be abandoned, destroyed, or sold off by their heirs.[26]

The potential ability of museums to enable people to study and preserve the cultural and historical heritage and make it accessible to the public is particularly important in the contemporary African context of political tragedies, tremendous political change, in addition to the ongoing looting of the cultural heritage. One misunderstanding about museums is the idea that they need be mainly focused on acquiring and centralizing collections of objects in their storerooms. Preserving the cultural heritage can and will certainly involve the local communities as active partners in preserving the archaeological sites and family and community patrimonies *in situ*. In this way, the preservation of cultural heritage is no longer the "mission" (an impossible one) of just a few specialized institutions, but is firmly rooted in the communities. To cite one example, in Mali, the National Museum and the Ministry of Culture have initiated an experiment with a family community that holds the possessions of a famous nineteenth-century personality of the Segou kingdom. The objects are kept by family members, who do not want them to be taken out or even shown to other people. The museum has documented the objects and is helping the family to improve their conservation without removing them.

The Educational Potential of Museums

For museums, education is an important area, since conservation is not an end in itself. Official education curricula pay little attention to the cultural and natural heritage and related issues. Local customs, history, and technological and artistic traditions are practically all ignored. This raises the issue of the limited content and the inadequate levels of educational materials and knowledge accessible to schools. These problems are having a very negative impact on the quality of education. In these circumstances, one can only wonder about the cultural background of these young people, whose environments are being wrecked by social and cultural problems and changes.

Another concern is the absence of any systematic information about contemporary science and technology, both within, and outside the official educational system. Moreover, there is a significant difference between information accessible in big townships and what is available in the small towns and rural areas. On the whole, there is insufficient access to local and national culture and history, to the culture of other countries, and to information about science and technology. The result is an increasing gap in education between Africa and the developed countries. The deficit affects the young who are enrolled in formal schooling, as well as urban, suburban, and rural youth growing up outside the official system. These problems are not only due to inadequacies of the school system, but also to the weakness and the scarcity of cultural institutions that ensure informal access to knowledge and information. It is crucial for the future that museums assume their role as informal educational institutions. The aim is, at the same time, to supplement school curricula, and also to offer—as specific institutions working with material artifacts and visual media—what school cannot offer.

Access to Scientific Research

One major task for museums is to increase knowledge and make it accessible to the communities that they are expected to serve. Museums in Africa have long confined themselves to reproducing an ethnographic vision that is ahistoric, if not downright folkloric. That vision does not reflect the complex and changing cultural and social reality of the past and the present, and almost entirely neglects natural history and environmental issues. At the same time, current research has generated a growing amount of knowledge in various disciplines. However, this knowledge remains locked within narrow circles of scholars in African countries and abroad—almost inaccessible to the national publics and inadequately incorporated into teaching programs. Along with other media, museums offer great potential to serve as active channels for making the results of research accessible to national audiences.

The history of the natural heritage and the environment are two fields that will serve to illustrate the importance of research.

In historical research, using material culture as a source will increase our understanding of Africa's history—social, cultural, political, economic, scientific, and technical—by complementing studies based on oral and written sources. Limiting historical research to oral traditions and written sources has led to a concentration of the official history of Africa mainly to those political states that have played a major role. Most of the remaining areas and societies are the focus of ethnographic and anthropological work, and have remained outside the scope of historical research. However, we now understand that, apart from its ethnographic interest, material culture contains important data about social processes, trade and circulation of goods, and other influences. Material culture is a source of data able to greatly increase our knowledge of Africa's social and cultural history, complementing oral and written sources, and enhancing our understanding of the present cultural, social, and political processes.

> The material culture *is an important source of data on history*, just like oral and written sources. It is essential that museums use their collections to enrich our knowledge of history under a different light and to make it accessible to all, especially to those who share a common heritage.[27]

The specificity of this research lies in its relation to material objects and works, as well as to such intangible sources as oral traditions, without which an understanding of the material culture is difficult.

The evolution of the natural environment is a crucial issue for the present and the future of African countries. Changes in the natural environment and ecology, as historical processes involving both natural factors and people's interaction with nature are to be studied, documented, and integrated into a strategy of public outreach, into formal and informal education.[28] Museum research and related outreach work in this field will increase awareness about the natural environment, ongoing processes, the impact on human activities, and make this knowledge accessible to the national audiences and schools.

Effect on Public Life

Museums are able to shed light on contemporary knowledge and information in the areas of science, technology, and health, and are able to promote reflection upon issues that are crucial for the present and the future. They also have the potential to promote cultural contacts and understanding of other cultures, as well as developing access to contemporary forms of the visual arts.

From these various perspectives, there is no doubt that museums can have a strong and multifaceted impact on public life as intellectual institutions. Moreover, experience shows that this potential can be used in various ways, including those that can lead to perverse consequences. Museums are powerful intellectual tools that must be used carefully. As institutions that can, and often do, have a strong authority, they affect people's minds, with intellectual representations, interpretations, knowledge, and information.[29] They should not be taken for granted; rather, the power of the instrument must be used for development to improve the quality of life.

LINKS TO SOCIETY

In order for museums to realize their potential impact on public life in Africa, they must be fully integrated into the development strategies *and* into the society. This means that they must be able to respond to the realities of the people and to reflect their interests, to interact with them, and to become part of their lives. Conversely, people and communities can become involved with the museums and use them for their development. The need for stronger links to the society at various levels—from the national to the local—was stressed at several professional meetings held by ICOM (Lomé, 1991), WAMP (Abidjan, 1993; Ouidah, 1995), and other institutions.

The intellectual focus of museum programs and activities must be diversified in order to cover fields encompassing past and contemporary periods, and to address issues relevant to people's realities and to be able to engage their interest. Museums must also find adequate and efficient policies and ways of communicating in each particular context with each public, without replicating models that may be appropriate elsewhere. In order to achieve this, the following will be necessary:

First, the types of museums should be diversified. A single "national" museum (even where there are local museums that, in fact, repeat the model on a smaller scale) cannot cover all fields as an all-purpose museum. Second, museums should be encouraged to diversify their intellectual focus and to address issues relevant to the development of their communities. This will lead museums to promote new professional and methodological approaches and work more closely with other disciplines and draw upon scientific research. It will also lead them to consider not only the material objects and works, but to integrate these into a more complex approach including oral traditions, without which entire aspects of history and culture—both past and contemporary—will not be properly understood or reach local publics. Third, museums should be established at the local level. In the future, the development of local museums and museum-related programs will lead to new forms of museum organization, on the basis of either community or private management. It is logical to think that the current classic structure—collections and displays centralized in a single area or even in one building—can be replaced with other forms better adapted to the local context.[30]

Finally, museums should play a more active role in public education and outreach activities, by using national languages and the existing local traditions and media of communication.[31] This will often involve various types of oral traditions and literature, and related performance forms. For example, local storytelling traditions have great potential as a communication medium. The performances of storytellers, either on stage or on the radio, usually attract significant audiences.[32]

The convergence of these perspectives will be decisive for the emergence of museums capable of having an impact on public life and national development. In Africa, the strategy is to develop new models of institutions and to change the philosophy of museum professionals and of the existing institutions. The aim is not to replicate imported models, but to develop museum institutions and traditions adapted to their environment, making the best use of local resources and potentials, interacting as partners with their publics and communities, and responding to their interests.

SUMMARY OF MAJOR PROBLEMS

In order for museums to realize their potential for having a positive impact on public life and development, a number of major problems have to be addressed.

Strategic Weaknesses

Although museums often remain a monopoly of the states, at the policymaking level there is commonly a lack of articulated overall views on museums and their possible connections with the life of the society. This leads, in most cases, to the absence or ineffectiveness of policies and of institutionalized approaches to museum development. These deficiencies impede the establishment of museums, particularly at the local and community level, and limit the institutional development of existing museums. Thus, while there is a general tendency to create new museums—in provincial cities as well as in rural areas—in the absence of an articulated overall perspective and framework able to address institution development issues, most of the newly established museums decline soon after their opening. Several examples can be pointed to—for example, Côte d'Ivoire (Musée municipal de Bonoua), Mali (Musée régional de Gao, which almost collapsed, and more recently, Musée de Tombouctou), and Senegal (Musée de Thiès).

Institutional Weakness

For most existing museums, institutional fragility is a serious obstacle to development and efficiency. In several cases, the weakness of the legal and institutional base goes together with the absence of an articulated institutional mission and purpose. This situation does not create favorable conditions for institutional development and makes the museums vulnerable, if not nonviable.[33]

A second important cause for the weakness of institutions comes from the lack of autonomy. In most French-speaking countries, where the majority of museums are under public administration, the main decisions relating to staff, budget, and even program activities are often taken by, or dependent on, public administrative structures outside the museums themselves. Thus, bringing in personnel from the outside, or sending experienced museum personnel out to other posts often depends on external administrative decisions. The same precarious state and lack of autonomy exist regarding budget expenditures for use of equipment and facilities. In contrast, in English-speaking countries, museums run by the state—which are in the majority—are integrated within institutional systems legally less dependent on central external administrative authorities.[34] However, experiences in West Africa show that those systems contain channels for strong administrative and political interference and often present a heavily centralized national pyramid structure from the national to the local levels, with one decision-making center. For museums, this results in the same lack of autonomy and in the same instability and fragility, particularly with respect to the movement of personnel within the system.[35]

Another aspect to be stressed is the absence or inadequacy of planning and programming. This increases the role of improvisation in museum activities. It also makes it difficult to plan specific focuses and priorities according to existing resources. In addition, the situation does not promote dynamic growth of institutions or their ability to secure additional resources. As for individual private initiatives, experience also shows that the lack of a sound legal base is an obstacle to moving from individual collections—be they the products of the passion to collect, or of art trade activities—to a situation with museums as non-profit-making institutions. For private museums, the issue of institution building stands as a critical condition of their development.

Professional Training Needs

For museums, the development of curatorial, managerial, and technical skills is one of the major conditions for achieving maximum efficiency in their activities, and making the best use of existing potentials and resources. Managerial and curatorial skills are essential for program and institutional development, management of resources, and financing. Conversely, the lack of adequately trained personnel weakens the professional base and keeps institutions from developing. In Africa, there is a strong need for museum training. However, the almost complete lack of professional training on the continent is a matter of serious concern. The issue of training of top and midlevel museum personnel has never been addressed effectively.

All the intergovernmental experiences of training in Africa have either failed or revealed significant limitations. The Center for Museum Studies established in 1963 and run by UNESCO in Jos, Nigeria, was eventually taken over by that country. Due to the economic crisis in the country, the training activities have greatly decreased in quality and intensity. In 1981, the Centre de Formation en Muséologie-Muséographie was initiated for French-speaking countries by UNESCO and the UN Development Programme. In 1986, it officially became the Institut Régional de Formation en Muséologie, and the ACCT (Agence de coopération culturelle et technique) joined the group of donors supporting the center. However, the initiative later collapsed, for several reasons, one of which was lack of attention to the issues of institution building and to the long-term financial security of the center. Other training programs for African museums initiated in Africa, such as the PREMA Program developed by ICCROM in Rome, may make a positive contribution if they succeed in avoiding the replication of imported models of museums and if they can develop a training approach that takes into consideration the need for dynamic changes in African museums.

At the moment, no appropriate response has been forthcoming at the national level. Training has to take place outside Africa, with several negative effects, such as creating a dependence on foreign training institutions and museums; the prohibitively high costs of that training; and insufficient adaptation to the cultural and economic context of most African countries. The result of the insufficiency and inadequacy of training is the weakness of the professional base of museums.

Lack of Funding Mechanisms

Most museums in West Africa are public-sector institutions. To support their activities, they depend almost entirely on public funds, mainly from state budgets. The possibility of obtaining public funds is often minimal, the priority being given over to meeting emergency problems, which rarely include cultural activities. Public funds, when available, are very limited, and used almost exclusively to cover staff and administrative expenses, while program activities remain largely unfunded. This is a critical problem for local museums. It has become a pattern that local museums are established, with a potential for having an impact on public life at a community or regional level, only to stagnate, or even collapse, due to a lack of financial resources and of alternative mechanisms of funding. At the same time, very little has been done to promote fund raising and income generating as important sources of support for museum activities. Even when positive initiatives take place, their development is jeopardized by the lack of institutionalized management, and by all the overall institutional environment.

At the moment, the only viable alternative is funding from bilateral and multilateral development agencies. However, alternative funding through foreign aid is sporadic, depending more on unplanned interventions of external political factors, and is rarely oriented to long-term systematic institutional and program development. Yet it would be dangerous to fall into dependence on outside donors.

That situation creates a series of obstacles for museum development in Africa. The first of them is a basic lack of financial resources to sustain program activities, which are the only way for museums to have an impact on public life and development, and to fulfill their raison d'être in research, preservation, public outreach, and education. Another consequence is that most available public funds are allocated to public museums of national status. That raises the issue of how other public and private museums can develop and operate on a local level, in order to make the services offered by museums accessible to citizens not living in the capital cities or in the large urban centers.

A second obstacle is the lack of institutionalized policies encouraging alternative mechanisms to secure financial resources. Thus, strategies for developing income-generating activities, one of the fundamentals for institutional autonomy, are rarely in evidence. Fund raising, both locally and internationally, is a sporadic activity. The standard practice is not to raise funds to implement a serious, well-integrated program activity set up by the museum, but to generate proposals for casual projects likely to attract donors. Finally, there is a lack of alternative and institutionalized nongovernmental mechanisms for funding.

Collaboration and Exchange within Africa

On several occasions, attention has been directed to the need to develop relations between museums. The weakness and the sporadic nature of exchanges of information; of collaborative programs; of the exchange of staff and experiences; of exhibitions, even within single countries, are important obstacles to the development of museums. The isolation of institutions and of professionals weakens both. It does not create the conditions in which various regional achievements, potentials, and resources complement and enrich each other, leading to the development of global practical and theoretical professional experience based on the realities and the context of different regions within Africa.

For a number of reasons—among them, the insufficient financial resources and the poor links with international professional networks—African museums have a limited access to professional information flows. Few periodical publications and books are available. Most local museums have no access at all to that information. The negative impact of this situation on institutional and professional development cannot be overestimated.

CURRENT DYNAMICS

Despite the many serious problems, there are changes underway that are making museums more dynamic institutions. Moreover, museum professionals are becoming increasingly focused on their institutions' role in society. New programs and initiatives are developing in various parts of the continent. At the same time, the intellectual approaches toward museum work and professional attitudes are evolving, which reflects the changes among the professionals themselves. Thus, museums in Kenya have developed strong research and educational activities and have introduced innovations in museum techniques, as well as exploring new approaches to establishing links with local communities. The SADCAMM network is establishing collaborative programs. In Mali, the Musée national has achieved good results in museum techniques, exhibition and audiovisual research, school education activities, and in developing links with local communities. Promising initiatives are developing in Cape Verde, such as the Museum of Special Documents, which is being established by the National Historical Archives. In Benin, a network of historical museums is developing, and, more recently, at the Historical Museum in Ouidah, an exhibition was organized exclusively on the historical heritage of local families.

In addition, there have been a number of international initiatives that will encourage museums to play an active role in the development of their societies. This process is supported by international professional organizations. In 1991, ICOM organized a series of workshops on "What Museums for Africa? Heritage in the Future," in Benin, Ghana, and Togo. Later, ICOM launched the AFRICOM Program, aimed at implementing some of the activities proposed during the workshops. Some of the issues discussed were the illicit traffic in cultural heritage, museum cataloging and documentation, and autonomy of museums.

At the same time, international nongovernmental professional organizations are developing within Africa itself. Thus, WAMP, which started in 1982 as a project of the International African Institute, in London, is now a fully established independent nongovernmental West African institution. Through its workshops,[36] regrant program, publications,[37] and international programs,[38] WAMP is working to support the development of new professional approaches, and links with research and education, to reinforce the institutional capacities, the professional network and collaboration in West Africa, and to promote the collaboration between West African museums and their partners in the North.

Other initiatives are working to promote systematic and long-term collaboration between African museums and their counterparts in the North, as in the case of the Swedish African Museum Program. This is a crucial avenue that will lead to a much-needed international institutional collaboration in various extremely relevant domains, such as the looting of cultural heritage and archaeological sites, and the related traffic. This collaborative work should also establish a tradition of exchange and loans of collections, exhibitions and documentation, thus helping to address some of the issues related to the debate on the repatriation of cultural heritage. Finally, these initiatives will ensure that African museums and professionals working in Africa will contribute, on the basis of their experiences, documentation, and collections, to studies on African cultural heritage and arts, which, at the moment, and in line with a long tradition, are completely dominated by external perspectives and intellectual conventions of Western institutions and scholars.

All these developments show that activities are under way that are fostering a new generation of museums and museum professionals in Africa. However, the problems noted above as obstacles to museum development in Africa need to be addressed. They require complex action on a number of different levels. Positive results will come from combined and systematic efforts, starting with the understanding that culture is a crucial issue for development in Africa; that cultural institutions and, among them, museums have an important contribution to make in improving the life of people and in addressing development issues at the local level and beyond. The efforts should first of all involve the African countries themselves, and not only governments, but also the channels within civil society and of nongovernmental sectors—the museum professional networks, local bodies and authorities, and private individuals. For culture is not a monopoly of the state, but is relevant to and relies on each citizen. Development agencies should be expected to support those efforts, first of all by integrating cultural criteria and sensitivity into their own approaches to development. Generally speaking, it might be appropriate to make a special effort to draw on local potentials and resources for solutions to development problems, instead of making exclusive use of external remedies. Support from development agencies must also help address some of the problems blocking museum development, particularly the reinforcement of the institutional capacities and of the professional base.

SUGGESTIONS FOR FUTURE ACTION

The need for training opportunities in Africa is crucial. Creating training opportunities does not necessarily imply maintaining a centralized training institution. The first task consists of formulating and supporting museum training curricula in existing national and local training institutions. Such efforts could be implemented through an international program of flexible training courses, using the existing facilities in museums. Thus, training in audiovisual techniques would be held in museums offering well-equipped audiovisual facilities, while training in museum education would take place in other appropriate institutions. The advantage of such an approach is that it does not require centralized facilities, structures, and staff. At the moment, priority should be given to curatorial and managerial training and to training in fund raising.

Attention should be paid to developing nongovernmental mechanisms for funding, operated within Africa, controlled and run by Africans. Nongovernmental institutional mechanisms for funding not only have the potential to constitute an important additional source of public funding but can also serve as flexible channels by which civil society can contribute to the development of museums, be they public or private, and promote specific areas of interest independently of government interference.

It might also be appropriate and useful to carry out international multidisciplinary research, focusing on the relation between cultural factors and cultural traditions and social stability, instability, cohesion, and division. Such research could be undertaken in various situations and countries, including developed areas. This research could clarify the role of culture in the development of social entities, which would be quite useful to the ongoing discussion of culture and development.

NOTES

1. One of the main concepts of French colonial ideology, "la mission civilisatrice," was aimed at changing the peoples of the colonies through French education and medicine, the imposition of Western law, and the creation of new local elites educated in the spirit of French culture and dedicated to France.

2. Henrika Kuklick, "Contested Monuments: The Politics of Archaeology in Southern Africa," in *Colonial Situations. Essays on the Contextualization of Ethnographic Knowledge,* ed. Georges W. Stocking, Jr. (Madison: University of Wisconsin Press, 1991), 137–38.

3. Ibid., 164.

4. See the publications of the Bureau International de Recherche sur les Implications Sociales du Progrès Technique, and also various publications of G. Balandier : G. Balandier, ed., *Les implications sociales du progrès technique* (Paris, 1959); G. Balandier, ed., *Les implications sociales du progrès technique* (Paris, 1962); G. Balandier, "Structures sociales traditionnelles et changements économiques," *Cahiers d'études africaines* no. 1 (January 1960).

5. See also Mamadou Dia, "Indigenous Management Practices: Lessons for Africa's Management in the '90s," in *Culture and Development in Africa,* ed. Ismaïl Serageldin and June Taborof, Proceedings of an International Conference held at the World Bank, Washington, D.C., April 2 and 3, 1992 (Washington, D.C.: Word Bank, 1994), 166–67.

6. Robert Klitgaard suggests an agricultural analogy: "Now the analogy I am suggesting says that "taking soil into account" resembles "taking culture into account." Culture is the symbolic soil in which development takes place." See Robert Klitgaard, "Taking Culture into Account: From 'Let's' to 'How'," in *Culture and Development in Africa,* ed. Serageldin and Taborof, 82. The question concerns the responsibility over development choices: who is the farmer and does the soil have any choice over what crops to grow?

7. Klitgaard, "Taking Culture into Account," 101.

8. Aaron Wildavsky, "How Cultural Theory Can Contribute to Understanding and Promoting Democracy, Science and Development" in *Culture and Development in Africa,* ed. Serageldin and Taborof, 164.

9. Klitgaard, "Taking Culture into Account," 101.

10. For instance, Mohammed Arkoun notes that: "In many Mus-

lim societies the crisis of cultural values, legitimacy, and legality is perhaps more dramatic than the economic regression. Wealthy countries may be able to help in improving the economy, but they cannot initiate cultural alternatives after the disastrous disintegration of the popular cultures and the urban traditional tissues as well as the old rural solidarities." (See Mohammed Arkoun, "Discussant Remarks," in *Culture and Development in Africa*, ed. Serageldin and Taborof, 124.)

11. Ismael Serageldin, "The Challenge of a Holistic Vision: Culture, Empowerment, and the Development Paradigm," in *Culture and Development in Africa*, ed. Serageldin and Taborof, 19.

12. For example, several historical and anthropological studies have stressed the flexibility and mobility of social identity in Africa. They have shown that most categories of rigid classification inherited from classical ethnography and anthropology and widely adopted by museum curators and scholars (and other experts) in African arts and humanities have to be reconsidered. Thus, based on his research in East Africa, Terence Ranger argues that: "almost all recent studies of nineteenth-century pre-colonial Africa have emphasized that far from there being a single "tribal" identity, most Africans moved in and out of multiple identities, defining themselves at one moment as subject to this chief, at another moment as a member of that cult, at another moment as part of this clan, and yet at another moment as an initiate in that professional guild. These overlapping networks of association and exchange extended over wide areas. Thus the boundaries of the "tribal" polity and the hierarchies of authority within them did *not* define conceptual horizons of Africans."(See Terrence Ranger, "The Invention of Tradition in Colonial Africa" in *The Invention of Tradition*, E. Hobsbawm and T. Ranger [Cambridge: Cambridge University Press, 1983], 248.)

     In West Africa, J. L. Amselle observes that every culture "is dissolved in a serial set or in a reservoir of conflictual or peaceful practices, the social actors of which use them to permanently renegotiate their identity. To stiffen these practices leads to an essentialist vision of culture. . . ." (See J. L. Amselle, *Logiques métisses: Anthropologie de l'identité en Afrique et ailleurs* [Paris: Payout, 1990], 10.)

13. Recognizing this complexity, the participants of the workshops organized in 1991 at Lomé (Togo) by the International Council of Museums (ICOM), cultural identities were seen as phenom-

ena subject to constant evolution and historical change, in relation with "material and non-material traits and phenomena characterizing the various social, economic, confessional, professional groups and communities in their local, regional, national or transnational specificities. Consequently, individuals as well as . . . communities, are involved in various types of relations at different levels, depending on situations and affinities, thereby creating a diversity of flexible and non-partitioned identities."

(See "Report of the Togo Workshop," in *What Museums for Africa? Heritage in the Future* [Paris: ICOM, 1992], 358.)

14. Ibid.

15. Among the issues to be considered: stability and cohesion. Why do migrants, from wherever they come, seek to recreate aspects of their cultural environment, even when the new social and political conditions do not tolerate it?

16. The question concerns the extent to which the existing communities and groups, including the minorities, have access to their own history and culture as an expression of their existence and to the history and cultures of other people within and outside the country. This relates closely to the issues of democracy and pluralism.

17. See, for instance: Mamadou Dia, "Indigenous Management and Practices," 165–91.

18. J. B. Kiethega, "Heritage and Contemporary Culture: Evolution of the Concept and Collections" in *What Museums for Africa? Heritage in the Future*, ed. Serageldin and Taborof, 273.

19. Philippe Garcia de la Rosa, "Protecting the Cultural Heritage: a Tool for Development" in *What Museums for Africa? Heritage in the Future*, 298.

20. Only a small part of it—rarely the best—is accessible to Africa. The international meeting on "Audience Africa," held under the auspices of UNESCO, reminded us that "the twenty-first century will be one of tremendous upheavals, accelerated change and unceasing renewal in a radically different economic, geopolitical and cultural context from that which humanity has known to the present day. Science, technology, communication and information technology will radically change the structure of knowledge and the individual and collective destiny of the earth's peoples." (*Audience Africa—Social Development: Africa's Priorities* [Final Report, UNESCO, Paris, February 6–10, 1995], 2.)

21. As to the issue of whether museums are an institution relevant to an African context, a proper history of museums on the continent still has to be written. The tradition of keeping and preserving did not begin with European colonization. From various parts of Africa there had been early reports of groups of objects (collections, in fact) or individual objects having apparently been maintained and preserved. Those collections served specific functions, upon which, to some extent, depended the equilibrium of the groups to which they were related.

22. *"Final Report,"* in *What Museums for Africa? Heritage in the Future,* 371.

23. Ibid.

24. ICOM—International Council of Museums—is a worldwide organization of museum professionals, based in Paris. WAMP—West African Museums Program—is a nongovernmental organization for museum development in West Africa, based in Dakar, Senegal. SADCAMM—Southern Africa Development Community Association of Museums and Monuments—is an intergovernmental network of Southern African countries. SAMP—Swedish-African Museum Program—is a collaborative program between Swedish and African museums, based in Stockholm.

25. Richard Handler speaks about "the nationalistic objectivation of culture." See Richard Handler, "On Having a Culture: Nationalism and the Preservation of Quebec's Patrimoine," in *Objects and Others: Essays on Museums and Material Culture,* ed. G. W. Stocking, Jr. (Madison: University of Wisconsin Press, 1985), 192–17.

26. Numerous similar cases can be cited throughout Africa. They are an indication that those objects mean something very important to the communities or individuals who own or keep them. See also Claude D. Ardouin, "Vers un trafic licite des biens culturels ? Quelques réflexions et questions à partir d'une perspective anthropologique," *International Journal of Cultural Property* 4, no. 1 (1995): 91–104.

27. Claude D. Ardouin, "What Models for African Museums? West African Prospects," in *Culture and Development in Africa,* ed. Serageldin and Taborof, 233.

28. An example would be the degradation of ecology in the Sahel and its impact on ways of life, with the disappearance during periods of drought of individual and collective heritage (e.g.,

family property) that must be sold by the owners.

29. Duncan F. Cameron reminds about the "terrifying power of the museum" to transform and even to invert the sense of things, to "manipulate" our spiritual sensitivity, and concludes that it can be a powerful arm that must be used with a profound awareness of its nature. See Duncan F. Cameron, "Marble Floors are Cold for Small, Bare Feet" (paper presented at the 1993 Commonwealth Association of Museums Triennial Congress at Ottawa, Canada) *Commonwealth Association of Museums Publications* 1 (1993): 2–27.

30. In some cases, problems with establishing a museum could arise, such as the very justified reluctance or hostility of the owners of family or community heritage to give up their property to the museum. More flexible forms of organization must be found that would enable each community to retain its heritage, with the necessary professional assistance to preserve and document the materials and make them available—when possible—for educational purposes and for public access. This will clearly create technical problems having to do with conservation, public access, legal, and financial arrangements.

31. See also Claude D. Ardouin, "National Languages and Communication in Museums," in *What Museums for Africa? Heritage in the Future*, 299–302.

32. See also Mwambayi Kalengayi, "The Use of Popular Story Tellers in the Transmission of Knowledge," in *What Museums for Africa? Heritage in the Future*, 311–15.

33. In West Africa, the inadequate resolution of issues related to institutional development has brought about the collapse of several initiatives to establish local museums.

34. A detailed study of the issue of autonomy in Africa was done and published by the ICOM. See Vincent Negri, *Etude sur l'autonomie juridique et financière des musées en Afrique* (Paris: ICOM, 1995).

35. The Nigerian case offers an example of such heavy centralization of the state museums within the National Commissions for Museums and Monuments, with one decision-making center at the top, and individual museums considered as "stations" of equal status. Thus, the museums in Jos and in Lagos have the same status as other stations, some of which have only offices, but no collections.

36. Thus, in 1985, a workshop on "Local Museums" was held in Lomé, Togo. In 1993, a series of workshops was begun on

"Museums, Research and Communication": "Museums and Archaeology" (Abidjan, Côte d'Ivoire, 1993); "Museums and History" (Ouidah, Benin, 1995), "Museums and Urban Culture" (Accra, 1996). The three workshops were sponsored by the Rockefeller Foundation.

37. WAMP publishes a bulletin that is distributed throughout Africa.

38. The most recent program is on "Identification, Classification, Preservation and Interpretation of Photographic Holdings in West African Archives and Museums," sponsored by the Getty Grant Program.

CHAPTER 10

Culture, the Economy, and Development in Africa

Basile T. Kossou

INTRODUCTION

Not many years have passed since the existence of a culture belonging to the "primitive tribes" or "savages" of Africa was commonly acknowledged. Today, one would be considered ignorant or racist to deny that the "African peoples" have constructed genuine civilizations, societies cemented by the belief in specific values and that bear witness to a legacy recognized as enriching the cultural inheritance of humanity.

One generation ago, speaking of culture in relation to economy seemed incongruous because culture was chiefly defined as the knowledge, production, and consumption of the fine arts. The plastic arts, literature, theater, music, dance, and other arts were what made up culture, in the common consciousness—the luxuries one can indulge in once the exigencies of economic life and material subsistence have been met. Living first, then philosophy.

Economic development, which has determined the way in which thinkers have considered the economy since the Enlightenment, notably in developed countries, was and to a great extent continues to be defined as economic and social progress. This progress is measured in terms of the following: material growth, a rise in the gross national product, the multiplication of modern infrastructures, advanced technologies, and other factors.

It has now been acknowledged that this concept is problematic. The wealthy nations themselves have experienced problems other than those of economic growth. And economic growth has manifested itself as a generative force, among others, of crises driven by noneconomic, *social and cultural* factors. African nations, the former colonies of developed countries, were drawn into the wake of the rich nations while within the process of development. Their "development," planned and carried out by their former colonial rulers, had inevitably consisted in becoming reflections and copies of those rulers. This is the origin of the *extroverted development* that can be observed today in African countries, and that some call "maldevelopment."

EXTROVERTED DEVELOPMENT IN AFRICA

Extroverted development in Africa is defined as a development conceived, organized, and planned outside of Africa to fulfill the economic needs and objectives of colluding nations, which in so doing drained Africa's natural resources and controlled African economic life. The issue here is one of *economic extroversion*—to which is added a *cultural extroversion*, which begins with the conception and the implementation of development projects that do not take into account the social and cultural realities of the concerned nations. From this perspective, African development possesses a double deficit, economic and cultural.

The maldevelopment in Africa, say the experts, results from the combination of a number of socioeconomic factors. Notable among these is the low per capita average income, the high percentage of the population that is rural, the low levels of productivity, the limited and precarious, fragmentary and dependent industrial infrastructures, the high illiteracy rates, the rise in unemployment (and emigration), widespread malnutrition and mediocre health services, and the predominance of foreign companies in banking, commerce, finance, industry, and management—all of which work to create a very serious economic vulnerability.

People have drawn up various scenarios for the immediate and long-term future of Africa. However, the shocking reality of the present seems, from a socioeconomic perspective, only to prefigure even more tragic prospects for Africa if the social dynamic of maldevelopment continues: a demographic explosion, increased illiteracy, high unemployment, food shortages, national debt, inequality in currency exchange, damage to the environment, and other problems.

Moreover, regardless of the future scenario envisioned or schemes proposed in order to move away from underdevelopment, it is apparent that, during the first four decades of development, all approaches to some extent failed to integrate the cultural components of the communities concerned—all the methods, systems of social values, and the innate potential (human, natural, and technical) that would enable each society to make its own fundamental choices and to achieve its freely chosen development objectives.

For example, agricultural development and nutrition are vital issues that have long been considered by all African nations as among their top priorities. The statistics on nutrition and agriculture in Africa are quite alarming. African agriculture cannot sufficiently cover the nutritional needs of the people. This is doubtless the result, it is said, of the continent's natural disasters and geoclimatic disturbances. Yet there are also contributing human factors, social and cultural, that plans for agricultural development often fail to address, and that act as obstacles to progress. Thus, for example, nutritional self-sufficiency depends not only on agricultural production, but equally on the interaction of a number of specific social and cultural elements.

According to the statistics, in 1975, Africa's population was approximately 401 million inhabitants. The United Nations estimates that in the year 2000 that number will reach 814 million, and double within twenty-five years. Much of the attention has focused on the African urban population, which numbered 100 million in 1975 and is projected to pass 306.5 million around the year 2000. The question to be posed is whether agriculture, which exists only outside the cities, will develop enough to satisfy the needs of the urban population.

This means, at least partially, that agriculture, which is the domain of rural populations, must be developed to meet the needs of urban populations. Will there, in this case, be an equitable redistribution of the fruits of labor between rural and urban dwellers inasmuch as the rural population represents more than 80 percent of the total population? This involves a human problem of ethics, which, if not resolved in the interest of greater justice, would justify the growing disaffection of the populations of the rural world with agriculture and reinforce the tendency toward emigration, of which the catastrophic consequences are known.

If 80 percent of the African population is rural, national development must be essentially a rural development, because it is a development that concerns and profits the majority. This implies the rejection of all politics of elitist development and a commitment to ameliorate the standard of living and working conditions for the rural populations.

It is a question of taking measures to further motivate the rural populations and allow them access to their rights, which will stimulate a conscious sense of national responsibility and solidarity. Measures susceptible to improving their material working conditions will progressively elevate the level of scientific culture and technology of rural populations, which in turn will act as a great impetus toward development in general. But how can this be achieved if 80 percent of the African population is illiterate?

Rural development is not possible without addressing the need for literacy education among rural populations. Moreover, the continuity of this development would be endangered if the rural world were to be left out of the redistribution of the fruits of the common efforts for national development. It is a question of reexamining and reorienting all policies for national development in African countries. Consequently, the partners in developing Africa must place the rural world and the eradication of illiteracy high on their list of common objectives.

At the same time, serious attention must be paid to the following sociocultural problem—one that is tied to nutrition issues and presents agricultural development with several paradoxes due to sociocultural differences. Agriculture, which is under environmental and geoclimatic restrictions, has an objective productivity that is determinable and limited. Nutrition, however, depends increasingly on foreign aid and is less and less locally controllable in developing nations.

It is a fact that industrial development has made fresh agricultural products consumable in African countries (products such as citrus fruits, meats, and fish, etc.), as well as canned and bottled products. This has had a positive effect on nutrition: such communities that formerly would eat only the meat of an animal killed according to a precise ritual are able to bypass this interdiction by eating frozen meat or smoked chicken. But there has been a significant negative effect as well—namely, *nutritional extroversion*.

Local agriculture cannot meet all the new nutritional needs of populations, notably the urban populations, due to growing demands to consume more and more of what the local agriculture does not produce. Moreover, the taste for products of foreign food crops, maintained by advertising and the seduction of packaging and brandnames, has created new nutritional habits that have progressively reduced markets for local products in favor of "arrivals" from former colonial nations.

The prerequisite sine qua non of nutritional self-sufficiency in Africa is to take into account the social and cultural aspects of nutrition, while correcting nutritional extroversion by a return to endogenous sources of nutrition. This could be achieved by:

- encouraging research into nutritional habits in African nations in order to convert the populations into consumers of local products;
- controlling publicity about nutrition to change nutritional traditions;
- instituting and encouraging the organization of regional food fairs to make known and exchange the products of the African nutrition industry.

This example shows that development in African communities has lost its original base and its cultural direction because the only framework used has been an economic one. Pulled by world market forces, the African model for development has taken on external elements that appear to be the only ones able to establish a dynamic for development. In addition, plans for development were often the replication of models conceived of in the context of other societies. Naturally, development plans conceived in strict material and statistical terms, or in terms of economic growth, are potentially transportable—that is, the imitation in one society of the social structures and administrative models of another. However, for more than thirty years now the replication of occidental models of development has led to inappropriate approaches to transforming the African economy and resolving its fundamental problems—basic human needs notable among them.

It is necessary to *"recenter"* economic development, to root it in the values of negritude (L. S. Senghor), to take charge of it and practice self-reliance (J. Nyerere), and imprint upon it an African personality and authenticity (Mobutu). Thus, the leading African authorities are beginning the preliminary affirmation of cultural identity—the necessary base of and irreplaceable compass for African development.

INTERACTION BETWEEN CULTURE AND ECONOMY

Those high officials responsible for African development were not wrong to propose that African cultural mores be considered and applied to economic development. There is definitely an interaction between culture and the economy within development. For example, an irrigation or well-drilling project in the field of agriculture protects the rural world from unpredictable weather changes; it also sets a definite timetable for work, which can change the life of the population for the better in various ways. This is because the time saved can be devoted to the making of crafts, but can also be used for other productive labor, as well as for leisure. These economies of time can transform and rationalize social attitudes by destroying religious myths that cast weather and natural disasters as manifestations of the will of the gods. Thus, an irrigation project could bring about a transformation within a rural community, leaving behind fatalistic, resigned views. Instead, a more positive perspective and the prospect of productive labor could raise the quality of life. It is necessary to recognize that these changes are not possible if the people's spirits are not possessed with the *fatum mahometanum.*

In any case, the time saved through irrigation may be used to generate new social and cultural realities. Thus, in the progression from preirrigation to postirrigation, intellectual, moral, spiritual, technological, and human resources are formed that will empower the beneficiaries of irrigation projects and assure them of mastery over such projects.

An economic development project can thus generate *cultural added value* when it creates a benefit that is well integrated with or consciously transforming of sociocultural values. On the other hand, it can also provoke social and cultural losses, structural imbalances, and detrimental ruptures to social cohesion, thus making the project work counter to its own initial objectives. To prevent this, it is essential to identify, in advance, the cultural implications of the project.

In the dialectical relationship that connects the factors involved, economic projects are not the only ones that engender cultural added value. Cultural projects that promote the dissemination of information and the full expression of creativity in a community have eminently beneficial effects on economic development. For example, the crafts industry, whose economic viability no longer needs to be proven, is an expression of the creative and inventive capabilities of a people. And in many civilizations, industrial development sprang from the crafts industry, which still sustains the cultural industries that are now in decline.

It has not always been accepted that culture produces economic results; the economy alone, it was thought, determined cultural life, making culture a consequence and even a product of the economy. Economic growth was considered sufficient to satisfy all the needs and aspirations of society, which could then taste the joys of culture. This superannuated definition of culture has been revised and rejected in favor of another approach that encompasses the overall quality of life. At the same time, the concept of heritage—traditionally restricted to material objects such as sites, edifices, monuments, and works of art—has been enlarged to include a people's sense of its common history, collective identity, and the continuity that exists between past and present.

Thus, culture is perceived as the individual's development of his or her own creative potential, with an awareness of the solidarity of individuals with their community and the potential benefit of their actions to society. However, development, and thus creativity, is a process of conception, invention, and production, which draws its resources and models from a collective history, its originality and specificity from a consciousness of an inherited identity; and its internal dynamism from the will to promote this creativity to ensure the continuity of individual and collective life.

Creativity is thus an essential dynamic in which the economy and culture interact dialectically. It is, therefore, the primary social fact that affects development, a process in which culture and the economy are intertwined in an intrinsic relationship.

THE WORLD DECADE OF CULTURAL DEVELOPMENT

At conferences in 1956 (Paris) and 1959 (Rome), intellectuals and artists of the Black world had advocated a "cultural policy" for the independence and rehabilitation of the continent. At the Pan-African Cultural Symposium in Algiers (1969), this became the clear and explicit position of the African governments who had come together under the aegis of the Organization of African Unity (OAU). At the intergovernmental conference of cultural policies in Africa (AFRICACULT), organized in 1975 by UNESCO in cooperation with the OAU, the necessary articulation of culture and the economy for indigenous and harmonious development was strongly reaffirmed. In 1977, the Cultural Charter of Africa was adopted by the OAU.

The exclusion of sociocultural factors from the process of development prevented the liberation and the mobilization of those forces, in each society, potentially capable of leading to global development or individual growth. Administrators (decision makers) have held the position that development must contribute to the well-being or improvement of individuals and communities; however, this improvement has often been measured in terms of quantitative growth and not qualitative improvement—as defined according to sociocultural value systems external to the concerned populations. The various problems brought on by the economic formulas recommended for emerging from the crisis have necesitated a new approach to development, informed by the perception that the world economic crisis was a crisis of civilization, a crisis of culture. In this context, it has been necessary to correct the process of development, to give it new balance and dimension.

In 1975, AFRICACULT had these recommendations for new directions:

> [I]f Africa intends to develop itself, it must also preserve its personality. Making this choice is to enter history with head held high and a steadfast heart; it also involves handling difficulties, which, without being artificial, are not simple to surmount. The dilemmas are only intractable as long as the problems of development are separated from those of culture.

In other words, Africa has decided never to consider an approach to the organization and administration of social and collective life that marginalizes culture in relation to development. There can be no development without culture.

At the 1979 OAU-sponsored Monrovia Colloquium on "perspectives on African development to the year 2000," a colloquium to reformulate the terms of development strategy, the radical change called for was one of innovations in analysis, method, and approaches to development. The demographic explosion, ideological tutelage, and external cultural domination in Africa were viewed as the lesser evils or secondary to the real danger, which was, above all else, cultural: "The primary objective of development can only be the creation of a material and cultural environment favorable for growth and creative participation."

In 1982, UNESCO, after a series of regional intergovernmental conferences on cultural policies, organized a World Conference on the question, in Mexico. The unanimous conclusion at the conference was that central to development was a spiritual and physical blooming of cultural and material well-being, from which sprang the idea of launching a campaign for full-scale development of all human beings. The conference in Mexico called for a mass effort—over a period of ten years—on the part of the international community, to give birth to a more just and creative humanity, one ultimately reconciled to itself. This led to the launching of the World Decade of Cultural Development in January 1988.

The positions defined within the framework of this decade-long effort are clear. Development was viewed in the following terms:

- to be conceived of as the totality of actions aimed at improving the quality of people's lives;
- to be based on the identities and cultures of the people themselves; and
- to take all aspects of economic and social transformation fully into account and maintain the participation of the concerned populations in the creation of their culture and in the search, according to the international plan, of a new understanding and new *solidarities* between all people and between all cultures.

In this spirit, real efforts were made by African governments to readjust their projects and plans for economic development: in 1984, the OAU adopted a Declaration of the Heads of State and Government on the cultural aspects of the Plan of Action for Lagos; the Economic Community of the States of West Africa (CEDEAO) outlined a framework of cooperation for a cultural agreement; the Tariff and Economic Union of Central Africa (UDEAC) agreed to undertake research into the social and cultural obstacles to economic growth. The Community for the Development of Southern Africa (SADC) founded a program for culture and information. Moreover, since Lomé III, the agreement that tied the European Community and the ACP Group of States (African, Caribbean, and Pacific) has included a chapter on cultural cooperation.

CULTURAL INDUSTRIES IN AFRICA[1]

To summarize, there is a dynamic rapport, essential and fertile, between culture and the economy. But the majority of African nations have not promoted endogenous creativity. Thus, they have continued to suffer economic as well as cultural domination by the industrialized countries; and their economies stagnated, were weakened, and turned outwards because they were characterized by the expensive consumption of foreign products. This produced an urgent need to redirect the focus of society from consumption to creativity, giving rise to and developing, among other things, cultural industries.

But what are the main issues? Cultural industries are composed of tools, technologies, and mechanisms, as well as the cultural resources that permit production on an industrial scale. Cultural industries involve products made for aesthetic, educational, informative, touristic, economic, and cultural ends. Included in this category are, for example, radio, television, films, advertising, records, cassette tapes, teaching aids (maps, diagrams, films, and pedagogical and didactic materials), objects of art, collectors' items (stamps, for example), crafts, and manufactured goods (tapestry, ceramics). Equally important, however, are the technologies that make these products possible as well as the distribution channels through which they acquire economic value and access to the international market.

If we accept this definition, cultural industries constitute a creative sector that, as much as any other, has an obvious impact on economic development. Cultural industries have manifold effects on cultural life and its transformation, as well as increasing relevance for development. In the world today, thanks to these industries, cultures are spreading and affirming themselves, preserving their own authenticity as well as engaging in dialogues with other cultures. The international market is no longer monopolized by economic products; there is now a large niche carved out for cultural products. Artistic biennials, film festivals, book and crafts fairs, and audiovisual demonstrations, are signs of technological achievement and national development in the world context. For the international market, however, African cultural industries remain insignificant and invisible.

The slow growth of African cultural industries springs from the lack of qualified personnel, as well as from problems of access to the equipment necessary for the manufacture of products. It is incontestably less expensive to buy foreign television series, sold at "dumping" prices, than it is to produce films and shows locally. Cultural industries obviously demand human resources and expensive infrastructures, putting pressure on the financial capacities of isolated developing nations. For these reasons, the 1982 UNESCO World Conference on Cultural Policies (MONDIACULT) made the following recommendations, which remain relevant today:

- the study of production capabilities and distribution of cultural goods in developing countries toward the goal of encouraging

development and the establishment of an inventory of their
needs;
- support, with regard to institutions aiding development, for the
installation of infrastructures for cultural goods, as well as the
promotion of the education of specialists and technicians who
are necessary for their functioning.

To this end, there remains a need:

- to make an inventory of the centers for the production of
cultural goods existing within the nations or in their subregions;
to look for ways of aiding the development of such centers (by
restoration, reinforcement, subregionalization, or region-
alization);
- after studying the market, to organize and rationalize the distribution and commercialization of the products of African
cultural industries, within the framework of the African
Common Cultural Market and on the international market;
- to encourage the coproduction of diverse films and television
programs by national television companies or by filmmakers
from different nations; and in view of the expansion of the film
market in Africa, to promote the use of international or African
languages (through dubbing or subtitles);
- to place production units in the various subregions (i.e., radio
and television receiving stations, printing presses, industrial
centers for manufacturing crafts, and centers for manufacture
of scholarly materials);
- to develop cooperation between publishing houses and
encourage the publication of collective and specialized works
that will contribute to national, regional, and subregional
integration; and
- to organize fairs to promote the products of African cultural
industries.

I close with the example of the crafts industry, which I would rank
among the cultural industries. This industry is critical, first, because it is within the reach of all African communities; and second,
because it is a domain of free activity in which rural communities
find significant financial rewards.

In all countries, the crafts industry plays a part in local traditional industry. A productive activity par excellence, the crafts industry bears witness to popular ingenuity, to attitudes toward the
world, and to local popular culture. The small size of the crafts
sector, its limited productivity, and the fact that it depends solely
on human capacity (manual labor) disqualify it from modern in-

dustrial competition. This does not diminish the value and price of the crafts industry's products. The more they are manufactured by hand, the more their value increases; they increase in market value (economic interest) and carry the stamp of human authenticity (cultural value and interest).

Craftsmanship, essentially a cultural activity, generates significant economic and cultural added value for social development. African crafts industries, although much sought after in the world, nonetheless have not experienced their full potential growth in terms of national or regional development. And this retardation seems all the more prejudicial to popular participation in development, for the crafts industry is the favored domain of creative initiatives of the working class, the peasantry, and rural populations in general. Crafts are the manifestation of creative and inventive capacities of the people, in the same way that they are a strong indicator of the technological level of a society and its need for new technologies. Indigenous development cannot do without the capital of knowledge, know-how, and technical skills belonging to local crafts industries, which constitute its basic potential. This is why the following steps remain essential:

- complete the inventory and the functional classification of African crafts industries, to measure their impact on national development and to improve, where needed, the local traditional technologies;
- put into place national policies for the development of local crafts industries that clearly define their cultural orientation and their economic contribution to national development, while mobilizing and supplying the financial means that will permit upgrading of the necessary infrastructures and the raising of standards, thereby enhancing the stature of craftspeople and their profession;
- implement educational programs for young craftsworkers overseen by veteran workers, in both beginning and advanced programs, as well as their instruction in new technologies and methods of management;
- reestablish manual labor and institute educational programs for craftsmanship within different settings, in a manner that will connect education to productive work and artistic creation and the crafts industry to economic viability; and
- create or reinforce subregional centers for the promotion of craftspeople and artists, encourage periodic organization of crafts fairs for laborers and artists (such as the International

Salon of Craftsmanship of Ouagadougou).
Just as the crafts industry was the industry of past African societies, it must continue today to be the spirit that marks modern industrialism as authentic by rooting in it the heritage of African knowledge and skills.

NOTE

1. See Basile T. Kossou, *The Cultural Dimension of Development toward Integrating Socio-Cultural Factors in the Plan of Action for Lagos* (Paris: UNESCO, 1985).

(Translated from the French by Daniel Halpern)

CONTRIBUTORS

Philip G. Altbach holds the J. Donald Monan, SJ, professorship of higher education and is director of the Center for International Higher Education, Boston College, Chestnut Hill, Massachusetts. He is also director of the Research and Information Center of the Bellagio Publishing Network.

Claude Daniel Ardouin is a consultant focusing on cultural development and, especially, on museums in Africa. He has been the director of the West African Museums Project in Bamako, Mali. He is based in Montpellier, France.

Walter Bgoya is managing director of Mkuki na Nyota Publishers, Dar es Salaam, Tanzania.

Salah M. Hassan is assistant professor of African art history and visual culture in the Africana Studies and Research Center, Cornell University, Ithaca, New York. He served as curator of several international exhibitions of African arts in Britain, South Africa, and the United States, and as a consultant to several museums and art-related institutions.

Jacques G. Katuala is program officer at the African Capacity Building Foundation, Harare, Zimbabwe. He holds a Ph.D from the University of California, Berkeley, and has extensive experience in development planning in the United States and Africa.

Basile T. Kossou is director, Africa Section, Bureau of External Relations, UNESCO, Paris, France.

Ali A. Mazrui is the Albert Schweitzer Professor of the Humanities at the State University of New York at Binghamton. He is also a senior scholar in African Studies at the Africana Studies and Research Center, Cornell University and the A. D. White Professor-at-Large Emeritus at Cornell University.

Gcina Mhlophe is founder of Zanendaba Storytellers, Johannesburg, South Africa.

J. H. Kwabena Nketia is emeritus professor and director of the International Center for African Music and Dance at the University of Ghana, Legon, Ghana. He is also Andrew Mellon professor emeritus at the University of Pittsburgh and professor emeritus at the University of California at Los Angeles.

Damien M. Pwono is senior program adviser, arts and humanities, The Rockefeller Foundation, Nairobi, Kenya. He holds a Ph.D in music from the University of Pittsburgh, where he launched and directed the International Center for Culture and Development.

Diana Senghor is director, Regional Program on West Africa, The Panos Institute, Paris, France.

Ben Zulu is executive director, Media for Develpment Trust, Harare, Zimbabwe.

Index